ISBN 978-1-330-60291-1
PIBN 10081099

1 MONTH OF
FREE
READING

at

www.ForgottenBooks.com

By purchasing this book you are eligible for one month membership to ForgottenBooks.com, giving you unlimited access to our entire collection of over 700,000 titles via our web site and mobile apps.

To claim your free month visit:

www.forgottenbooks.com/free81099

English
Français
Deutsche
Italiano
Español
Português

www.forgottenbooks.com

Mythology Photography **Fiction**
Fishing Christianity **Art** Cooking
Essays Buddhism Freemasonry
Medicine **Biology** Music **Ancient**
Egypt Evolution Carpentry Physics
Dance Geology **Mathematics** Fitness
Shakespeare **Folklore** Yoga Marketing
Confidence Immortality Biographies
Poetry **Psychology** Witchcraft
Electronics Chemistry History **Law**
Accounting **Philosophy** Anthropology
Alchemy Drama Quantum Mechanics
Atheism Sexual Health **Ancient History**
Entrepreneurship Languages Sport
Paleontology Needlework Islam
Metaphysics Investment Archaeology
Parenting Statistics Criminology
Motivational

[FIFTIETH EDITION.]

14

THE PLAIN MAN'S
PATHWAY TO HEAVEN;

WHEREIN

EVERY MAN MAY CLEARLY SEE WHETHER HE
SHALL BE SAVED OR DAMNED.

SET FORTH DIALOGUE-WISE,

FOR THE BETTER UNDERSTANDING OF THE SIMPLE

By ARTHUR DENT,

Preacher of the Word of God at South-Shoobery in Essex, 1590.

CORRECTED AND MUCH AMENDED; WITH A TABLE OF ALL THE
PRINCIPAL MATTERS; AND THREE PRAYERS,
NECESSARY TO BE USED IN PRIVATE FAMILIES, HEREUNTO
ADDED BY THE SAME AUTHOR.

" Every morning the Lord bringeth his judgment to light, he falleth not; but
the wicked will not learn to be ashamed."—ZEPHANIAH iii. 5.

BELFAST:
NORTH OF IRELAND BOOK & TRACT DEPOSITORY,
7 QUEEN'S SQUARE.
EDINBURGH: J. MACLAREN. A. ELLIOT.
GLASGOW: M. OGLE & SON. J. MACKIE. D. BRYCE.
STIRLING: PETER DRUMMOND. GREENOCK: J. M'KELVIE.
BRIGHTON (ENGLAND): GEO. STEDMAN.
1859.

CONTENTS OF THIS DIALOGUE.

It sheweth Man's Misery in Nature with the means of recovery.

II.

It sharply inveigheth against the Iniquity of the Time, and common Corruption of the World.

III.

It sheweth the marks of the Children of God, and of the Reprobates, with the apparent signs of Salvation and Damnation.

IV.

It declareth how hard a thing it is to enter into life, and how few shall enter.

V.

It layeth open the ignorance of the World, with the objections of the same.

LASTLY,

It publisheth and proclaimeth the sweet promises of the Gospel, with the abundant mercies of God to all that repent, believe, and truly turn unto him.

TO THE READER.

PROVIDENTIAL leadings are often pleasing to observe. The re-appearing of " THE PLAIN MAN'S PATHWAY TO HEAVEN " came about on this wise.

A man in Christ, reading " Bunyan's Grace Abounding to the Chief of Sinners," came upon the following:—

" Presently after this, I changed my condition into a married state, and my mercy was to light upon a wife whose father was counted godly. This woman and I, though we came together as poor as might be (not having so much household stuff as a dish or spoon betwixt us both), yet this she had for her part, ' The Plain Man's Pathway to Heaven,' and ' The Practice of Piety,' which her father had left her when he died. In these two books I would sometimes read with her; wherein I also found some things that were somewhat pleasing to me; but all this while I met with no conviction. She, also, would be often telling me what a godly man her father was, and how he would reprove and correct vice, both in his house and among his neighbours; and what a strict and holy life he lived in his days, both in word and deeds. . . . Wherefore, these books, with the relation, though they did not reach my heart, to awaken it about my sad and sinful state, yet they did beget within me some desires to reform my vicious life, and fall in very eagerly with the religion of the times, to wit, to go to church twice-a-day, and that too with the foremost; and there would very devoutly both say and sing as others did, yet retaining my wicked life."

To see this book, " The Plain Man's Pathway to Heaven," the reader felt a great desire.

When the desire was forgotten, unexpectedly he alighted upon an old copy, in black letter, without the title-page, and a leaf. The desire came to remembrance, and the book was eagerly purchased.

Years rolled away, and the book had been to the uttermost parts of the earth, and back again.

That God had directed John Bunyan to write the " Pilgrim's Progress," in allegory, through the means of this book, appeared not at all improbable; and as savoury meat was in it which is agreeable to the taste of many, a re-publication, for the good of the "household," was fondly entertained. It was not so favourable to do this abroad; but, returning home again, Mr. Wilson kindly undertook to bring it forth in a new dress. Efforts not a few were made to find another copy, but in vain: and the Prospectus informed subscribers that, "although it is minus the title-page, and one leaf, yet all the gold is preserved." A friend in England wrote that he had an incomplete copy, in plain type, and sent the same, containing the dedication by the author, and the leaf awanting. Another servant of Christ also wrote that he had the book, and sent a copy of the title-page.

Thus, from three copies, it now appears entire. The Lord, the God of Israel add his blessing— "To feed the Church of God, which he hath purchased with his own blood." Amen.

In an edition of the " Plain Man's Pathway," published in 1704, it is stated to be the fortieth edition, and that, upon a computation, one hundred thousand copies of this work had been sold. At a more recent date, we learn that it was again reprinted as the forty-first edition;

and from what we have heard concerning other editions, we think it probable that this will be the fiftieth edition. In the old editions, there is no division in the work: though embracing a great variety of topics, the heading of all the chapters were the same. We trust the liberty taken in giving the title to each new subject will prove helpful to the reader, as it will enable him more easily to refer to any particular in the book. The only other liberty taken has been to modernise the spelling: in all other respects it is *bona fide* as first issued in 1601.

ITS AUTHOR.

The Author, ARTHUR DENT, was minister of South Shooberry, a village near to Southend, in Essex, but persecuted by Bishop Aylmer for nonconformity. About the year 1584 he endured many troubles from this prelate, for refusing to wear the surplice, and omitting the sign of the cross in baptism. With several of his persecuted brethren, many of whom were suspended and in prison, he thus petitions the lords of the Queen's Council:—

"We cheerfully and boldly offer this our humble suit unto your honours, being our only sanctuary upon earth. next to her Majesty,* to which we repair in our present

* Queen Elizabeth.

necessity; and, most of all, we are encouraged when we
consider how richly God hath adorned your honours with
knowledge, wisdom, and zeal for the gospel, and with godly
care and tender love to those who profess the same.   Most
humbly, therefore, we beseech your honours, with your
accustomed favour in all godly and just causes, to hear and
to judge of our matters.   We have received the charge, as
loyal and faithful men, to instruct and teach our people in
the way of life; and every one of us hearing this sounded
from the God of heaven, ' *Woe be unto me, if I preach not
the gospel!*' we have all endeavoured to discharge our
duties, and to approve ourselves both to God and man.
Notwithstanding this, we are in great heaviness, and some
of us already put to silence, and the rest living in fear; not
that we have been, or can be charged, we hope, with false
doctrine, or slanderous life; but because we refuse to subscribe 'that there is nothing contained in the book of
Common Prayer contrary to the word of God.'   We do
protest, in the sight of God, who searcheth all hearts, that
we do not refuse from a desire to dissent, or from any sinister
affection, but in the fear of God, and from the necessity of
conscience.   The apostle teacheth, that a person who
doubteth is condemned if he eat: if a man, then, be condemned for doing a lawful action, because he doubts whether
it be lawful; how much more should we incur the displeasure
of the Lord, and justly deserve his wrath, if we should
subscribe, being fully persuaded that there are some things
in the book contrary to his word!   If our reasons might
be so answered by the doctrine of the Bible, and we could
be persuaded that we might subscribe lawfully, and in the
fear of God, we would willingly consent.   In these and
other respects, we humbly crave your honourable protection,
as those who from the heart do entirely love, honour, and
obey her excellent Majesty, and your honours, in the Lord.
Giving most hearty thanks to God for all the blessings we
have received from him, by your government; constantly
praying, night and day, that he will bless and preserve her

Majesty and your honours to eternal salvation, your honours'
poor and humble supplicants."*

In a work of ARTHUR DENT's, called "The
Ruin of Rome, or an Exposition of Revelations,"
his friend EZEKIEL CULVERWELL, gives the
following account of him:—

"To give some public testimony of my love towards him,
and reverence of the rare grace which we all who enjoyed
his sweet society did continually behold in him, whose
learning his labours do shew; and whose diligence, yea,
extreme and unwearied pains in his ministry, publicly,
privately, at home, and abroad, for at least four-and-twenty
years, all our country can testify: all which being adorned
with such special humility, do make his name the greater,
and our loss the more grievous. I may not leave out this—
which I avow to be as certain as it is singular—that, besides
all others his great labours, he had a special care of all the
churches night and day, by study and fervent prayer,
procuring the prosperity of Zion and the ruin of Rome.
And, to end with his blessed end, his life was not more
profitable to others, than his death was peaceable to himself:
scarcely a groan was heard, though his fever must have

* This petition is signed by

G. GYFFARD.	R. HAWDEN.	R. BLACKWELL.
R. ROGERS.	J. JESSELIN.	T. HOWELL.
N. COLPOTTS.	T. UPCHE.	M. WIRSDALE.
L. NEWMAN.	R. CARR.	R. EDMUNDS.
W. DIKE.	J. WILTON.	A. PIGOT.
T. CHAPLAIN.	S. COTESFORD.	C. RUSTICUS.
A. DENT.	R. ILLISON.	J. HUCKLE.
T. REDRICH.	W. SERDGE.	T. CAREW.
G. WHITING.	E. BARKER.	J. BISHOP.

The first in this honourable list, Mr. Gyffard, was vicar of Maldon, a
most eminent man, and a very noted preacher of God's word. He
endured heavy persecutions and grievous troubles. The lord high
treasurer, Burleigh, wished to favour him, but the bishops were too
many for the minister of state. He was a voluminous writer. His
works are recommended by Dent, page 256. See "Brook's Lives of
of the Puritans," Vol. II. 273-8.

been violent, which despatched him in three days. Having made a pithy confession of his faith, 'This faith,' said he, 'have I preached; this faith have I believed in; this faith I do die in; and this faith would I have sealed with my blood, if God had so thought good; and tell my brethren so.' He afterwards said, 'I have fought a good fight, I have finished my course, I have kept the faith; henceforth there is laid up for me the crown of righteousness:' and, with his last breath, added, 'I have seen an end of all perfection, but thy law is exceeding broad.'"

SIR JULIUS CÆSAR, KNIGHT,

*One of the Masters of the Requests to the King's Majesty, Judge of the
High Court of Admiralty, and Master of St. Catherine's,
wisheth all good things in Christ Jesus.*

HAVING finished, Right Worshipful, and made
ready for the press this little Dialogue, I be-
thought me, since the common manner of all that
write any books in this age, is to dedicate the
same to one or to other of great place, to whom
I might dedicate these my poor labours. At
last I did resolve with myself, none to be more
fit than your Worship; both in regard of some
affinity in the flesh, as also because of those
manifold good parts wherewith the Almighty
hath endued you. Having therefore none other
thing to present your Worship withal, in token
of a thankful heart for your courtesies shewed
towards me, behold, I do here send unto you this
third fruit of my labours now published. Most
humbly beseeching you to take it in good worth;
not weighing the value of the thing, which is of
no value, but the simple and good meaning of the
giver. This work doth sharply reprove and evict
the world of sin, and therefore is likely to find
many deadly enemies, which with cruel hatred
will most eagerly pursue it unto death. Zoilus
also, and his fellows, I know will bitterly carp at
it. Therefore, it flieth unto your Worship for

protection, and humbly desireth to take sanctuary under your wings. Wherefore, I humbly intreat you, to take upon you the patronage and defence of it; that by your means it may be delivered both from the calumnious obloquies of evil-disposed persons, and also from the world's malignity; so as it may take no injury. And concerning this little volume, the sum of the matter of it, you shall find in the Epistle to the Reader. As concerning the manner, here is no great matter in learning, wit, art, eloquence, or ingenious invention; (for I have herein specially respected the ignorant and vulgar sort, whose edification I do chiefly aim at) yet somewhat there is, which may concern the learned, and give them some contentment. Whatsoever it be, I leave it with your Worship, beseeching you to give it entertainment. And so I do most humbly take my leave, commending both yourself, your good wife, and your whole family to the merciful protection of the ever living God.

Your Worship's, to command in the Lord,

ARTHUR DENT.

South Shooberry, Essex,
April 10, 1601.

EPISTLE TO THE READER.

GENTLE Reader, seeing my little Sermon of repentance, some few years since published, hath been so well accepted of, I have, for thy further good, published this Dialogue, being the third fruit of my labour, wishing to it the like success, that God thereby may have the glory, and thou who art the reader comfort. I have, in one part of this Dialogue, produced some of the ancient writers, and some of the wise heathen also, to testify upon their oath in their own language, and to bear witness of the ugliness of some vices, which we in this age make light of, which I wish may not be offensive to any. In other parts of this work, I do in a manner relinquish them. But in this case I have, in my weak judgment, thought them to be of some good use, to shew forth thus much, that if we do not in time repent, forsake our sins, and seek after God, both the ancient Christian fathers, whose eyes saw not that we see, nor their ears heard that we hear, yea, the very heathen also, shall rise up in judgment against us. Let none, therefore, stumble at it; but if any do, let them remember I am in a Dialogue, not in a sermon. I write to all of all sorts; I speak not to some few of one sort. But that which is done herein, is not much more than that of the Apostle, "as some of your own poets have said," Acts xvii. which is warrantable. One thing, dear Christian, I pray thee let me beg of thee; to wit, that thou wouldest not read two or three leaves of this book, and so cast it from thee; but that thou wouldest read it throughout even to the end; for I do assure thee, if there be anything in it worth the reading, it is bestowed in the latter part thereof, and most of all towards the conclusion. Be not discouraged therefore at the harshness of the beginning, but look for smoother matter in the midst, and most smooth in the perclose and wind-up of all; for this Dialogue hath in it, not the nature of a tragedy, which is began with joy, and ended with sorrow; but of a comedy, which is began with sorrow, and ended with joy. This book meddleth not at all with any controversies in the Church, or anything in the state Ecclesiastical, but only entereth into a controversy with Satan and sin. It is contrived into six principal heads; first, it sheweth man's misery in nature, with the means of recovery; secondly, it sharply inveigheth against the iniquity of the time, and common corruptions of the world; thirdly, it sheweth the marks of the children of God, and of the reprobates, together with the apparent signs of salvation and damnation; fourthly, it declareth how hard a thing it is to enter into life, and how few shall enter; fifthly, it layeth open the ignorance of the world, with the objections of the same; last of all, it publisheth and proclaimeth the sweet promises of the gospel, with the abundant mercy of God, to all that repent, believe, and truly turn unto him. The Author of all blessing give a blessing unto it. The God of peace, which brought again from the dead our Lord Jesus, that great Shepherd of the sheep, through the blood of the everlasting covenant, make us perfect in all good works, sanctify us throughout, amend all our imperfections, and keep us blameless until the day of his most glorious appearing. Amen.

Thine, in the Lord,

A. DENT.

CONTENTS.

---

2 A

CONTENTS.

THE PLAIN MAN'S
PATHWAY TO HEAVEN.

INTERLOCUTORS.

THEOLOGUS,......................A Divine.
PHILAGATHUS,..................An Honest Man.
ASUNETUS,........................An Ignorant Man.
ANTILEGON,......................A Caviller.

MAN'S CORRUPTION & MISERY.

Phil. Well met, good master, Theologus.

Theol. What my old friend, Philagathus! I am glad to see you in good health.

Phil. Are you walking, sir, here all alone in this pleasant meadow?

Theol. Yea; for I take some pleasure at this time of the year to walk abroad in the fields for my recreation, both to take the fresh air, and to hear the sweet singing of birds.

Phil. Indeed, sir, it is very comfortable, especially now in this pleasant month of May: and thanks be to God, hitherto we have had a very forward spring, and as kindly a season as came this seven years.

Theol. God doth abound towards us in mercies; Oh that we could abound towards him in thanksgiving.

Phil. I pray you, sir, what a clock hold you it?

B

Theol. I take it to be a little past one; for I came but even now from dinner.

Phil. But, behold, yonder cometh two men towards us: what be they I pray you?

Theol. They be a couple of neighbours of the next parish: the one of them is called Asunetus, who in very deed is a very ignorant man in God's matters: and the other is called Antilegon, a notable atheist, and caviller against all goodness.

Phil. If they be such, it were good for us to take some occasion to speak of matters of religion; it may be we shall do them some good.

Theol. You have made a good motion: I like it well. If therefore you will minister some matter, and move some questions, I will be ready to answer in the best sort I can.

Phil. But stay, sir, lo here they come upon us.

Theol. Welcome, neighbours, welcome. How do you Asunetus, and you Antilegon?

Asun. Well, God be thanked; and we are glad to see your mastership in good health.

Theol. What makes both of you here at this time of the day? There is some occasion I am sure draweth you this way.

Asun. Indeed, sir, we have some little business; for we came to talk with one of your parish, about a cow we should buy of him.

Theol. Hath my neighbour a cow to sell?

Antil. We are told he hath a very good one to sell; but I am afraid at this time of the year, we shall find dear ware of her.

Theol. How dear? what do you think a very good cow may be worth?

Antil. A good cow indeed, at this time of the year, is worth very near four pounds, which is a great price.

Theol. It is a very great price indeed.

Phil. I pray you, Mr. Theologus, leave off this talking of kine, and worldly matters; and let us enter into some speech of matters of religion, whereby we may do good, and take good one of another.

Theol. You say well: but it may be these men's business requireth haste, so as they cannot stay.

Asun. No, sir, we are in no great haste, we can stay two or three hours, for the days are long; if we dispatch our business by night it will serve our turn well enough.

Theol. Then if it will please you to walk to yonder oak tree, there is a goodly arbour, and handsome seats, where we may all sit in the shadow, and confer of heavenly matters.

Asun. With a good will, sir.

Phil. Come, then, let us go.

Asun. This is a goodly arbour indeed, and here be handsome seats.

Theol. Sit you all down, I pray you. Now friend Philagathus, if you have any questions to move of matters of religion, we are all ready to hear you.

Phil. It may be these men are somewhat ignorant of the very principles of religion; and therefore I think it not amiss to begin there, and so to make way for further matters.

Theol. I pray you do so then.

Phil. First, then, I demand of you, in what state all men are born by nature?

Theol. In the state of condemnation, as appeareth, Eph. ii. 3. We are by nature the children of wrath as well as others. And again it is written, "Behold I was born in iniquity, and in sin hath my mother conceived me," Psal. ii. 5.

Phil. Is it every man's case? Are not dukes and nobles, lords and ladies, and the great potentates of the earth exempted from it?

Theol. No, surely, it is the common case of all, both high and low, rich and poor, as it is written, "What is man that he should be clean, and he that is born of a woman, that he should be just?" Job xv. 14.

Phil. From whence cometh it, that all men are born in so woful a case?

Theol. From the fall of Adam, who thereby had not only wrapt himself, but all his posterity, in extreme and unspeakable misery; as the apostle saith, "By one man's disobedience, many were made sinners: and by the offence of one, the fault came on all men to condemnation."

Phil. What reason is there that we all should thus be punished for another man's offence?

Theol. Because we were then all in him, and are now all of him: that is we are so descended out of his loins, that of him we have not only received our natural and corrupt bodies, but also by propagation have inherited his foul corruptions, as it were by hereditary right.

Phil. But forasmuch as some have dreamed that Adam by his fall hurt himself only, and not his posterity, and that we have his corruption derived unto us by imitation, and not by propagation; therefore I pray you shew this more plainly.

Theol. Even as great personages, by committing treason, do not only hurt themselves, but also stain their blood, and disgrace their posterity, for the children of such nobles are disinherited, whose blood is attainted, till they be restored again by act of parliament; even so our blood being attainted by Adam's transgression, we can inherit nothing of right, till we be restored by Christ.

Phil. Doth this hereditary infection and contagion overspread our whole nature?

Theol. Yes, truly, it is universal, extending itself throughout the whole man, both soul and body, both reason, understanding, will and affections; for the scriptures avouch that we are dead in sins and trespasses, Eph. ii. 1; Col. i. 21, ii. 13.

Phil. How understand you that?

Theol. Not of the deadness of the body, or the natural faculties of the soul, but of the spiritual faculties.

Phil. Did Adam then lose his nature and destroy it by his fall? or is our nature taken away by his fall?

Theol. Not so. Our nature was corrupted thereby, but not destroyed: for still there remaineth in our nature, reason, understanding, will, and affections, and we are not as a block, or a stock; but by Adam's disobedience we are blemished, maimed, and spoiled of all ability to understand aright, or to will and do aright. As it is written, "We are not sufficient of ourselves, to think any thing as of ourselves: but our sufficiency is of God," 2 Cor. iii. 5. And again, "It is God which worketh in you both the will and the deed; even of his good pleasure," Phil. ii. 13. And, as concerning the other point, St. James saith, "That all men are made after the similitude of God," James iii. 9, meaning thereby that there remain some relics and parts of God's image, even in the most wicked men; as reason, understanding, &c. so that our nature was not wholly destroyed.

Phil. Then you think there be some spark and remnants left in us still of that excellent image of God, which was in our first creation.

Theol. I think so indeed: and it may plainly appear unto us in the wise speeches and writings of heathen poets and philosophers; in all which we may, as by certain ruins, perceive what was the excellent frame and building of man's creation.

Phil. Can a man please God in any thing which he doth, so long as he continueth in the state of nature?

Theol. No, not in any thing: for till we be in the state of grace, even our best actions are sinful; as preaching, prayer, alms deeds, &c. As it is written, "Who can bring a clean thing out of that which is unclean?" Job xiv. 4. The apostle also saith, "They which are in the flesh cannot please God," Rom. viii. 8; that is, such as are still in their natural corruption. And our Lord Jesus himself saith, "Do men gather grapes of thorns, or figs of thistles?" Matt. vii. 16; meaning thereby, that mere natural men can bring forth no fruits acceptable to God.

Phil. This is a very harsh and hard saying; I pray you, for my further instruction, make it more plain.

Theol. Men in the state of nature may do those things which of themselves are good, but they do utterly fail in the manner of doing them: they do them not as they should be done; that is, in faith, love, zeal, conscience of obedience, &c. neither yet with any cheerfulness, delight or feeling, but even as it were, forcing themselves to do the outward actions. Thus did Cain sacrifice, the pharisees pray, Ananias and Sapphira give alms, and the Jews offer up their oblations and burnt-offering.

Phil. Have men any true sight, or lively and sound feeling of this misery and woful estate, so long as they be merely natural?

Theol. No, surely, but are altogether blinded and hardened in it, being nothing desirous to come out of it, but do greatly please themselves in it, and can hardly be persuaded that they are in any such woful case; as appeareth plainly in the example of that ruler, who being commanded or rather required of our Saviour Christ to keep the commandments, answered, "All these have I kept from my youth," Luke xviii. 21. And again, although the church of Laodicea was wretched, miserable, poor, blind, and naked, yet she thought herself rich, increased with goods, and wanting nothing. It followeth then, that so long as men are in the state of nature, they have no true sight and feeling of their misery.

Phil. Do you not think that all men being merely natural, are under the curse of the law?

Theol. Yes, certainly; and not only so, but also under the very tyranny and dominion of Satan, though they know it not, see it not, feel it not, or perceive it not; for all that are not in Christ, are under the curse of the law, and the power of darkness and the devil, as appeareth, Eph. ii. 2, where the devil is called the prince that ruleth in the air, even the spirit that now worketh in the children of disobedience, 2 Cor. iv. 4. In another place, he is called the god of this world, who blindeth the eyes of all unbelievers. And again, it is said, that all men naturally are in his snare, being taken captive of him at his will, 2 Tim. ii. 26.

Phil. Few will be persuaded of that; they will say they defy the devil, and thank God they were never troubled with him.

Theol. Their hot words do nothing amend the matter; for the devil is no more driven away with words, than with holy water, but he sitteth in the tongues and mouths; nay, possesseth the very heart and entrails of thousands which say they defy him, and are not troubled with him, as appeareth manifestly by their particular actions, and the whole course of their life.

Phil. Methinks, if the devil do so inwardly possess the hearts and consciences of men, they should have some sight and feeling of it.

Theol. The working of the devil in men's souls (being an invisible spirit) is with such inconceivable sleight and crafty conveyance, that men in the estate of nature cannot possibly feel it, or perceive it: for how can a blind man see, or a dead man feel?

Phil. Shew this more plainly.

Theol. Even as a crafty juggler doth deceive, and blind men's outward senses by the delusions of Satan, that they think they see that which they see not, and feel that which they feel not: even so the devil doth so delude and bewitch our inward senses, and the natural faculties of our souls, that we having a mist cast before our eyes, think we are that which we are not, see that which we see not, and feel that which we feel not. For the deep cunning of Satan lieth in this, that he can give us our death's wound, and we shall never know who hurt us.

Phil. Few will believe this to be true.

Theol. True indeed: for few will believe the scriptures: few will believe this, because few feel it: where it is not felt, it can hardly be believed: only the elect do feel it, and therefore only the elect do believe it. As for all others, they are the very apprentices and bond-slaves of the devil, which is a thousand times worse than to be a galley-slave.

———

REGENERATION.

Phil. How long do men continue in this woful state of nature, being under the curse of the law, and the very slavery of Satan and sin?

Theol. Till they be regenerate and born again, and so brought into the state of grace: as our Lord Jesus saith, "Except a man be born again, he cannot see the kingdom of God," John iii. 3.

Phil. Do not many die and depart this life, before they be born again, and consequently before they be brought into the state of grace?

Theol. Yes, no doubt, thousands: for many live forty or threescore years in this world, and in the end die, and go out of this life before they know wherefore they come into it: as it is written, "My people perish for want of knowledge."

Phil. What may we think of such?

Theol. I quake to speak what I think; for surely I do not see how such can be saved. I speak not now of infants and children, whereof some no doubt are saved by virtue of the promise and covenant, through the election of grace.

Phil. It seemeth then that you think none can be saved, but those only which are born again.

Theol. I think so indeed.

Phil. I pray you tell me what the same regeneration and new birth is, whereof you speak.

Theol. It is a renewing and repairing of the corrupted and decayed estate of our souls. As it is written, "Be ye changed by the renewing of your mind," Rom. xii. 2. And again, "Be renewed in the spirit of your mind," Eph. iv. 2, 3.

Phil. Explain this more fully.

Theol. Even as the wild olive retaineth his old nature, till it be grafted into the sweet olive, but afterward is partaker of a new nature; so we, till we be grafted into Christ, retain our old nature, but afterward are turned into a new nature, as it is written, "If any man be in Christ, he is a new creature," 2 Cor. v. 17.

Phil. I understand not what you say.

Theol. You must know this, that as there is a natural birth of the whole man, so there is also a spiritual birth of the whole man.

Phil. How is that?

Theol. When as the natural faculties of the soul, as reason, understanding, will and affections, and the members of the body also, are so sanctified, purged, and rectified by grace, that we understand, will, and desire that which is good.

Phil. Cannot a man will and desire that which is good before he be born again?

Theol. No more than a dead man can desire the good things of this life. For man's will is not free to consent unto good till it be enlarged by grace; and an unregenerate man doth sin necessarily, though not by constraint: for man's will is free from constraint (for it sinneth of itself) but not from thraldom unto sin.

Phil. You speak as if a man could do no other thing but sin, till the new work be wrought in him.

Theol. That is my opinion indeed: for a man and his flesh are all one, till he be regenerate; they agree together like man and wife, they join together in all evil, they live and die together: for when the flesh perisheth, the man perisheth.

Phil. Is not this regeneration a changing or rather a destroying of human nature?

Theol. Nothing less: it is neither an abolishing, nor changing of the substance of body or soul, or any of the faculties thereof; but only a rectifying and repairing of them by removing* the corruption.

Phil. Is then our natural corruption so purged and quite removed by the power of grace, as that it remaineth not at all in us, but that we are wholly freed of it?

Theol. Not so. For the relics and remnants of our old nature, which the scripture calleth the old man, do hang about us, and dwell in us, even until our dying day: as it is plainly proved in the last ten verses of the seventh to the Romans.†

Phil. Then you affirm that this new man, or new work of grace and regeneration, is imperfect in this life.

Theol. Yea. For the new creature, or new work of grace, can never be fully fashioned in this life, but is always in fashioning. And as our faith and knowledge in this life are imperfect, so is our regeneration and sanctification.

Phil. You said before that the regeneration or new birth is of the whole man, which speech

---

* The word subduing is more scriptural. See Mic. vii. 19. Rom. vi. 14.

† The scriptures not only speak of a remnant of evil, but of the body of sin and death; this is called, even in believers, the old man, there being no member lacking.

seemeth to imply, that the new work of grace is entire and perfect.

Theol. You mistake the matter.   For although the new birth is universal, and of the whole man, yet it is not entire, perfect, pure, and without mixture of corruption.   For it is written, "The flesh lusteth against the Spirit, and the Spirit against the flesh," Gal. v. 17   The apostle also prayeth, that the Thessalonians may be sanctified throughout, in spirit, soul, and body.

Phil. This seemeth very obscure—I pray you make it more plain.

Theol. You must note this, that the new works and the old, flesh and spirit, grace and corruption, are so intermingledly joined together in all the faculties of the soul and body, as that the one doth ever fight against the other.

Phil. But tell me, I pray you, how you under-stand this intermingling of grace and corruption in the soul?   Do you mean that grace is placed in one part of the soul, and corruption in another, so as they be sundred in place?

Theol. No, that is not my meaning, but this, that they be joined and mingled together (as I said) in and throughout the whole man.   For the mind, or understanding part, is not one part flesh and another part spirit; but the whole mind is flesh, and the whole mind is spirit, partly one, and partly another.   The same is to be said of the will and affections.

Phil. I pray you express it more plainly.

Theol. Even as the air in the dawning of the day is not wholly light, or wholly dark, as at midnight, or at noon day, neither is it in one part light, in another part dark; but the whole air is partly light, and partly dark throughout:

and as in a vessel of luke-warm water, the water itself is not only hot, nor only cold, but heat and cold are mixed together in every part of the water: so is the flesh and the spirit mingled together in the soul of man. And this is the cause why these two contrary qualities fight together.

Phil. Out of doubt this doctrine of regeneration is a very great mystery.

Theol. Yes, certainly: it is a secret of secrets, which the wise of this world cannot comprehend.

Phil. Some think that courtesy, kindness, good nurture, good nature, and good education, are regeneration, and that courteous and good-natured men must be saved.

Theol. They are greatly deceived; for these things do not necessarily accompany salvation, but are to be found in such as are altogether profane and irreligious: yet we are to love such good outward qualities, and the men in whom we find them.

Phil. What say you then to learning, wit and policy; are not these things of the essence of religion, and prove a regeneration?

Theol. No, no; for they be external gifts, which may be in the most wicked men, as in papists, heathen poets, and philosophers: yet we are greatly to reverence learned and wise men, although the new and inward work be not as yet wrought; for that is only of God, that is from above.

Phil. The common people do attribute much to learning and policy: for they will say, such a man is learned and wise, and knoweth the scripture as well as any of them all, and yet he doth not thus and thus.

Theol. It is one thing to know the history and letter of the scriptures, and another thing to believe and feel the power thereof in the heart, which is only from the sanctifying Spirit, which none of the wise of the world can have.

Phil. It is a common opinion, that if a man hold the truth in judgment, be no papist, or heretic, but leadeth an honest civil life, then he must of necessity be saved.

Theol. That followeth not: for many come so for, which yet notwithstanding have not the inward touch.

Phil. That seemeth strange. For many will say, as long as they be neither whore nor thief, nor spotted with such like gross sins, they trust in God they shall be saved.

Theol. They err not knowing the scriptures. For many thousands are in great danger of losing their souls for ever, which are free from such notorious and horrible vices: nay, many which in the world are counted good honest men, good true dealers, good neighbours, and good townsmen.

Asun. I pray you, sir, give me leave a little. I have heard all your speech hitherto, and I like reasonably well of it; but now I can forbear no longer, my conscience urgeth me to speak. For methinks you go too far, you go beyond your learning in this, that you condemn good neighbours, and good townsmen. You say, many such men are in danger of losing their souls; but I will never believe it while I live. For if such men be not saved, I cannot tell who shall.

Theol. But you must learn to know out of the scriptures that all outward honesty and righteousness, without the true knowledge and inward feeling of God, availeth not to eternal life. As our Saviour Christ saith, "except your righteousness exceed the righteousness of the scribes and pharisees, ye cannot enter into the kingdom of heaven," Matt. v. 20. It is also written that when Paul preached at Berea, many honest men and honest women did believe, Acts xvii. 12; that is, such as were outwardly honest, or honest to the world only; for they could not be truly and inwardly honest before they did believe. Therefore you see that this outward honesty and civility, without the inward regeneration of the Spirit, availeth not to eternal life; and then consequently, all your honest worldly men are in great danger of losing their souls for ever.

Asun. What sound reason can you yield why such honest men should be condemned?

Theol. Because many such are utterly void of all true knowledge of God, and of his word. Nay, which is more, many of them despise the word of God, and hate all the zealous professors of it. They esteem preachers but as prattlers, and sermons as good tales; they esteem a preacher no more than a shoe-maker: they regard the scriptures no more than their old shoes. What hope is there then, I pray you, that such men should be saved: doth not the Holy Ghost say, "how shall we escape if we neglect so great salvation?" Heb. ii. 3.

Asun. You go too far—you judge too hardly of them.

Theol. Not a whit. For all experience showeth, that they mind, dream, and dote of nothing else day and night, but this world, this world's lands and leases, grounds and livings, kine and sheep, and how to wax rich. All their thoughts,

words, and works, are of these and such like
things; and their actions do most manifestly declare that they are of the earth, and speak of the
earth; and that there is nothing in them but
earth, earth.   As for sermons, they care not how
few they hear.   And for the scriptures they regard them not, they read them not, they esteem
them not worth the while: there is nothing more
irksome unto them; they had rather pick straws,
or do any thing, than hear, read, or confer of the
scriptures.   And as the prophet saith, "The
word of the Lord is as a reproach unto them, that
have no delight in it," Jer. vi. 10.

Phil. I marvel much that such men should
live so honestly to the world-ward.

Theol. No marvel at all; for many bad men
whose hearts are worm-eaten within, yet for some
outward and carnal respects, do abstain from the
gross act of sin; as some for credit, some for
shame, some for fear of law, some for fear of
punishment; but none for love of God, for zeal,
or conscience of obedience.   For it is a sure thing,
that the wicked may have that spirit which doth
repress; but not that which doth renew.

Phil. It seemeth then by your speeches that
some which are not regenerate do in some things
excel the children of God.

Theol. Most certain it is that some of them in
outward gifts, and the outward carriage of themselves, do go beyond some of the elect.

Phil. Shew me I pray you in what gifts.

Theol. In learning, discretion, justice, temperance, prudence, patience, liberality, affability,
kindness, courtesy, good nature, and such like.

Phil. Methinketh it should not be possible.

Theol. Yes, truly.   For some of God's dear

children, in whom no doubt the inward work is truly and soundly wrought, yet are so troubled and encumbered with a crabbed and crooked nature, and so clogged with some master sin; as some with anger, some with pride, some with covetousness, some with lusts, some one way, some another; all which breaking out in them, do so blemish them and their profession that they cannot so shine forth unto men as otherwise no doubt they would; and this is their wound, their grief, and their heart smart, and that which costeth them many a tear, and many a prayer: and yet can they not get the full victory over them, but still they are left in them, as the prick in the flesh, to humble them.

Phil. Yet love should cover a multitude of such infirmities in God's children.

Theol. It should do so indeed: but there is great want of love, even in the best; and the worst sort espying these infirmities in the godly, run upon them with open mouth and take upon them to condemn them utterly, and to judge their hearts, saying they be hypocrites, dissemblers, and there is none worse than they.

Phil. But do you not think that there be some counterfeits, even amongst the greatest professors?

Theol. Yes, no doubt there be, and always have been some very hypocrites in the church: but we must take heed of judging and condemning all for some. For it were very much to condemn Christ and his eleven disciples, because of one Judas; or the whole primitive church, for Ananias and Sapphira.

Phil. But I hope you are of this mind, that some regenerate men, even in outward gifts, and their outward carriage, are comparable with any others.

Theol. Questionless, very many. For they being guided by God's Spirit, and upheld by his grace, do walk very uprightly and unblameably towards men.

Phil. Yet there resteth one scruple: for it seemeth very strange unto me, that men of so discreet carriage as you speak of, and of so many good parts, should not be saved. It is a great pity such men should be damned.

Theol. It seemeth so unto us indeed; but God is only wise; and you must note that as there be some infirmities in God's children, which he correcteth with temporal chastisements, and yet rewardeth their faith, love, and inward service and obedience, with eternal life; so there be some good things in the wicked, and them that are without Christ, which God rewardeth with temporal blessings, and yet punisheth them eternally for their unbelief and hardness of heart.

Phil. Now you have reasonably well satisfied me touching the doctrine of regeneration, and the manifold errors and deceits that are in it, and of it—I pray you let us now proceed: and first of all tell me, by what means the new birth is wrought?

Theol. By the preaching of the word, as the outward means; and the secret work of the Spirit, as the inward means, 1 Peter, i. 23; John xv. 3; Acts x. 44.

Phil. Many hear the word preached and are nothing the better, but rather the worse; what I pray you is the cause of that?

Theol. Men's own incredulity, and hardness of heart; because God in his wrath leaveth them to themselves, and depriveth them of his Spirit, without the which, all preaching is in vain: for except the Spirit do follow the word into our hearts, we can find no joy, taste, nor comfort therein, Acts xvi. 14.

Phil. Cannot a man attain unto regeneration and the new birth without the word and the Spirit?

Theol. No, verily: for they are the instruments and means* whereby God doth work it.

Asun. Why may not a man have as good a faith to God-ward, that heareth no sermons, as he that heareth all the sermons in the world?

Theol. Why may not he, which eateth no meat, be as fat and as well liking, as he that eateth all the meat in the world? For is not the preaching of the word, the food of our soul?

Asun. I like not so much hearing of sermons, and reading of the scriptures, except men could keep them better.

Theol. Faithful and honest hearers do therefore hear, that they may be more able to observe and do. For a man cannot do the will of God before he know it; and he cannot know it without hearing and reading.

Antil. I marvel what good men do get by gadding to sermons, and poring so much in the scriptures; or what are they better than others? there are none more full of envy and malice than they. They will do their neighbour a shrewd turn as soon as any body; and therefore, in my opinion, they be but a company of hypocrites and precise fools.

Theol. You judge uncharitably. Full little do

---

* Is it not more correct to say the Spirit is the efficient, the word the instrumental cause?

you know what they feel, or what good God's people get by hearing of his word. For the work of the Spirit in the heart of the elect is very secret and altogether hid from the world, as it is written, "The wind bloweth where it listeth, and thou hearest the sound thereof, but canst not tell whither it goeth, or whence it cometh; so is every man that is born of the Spirit," John iii. 8. And again, "The things of God knoweth no man, but the Spirit of God."

Asun. Tush, tush; what needs all this ado? If a man say his Lord's prayer, his ten commandments, and his belief, and keep them, and say nobody no harm, nor do nobody no harm, and do as he would be done to, have a good faith to Godward, and be a man of God's belief, no doubt he shall be saved, without all this running to sermons, and prattling of the scriptures.

Theol. Now you pour it out indeed. You think you have spoken wisely. But, alas, you have bewrayed your great ignorance. For you imagine a man may be saved without the word, which is a gross error.

Asun. It is no matter, say you what you will, and all the preachers in the world besides: as long as I serve God, and and say my prayers duly and truly, morning and evening, and have a good faith in God, and put my whole trust in him, and do my true intent, and have a good mind to Godward, and a good meaning, although I am not learned, yet I hope it will serve the turn for my soul's health. For that God which made me must save me. It is not you that can save me, for all your learning, and all your scriptures.

Theol. You may very fitly be compared to a

sick man, who having his brain distempered with heat, raveth, and speaketh idly, he cannot tell what. For the Holy Ghost saith, "He that turneth away his ear from hearing the law, even his prayer shall be abominable," Prov. xxviii. 9. And again, "He that despiseth the word, he shall be destroyed," Prov. xiii. 13. So long therefore as you despise God's word, and turn away your ear from hearing his gospel preached, all your prayers, your fantastical serving God, your good meanings, and your good intents, are to no purpose; but most loathsome and odious in the sight of God: as it is written, " My soul hateth your new moons, and your appointed feasts, they are a burthen unto me, I am weary to bear them. When you stretch out your hands, I will hide mine eyes from you: and though you make many prayers, I will not hear; for your hands are full of blood," Isa. i. 14, 15. And again the Lord saith by the same prophet, "He that killeth an ox, is as if he slew a man: he that sacrificeth a lamb, as if he cut off a dog's neck: he that offereth an oblation, as if he offered swine's blood: and he that burneth incense, as if he blessed an idol," Isa. lxvi. 3; where you see, the Lord telleth you his mind touching these matters, to wit, that all your prayers, services, good meanings, &c. are abominable unto him, so long as you walk in ignorance, profaneness, disobedience, and contempt of the gospel. For he saith in the words immediately going before, "To him will I look, even to him that is poor and of a contrite spirit, and trembleth at my words," v. 2.

Asun. I grant indeed for them that are idle and have little to do, it is not amiss now and then to hear a sermon, and read the scriptures: but we have no leisure, we must follow our business, we cannot live by the scriptures; they are not for plain folks, they are too high for us, we will not meddle with them. They belong to preachers and ministers.

Theol. Christ saith, "My sheep hear my voice, and I give unto them them eternal life," John x. 27, 28. If therefore you refuse to hear the voice of Christ, you are none of his sheep, neither can you have eternal life. And in another place our Lord Jesus saith, "He that is of God, heareth God's word. Ye therefore hear it not, because ye are not of God," John viii. 47. Paul writing to all sorts of men, both rich and poor, high and low, men and women, young and old, exhorteth that "the word of Christ may dwell plenteously in them all, in all wisdom," Col. iii. 16. You see therefore that the apostle would have all sorts of people, that have souls to save, to be well acquainted with the scriptures. Therefore you may as well say you will not meddle with God, with Christ, nor with everlasting life, as to say you will not meddle with the scriptures.

Asun. Well, I cannot read, and therefore I cannot tell, what Christ or what Paul may say; but this I am sure of, that God is a good man, (worshipped might he be) he is merciful, and that we must be saved by our good prayers, and good serving of God.

Theol. You speak foolishly and ignorantly in all that you say, having no ground for any thing you speak but your own fancy, and your own conceit: and yet you will believe your own fancy against all preachers, and against all that can be spoken out of the word. But I pray you give me leave a little. If a man dream that he shall be a king, and in the morning when he is awake persuadeth himself it shall be so, may he not be justly laughed at, as having no ground for it? even so may all they which believe their own dreams and phantasies touching salvation; but it is true which Solomon saith, "A fool believeth every thing," Prov. xiv. 15, that copper is gold, and a counter* an angel.† And assuredly, great reason there is that he which will not believe God should be given over to believe the devil, his dream, and his fancy.

Asun. I pray you instruct me better then.

Theol. You had need indeed to be better instructed: for the devil hath slily deluded your soul, and cast a mist before your eyes, making you believe the crow is white, and that your estate is good before God, whereas indeed it is most woful and miserable.

Asun. Nay, I defy the devil, with all my heart. But I pray you tell me how it cometh to pass that I am thus deceived.

Theol. This it is that deceiveth you, and many others, that you measure yourselves by yourselves, and by others, which is a false mete-wand. For you seem to lie straight so long as you are measured by yourselves, and by others; but lay the rule of God's word unto you, and then you lie altogether crooked.

Asun. What other thing is there that deceiveth me?

Theol. Another thing that deceiveth you, is your own heart; for you know not your own heart, but are altogether deceived therein, "For

---

* Counter, a small piece of false money.
† Angel, a gold coin worth ten shillings.

the heart is deceitful above all things," Jer. xvii. 9. He is a wise man, and greatly enlightened, that knoweth his own heart. But you are blind, and know not what is within you; but dimly imagine you shall be saved, and hope you know not what of eternal life. And because blindness maketh you bold, you will seem to be resolute in words, and say it is a pity he should live, which doth any whit doubt of his salvation. And assuredly you speak as you think, and as you know. For ought that you know to the contrary it seemeth so; though indeed, and in truth it is not so; for you are deluded with a false light. And sometimes, no doubt, you have pricks, gripes, terrors, and inward accusations of conscience, for all your bold and resolute speeches.

Asun. Truly I never heard so much before.

Theol. That is, because you shut your eyes, and stop your ears against God, and all goodness. You are "like the deaf adder, which heareth not the voice of the charmer, though he be most expert in charming," Psal. lviii. 45.

Asun. Well then, if it be so, I would be glad now to learn, if you would teach me. And as you have shewed me the means whereby the new birth is wrought, so now shew me the certain signs and tokens thereof, whereby all men may certainly know that they are sanctified, regenerate, and shall be saved?

Theol. There be eight infallible notes and tokens of a regenerate mind, which may well be termed the eight figures of salvation; and they are these:—

A love to the children of God—a delight in his word—often and fervent prayer—zeal of

God's glory — denial of ourselves — patient bearing of the cross, with profit and comfort— faithfulness in our calling—honest, just, and conscionable dealings in our actions amongst men. 1 John iii. 14, ii. 5; Psalm cxix; cxlv. 18; Rom. xii. 11; Rev. iii. 19; Matt. xvi. 24; Job i. 21; Eph. iv. 21. 32; Phil. iv. 8.

Phil. Now that you have shewed us the evident signs of man's salvation: shew us also the signs of condemnation.

Theol. The contraries unto these are manifest signs of damnation: no love to the children of God—no delight in his word—seldom and cold prayers — coldness in God's matters — trusting to our selves—impatience under the cross—unfaithfulness in our calling—dishonest and unconscionable dealing.

Phil. No doubt, if a man be infected with these, they may be shrewd signs that a man is extremely soul-sick and in a very dangerous case. But are there not yet more evident and apparent signs of condemnation than these?

Theol. Yes, verily. There be nine very clear and manifest signs of a man's condemnation.

Phil. I pray you let me hear what they be.

Theol. Pride, whoredom, covetousness, contempt of the gospel, swearing, lying, drunkenness, idleness, oppression.

Phil. These be gross things indeed.

Theol. They may not be unfitly termed the nine Beelzebubs of the world: and he that hath these signs upon him is in a most woful case.

Phil. What if a man be infected with some two or three of these?

Theol. Whoever is infected with three of them, is in great danger of losing his soul. For all these are deadly venom, and rank poison to the soul: and either the three first, or the three last, or the middle three, are enough to poison the soul, and sting it to death. Nay, to say the truth, a man had as good gripe a toad, and handle a snake, as meddle with any one of these.

Phil. Is every one of them so dangerous?

Theol. Questionless. For they be the very plague sores of the soul. If any man have a plague sore upon his body, we used to say God's tokens are upon him, Lord, have mercy upon him. So we may truly say, if any man be thoroughly and totally infected at the heart with any one of these, God's tokens are upon his soul, Lord, have mercy on him.

Phil. Many do not think these to be so dangerous matters as you make them, and many there be which make light of them.

Theol. True indeed: for the most part of men are altogether shut up in blindness, and hardness of heart, having neither sight nor feeling of their sins; and therefore make light of them, thinking there is no such danger.

Phil. It is most certain that men are given to lessen and extenuate their sins; or else, to hide them, and daub them over with many cunning shifts and vain excuses. For men are ever ready to take covert, and will writhe and wreath (like snakes) to hide their sins: yea, if it were possible, to make sin no sin, to make virtue vice, and vice virtue. Therefore I pray you lay open unto me, out of the scriptures, the grievousness and ugliness of their sins?

Theol. The stinking filthiness of these sins is so great and horrible that no tongue or pen of man is sufficient fully to manifest and lay open the same, according to the proper nature and being thereof: yet notwithstanding I will do my endeavour to lay them open in some measure, that all men may the more loathe them.

PRIDE.

Phil. I pray you then, first of all begin with pride.

Theol. You say well: for that indeed may well stand in the fore-front, since it is a master-devil, and the master-pock of the soul.

Phil. Shew me out of the scriptures that pride is so grievous and loathsome.

Theol. Solomon saith, "Every one that is proud in heart, is an abomination to the Lord," Prov. xvi. 5; which plainly sheweth that God doth detest and abhor proud men. And is it not a fearful thing, think you, to be abhorred of God? And in the same chapter, verse 18, he saith, "Pride goeth before destruction, and an high mind before the fall;" wherein he sheweth that pride is the forerunner of some deadly downfall, either by disgracing or displacing; for it is an old and true proverb, "pride will have a fall." And oftentimes when men are most lifted up, then are they nearest unto it: as the examples of Haman, Nebuchadnezzar, and Herod, do plainly declare. When the milt swelleth, the rest of the body pineth away: even so, when the heart is puft up with pride, the whole man is in danger of destruction. Moreover, the Holy Ghost saith, ·

"The Lord will destroy the house of the proud,"
Prov. xv. 25.   Job saith of such kind of men,
"The spark of his fire shall not shine; fear shall
dwell in his house, and brimstone shall be scattered upon his habitation," xviii. 5. 15.   And
in another place, he saith, "The fire which is not
blown shall devour him," xx. 26.   Methinketh,
therefore, if there were any spark of grace in us,
these terrible speeches of the Holy Ghost might
serve to humble us, and pull down our pride;
especially as the scriptures do affirm that God
resisteth the proud, and setteth himself, *ex pro-
fesso,** against them; and therefore woe unto
them: for if God take against a man, who can
reclaim him? for he doth whatsoever he will,"
Job xxiii. 13.

Phil. But tell me, I pray you, when you speak
against pride, what pride it is that you mean?

Theol. I mean all pride, both that which is inward in the heart, and that also which breaketh
out in men's foreheads: I mean that which apparently sheweth itself in men's words and works.

Phil. Do you mean also pride of men's
gifts?

Theol. Yes, surely; for there is no pride worse
or more dangerous than that.   Beware, saith one,
of spiritual pride, as to be proud of our learning,
wit, knowledge, reading, writings, sermons,
prayers, godliness, policy, valour, strength, riches,
honour, birth, beauty, authority; for God hath
not given such gifts unto men, to the end they
should make sale-ware of them, and set them a
sunshining, to behold, seeking only themselves
with their gifts, the vain praise of the multitude,

* Professedly, avowedly.

and applause of the people, so robbing God of his honour, and proudly arrogating to themselves that which is due unto God, which is the praise of his gifts; but he hath given his gifts to another end, namely, that we should use them to his glory, and the good of others (either in church or common-wealth) especially of those which do most concern us.

Phil. Yet we see commonly men of greatest gifts are most proud.

Theol. True indeed: for the finest cloth is soonest stained. And as worms engender sooner in soft and tender wood than in that which is more hard and knotty, and as moths do breed sooner in fine wool than in course flocks, even so pride and vain-glory do sooner assault an excellent and rare man in all kind of knowledge and virtue, than another of meaner gifts. And therefore pride is said to spring out of the ashes of all virtues: for men will be proud, because they are wise, learned, godly, patient, humble, &c. Pride, therefore, may very fitly be compared to the crab-stock speins, which grow out of the root of the very best apple-tree. Therefore to say the truth, this is one of the last engines and weapons which the devil useth for the overthrowing of God's own children; even to blow them up with pride as it were with gunpowder. For as we see it come to pass in the siege of strong-holds, when no battery or force of shot will prevail, the last remedy and policy is to undermine it, and blow it up with trains of gunpowder; so when Satan can no way prevail against some excellent servants of God, his last device is, to blow them up with pride, as it were with gunpowder.

Phil. I see it is a special grace of God for men

of great gifts to be humble-minded; and he is an old man of a thousand, which excelling in gifts doth excel in humility; and the more gifts he hath, the more humbly he walketh; not contemning others, but esteeming them better than himself: for commonly, we are the worse of God's gifts, because we have not the right use of them; and again, because they engender so much proud flesh in us, that we had need daily to be corized.* Therefore God sheweth great favour and mercy to that man whom he humbleth and taketh down by any afflictions or infirmities whatsoever; for otherwise, it is sure proud flesh would altogether overgrow us.

Theol. You have spoken the truth; for the apostle himself confesseth that he was tempted and troubled this way, (2 Cor. xii.) I had like to have been puffed up out of measure with the abundance of his revelations; but that God, in great mercy sent him a cooler, and a rebater; to wit, a prick in the flesh, (which he calleth the messenger of Satan) whereby the Lord cured him of his pride.   And even so doth he cure many of us of our pride, by throwing us to Satan, leaving us to ourselves, and giving us over to commit some gross evil, even to fall down and break our necks; and all to the end he may humble us, tame us, and pull down our pride, which he seeth we are heart-sick of.   It is good for us, therefore, to be humble in the abundance of graces, that we be not proud of that which we have, or that which we have done.   For humility in sin† is better than pride in well-doing.

---

* Cauterized.

† It is better to be humbled for our sins, than proud of well-doing,
2 Chron. xxxii. 31.

Phil. Herein surely appeareth the great wisdom and mercy of God, that he so graciously bringeth good out of evil, and turneth our afflictions, infirmities, falls and downfalls to his glory and our good.

Theol. It is most true. For even as of the flesh of a viper is made a sovereign medicine, to cure those which are stung of a viper;* and as physicians expel poison with poison; so God, according to his marvellous wisdom, doth, of the infirmities which remain in us after regeneration, cure other more dangerous diseases; as pride, vain-glory, and presumption. Oh, blessed therefore, be his name for ever, who thus mercifully causeth all things to work together for the good of his own people: of whom these things are specially to be understood!

Phil. Is there no cause why men of great gifts should glory in their gifts?

Theol. No, surely, none at all. For the apostle saith, "Who separateth thee? and what hast thou, that thou hast not received? If thou hast received it, why boasteth thou, as though thou hadst not received it?" 1 Cor. iv. 7. Where the apostle plainly sheweth, that no man is to be proud of his gifts, because they are none of his own; he hath but receive them to use. We count him worthy to be laughed at as a fool, who having borrowed brave apparel of others, (as a silk gown, a satin doublet, a chain of gold, velvet breeches, &c.) should proudly jet in the streets in them, as if they were his own; even so they are worthy to be chronicled for fools, which are proud of good gifts, which are none of

* Flesh of the viper, anciently reckoned a sovereign remedy for the viper's bite.

their own. Therefore the prophet Jeremiah saith, ix. 23, "Thus saith the Lord: let not the wise man glory in his wisdom, nor the strong man in his strength, neither the rich man in his riches; but let him that glorieth glory in this, that he understandeth, and knoweth me." To this point also, well saith the heathen poet, Theocritus, "No man can escape the punishment of pride, therefore, in greatest prosperity be not puffed up."

Phil. Yet it is a world to see how proud, surly, haughty, stately, insolent, and thrasonical some be, because of their gifts; they think they touch the clouds with their heads, and that the earth doth not bear them; they take themselves to be petty angels, or some wonderful wights.* They contemn and disdain all others which have not the like gifts. They do contemptuously overlook them, as a lion would overlook a mouse, a king a beggar; or, as we say in a proverb, "as the devil overlooked Lincoln."

Theol. Oh proud dust! Oh haughty worm's meat! If they would bring their hearts before God, and their consciences, thoughts, and affections to be judged by this law, it would soon cool them, and take them down well enough; they should see their wants and imperfections to be so great, that they indeed should have no more cause to boast of their gifts, than the black Moor hath of his whiteness, because his teeth are white. The Holy Ghost cuts all our combs, and pulleth down all pride of flesh, when he saith, "How small a thing doth man understand of God!"

Phil. I pray you, let us proceed to speak of

---

* Creatures, beings.

the outward and gross pride of the world: and first of all, tell me what you think of pride in apparel.

Theol. I think it to be a vanity of all vanities, and a folly of all follies; for to be proud of apparel, is, as if a thief should be proud of his halter, a beggar of his clouts, a child of his gay toys, or a fool of his bauble.

Phil. Yet we see how proud many (especially women) be of such baubles. For when they have spent a good part of the day in tricking and trimming, pricking and pinning, pranking* and pouncing,† girding and lacing, and braving up themselves in most exquisite manner, then out they come into the streets, with their pedlar's shop upon their back, and carry their crests very high, taking themselves to be little angels. or at least somewhat more than other women. Whereupon they do so exceedingly swell with pride, that it is to be feared they will burst with it, as they walk in the streets. And truly we may think the very stones in the street, and the beams in the houses do quake, and wonder at their monstrous, intolerable, and excessive pride. For it seemeth that they are altogether a lump of pride, a mass of pride, even altogether made of pride, and nothing else but pride, pride.

Theol. You seem to be very hot in the matter.

Asun. Marry, sir, I like him the better: for the world was never so full of pride as it is now-a-days.

Theol. Alas! alas! indeed, who can hold his peace at the pride of this age! What a thing is it, that flesh and blood, worms' meat. dust and ashes, dirt and dung, should so brave it out with

---

* Dressing up smartly.   † Cutting in and out in jags or scollops

D

their trim clouts, and that in the sight of God, angels and men! For the time will come, when both they, and all their gay clouts shall be buried in a grave: yea, as Job saith, xvii. 13, 14, "The grave shall be their house, and they shall make their bed in the dark. And then shall they say to corruption, thou art my father; and to the worm, thou art my mother and my sister." What then shall it avail them thus to have ruffled it out in all their bravery, when as suddenly they shall go down to destruction? What did it profit the rich man to be sumptuously clothed, and fare deliciously every day, when his body was buried in the dust and his soul in hell fire?

Asun. I pray you, sir, what say you to these great ruffs, which are borne up with supporters and rebatoes,* as it were with post and rail?

Theol. What should I say? but God be merciful unto us. For such things do draw down the wrath and vengeance of God upon us all: and as the apostle saith, Col. iii. 6, "For such things' sake, the wrath of God cometh upon the children of disobedience." And truly, truly, we may well fear that God will plague us for our abominable pride.

Asun. What say you then to these doubled and redoubled ruffs which are now in common use, strouting fardingales,† long locks, fore tufts, shag hair, and all these new fashions which are devised and taken up every day?

Theol. I say, they are far from that plainness, simplicity, and modesty which hath been in former ages: our forefathers knew no such things. It is recorded of William Rufus, some-

---

* Head dresses.   † Hoops.

time king of this land, that when his chamberlain on a time brought him a new pair of hose, he demanded of him what they cost: who answered, three shillings. Whereat the king, being somewhat moved, commanded him to prepare him a pair of a mark. If kings were then thought to exceed that bestowed more than a mark upon a pair of hose, what is to be thought of many mean men in these our days (yea, such as have nô living, and are scarce of any good calling) which bestow as much upon one pair as the king did upon two, when he was thought most of all to exceed? But, alas! alas! we have passed all bounds of modesty and measure: there is no hoe* with us. Our land is too heavy of this sin. For the pride of all nations, and the follies of all countries are upon us: how shall we bear them? And as for these new fashions, the more new they be the more foolish and ridiculous are they: for with our new fashions we are growing clean out of fashion. If we had as many fashions of our bodies as we have of our attire, we should have as many fashions as fingers and toes. But vain men and women do apparently shew their vain minds by following so greedily such vain toys and fashions.

Asun. It was never good world since starching and steeling, busks and whalebones, supporters and rebatoes, full moons and hobby-horses, painting and dying, with selling of favour and complexion, came to be in use; for since these came in covetousness, oppression, and deceit have increased. For how else should pride be maintained? And sure it is, within these thirty years

* First measure.

these things were not known, nor heard of. And what say you then to painting of faces, laying open of naked breasts, dying of hair, wearing of perriwigs, and other hair coronets and top-gallants? And what say you to our artificial women, which will be better than God hath made them? They like not his handy-work: they will mend it, and have other complexion, other faces, other hair, other bones, other breasts, and other bellies than God made them.

Theol. This I say, that you and I, and all the Lord's people, have great and just cause of mourning, weeping, and lamentation, because such abomination is committed in Israel, *P*salm cxix. 119. David's eyes gushed out with rivers of tears because men kept not God's laws; and an horrible fear came upon him because men forsook the law of God. Jeremiah (ix. 1) did sigh in secret, wishing that his head were full of water, and his eyes a fountain of tears, because of the sins of the people. Nehemiah mourned for the transgression of God's people. Lot's just soul was vexed with the unclean conversation of the Sodomites; and shall we mourn nothing at all for these things? shall we be no whit grieved for the pride of our land? shall we shed no tears for such horrible and intolerable abomination? They are odious in the sight of God and men: the air stinketh of them. It is God's marvellous patience that the devil doth not carry them away quick, and rid the earth of them; or that fire and brimstone doth not come down from heaven and consume them.

Antil. You are too hot in these matters of attire: you make more of them than there is cause.

Asun. I con* him thanks. God's blessing on his heart: I shall love him the better while I know him, because he is so earnest against such shameful and detestable pride. Is it not a shame that women, professing true religion, should make themselves such pictures, puppets, and peacocks, as they do? and yet I hear few preachers in the pulpit speak against it.

Antil. I marvel you should be so earnest in matters of apparel. You know well enough that apparel is an indifferent thing; and that religion and the kingdom of God do not consist in these things.

Theol. I know right well that apparel in its own nature is a thing indifferent; but lewd, wanton, immodest, and offensive apparel is not indifferent; for all such abuse taketh away the indifferency of them, and maketh them sinful and evil by circumstance; for, otherwise, why should the Lord threaten by his prophet that he would visit the princes, and the king's children, and all such as were clothed with strange apparel, that is the fashions of other countries, Zeph. i. 8. Again; why should the Lord so plague the proud dames and mincing minions of Jerusalem for their pride and vanity in attire, if there were no evil in such kind of abuse? The Lord saith thus, in the third of Isaiah, against those brave and gallant dames, " Because the daughters of Zion are haughty, and walk with stretched-out necks, and with wandering eyes, walking and mincing as they go, and make a tinkling with their feet: therefore shall the Lord make the heads of the daughters of Zion bald, and the Lord shall discover their secret parts. In that day shall the Lord take away the ornament of the slippers, and the calls, and the round tires, the sweet balls, and the bracelets, and the bonnets, the tiers of the head, and the stops, the head-bands, and the tablets, the ear-rings, the rings, and the mufflers, the costly apparel, and the veils, and the wimples, and the crisping pins, and the glasses, and the fine linen, and the hoods, and the lawns. And instead of sweet savour, there shall be stink; and instead of a girdle, a rent; and instead of dressing of the hair, baldness; and instead of a stomacher, a girding of sackcloth, and burning instead of beauty. Then shall her gates mourn and lament: and she, being desolate, shall sit upon the ground." Thus we see how terribly the Lord threateneth the gallant dames of Jerusalem for their excessive and abominable pride. And this may well be a mirror for the proud minions of our age, which assuredly may well fear the Lord will bring some such judgment upon them as he did upon the daughters of Jerusalem: for their sin is as great in this kind as was the daughters' of Zion; and God is the same God now that he was then to punish it.

Antil. Tush: never speak so much of these matters of apparel; for we must do as others do, and follow the fashion, or else we shall not be esteemed.

Theol. If you follow them not you shall be more esteemed of God, of his angels, saints, and all good men. As for all others, if you esteem them more than these you shew what you are.

Antil. Well, for all that, say you what you will, pride is in the heart, and not in the apparel; for one may be proud of plain apparel, as well as of costly; and some are as proud of their falling bands, and little sets, as others are of their great ruffs.

Theol. You speak foolishly. For how know you that you can judge men's hearts and inward affections? Can you say, when men's and women's apparel is sober, modest, and Christianlike, that they have proud hearts, and are proud of that attire? You go very far, indeed, to judge the heart. You ought to judge charitably of such as go soberly and modestly attired; even that their heart is according to their attire. As for you, we may rather think your heart is vain, light, and foolish; because your attire doth strongly argue it; and as the prophet saith, "The shew of your countenance testifieth against you; you declare your sins as Sodom, and hide them not," Isa. iii. 9.

Antil. I pray you then set down some rules for apparel out of the scriptures.

Theol. I may well set down what I will; but surely most men and women will do what they list. For verily it may be thought that many of this age have forsworn God, and his word, and all goodness; for they are come to this point, let God say what he will, they will do what they list. For as the prophet saith, "They have made a covenant with hell, and with death, and are grown to an agreement," Isa. xxviii. 15. And I do verily think, if God himself should come down from heaven in his own person, and dissuade men and women from this vanity of apparel yet would they still use it, as it were in despite of God and as it were to anger him the more. For they are so extraordinarily enamoured, and so immoderately delighted with it, and do so continually, and altogether dote on it, and are so wood mad* of it, that they will have it, though men and angels, and all the world say nay; nay, which is more, though they should go to the devil quick with it. And therefore it is but lost labour to speak against it, preach against it, or write against it. It is but even to plough the sea, or knock at a deaf man's door; for there is no hope of any reformation. Only this we gain, that the world is reproved and convicted of sin; and these things shall stand in record against them in the last day: so that they may say, they had a fair warning, and that there was a prophet amongst them.

Phil. Yet for all this, I pray you set us down some directions and rules, out of God's holy book, concerning attire. For albeit some be very bad and outrageous in these things, yet there be some others which are well-disposed, and will (no doubt) make some conscience to frame themselves according to the rules of God's word.

Theol. Well, then, for their sakes which are well-disposed, I will set down some few directions. St. *P*aul, in 1 Tim. ii. 9, willeth that "women should array themselves in comely apparel, with shamefacedness and modesty, as becometh women that profess the fear of God: and not with braided hair, or gold or pearls, or costly apparel." The apostle Peter giveth like rules also: for he saith, 1 Pet. iii. 3–6, speaking of Christian matrons, and professors of holy religion, that their apparel must not be outward, that is, not consist so much in outward bravery, (as braided hair, gold put about, &c.) as it must be inward, that the hidden man of the heart may be clothed with a meek and

---

* Furiously mad.

quiet spirit, which is a thing before God much set by. "For after this manner," saith he, "in times past, the holy women, which trusted in God, did attire themselves:" as Sarah, Rebecca, Rachel, and such like ancient and grave matrons.

Phil. Wherein doth this inward clothing specially consist?

Theol. In four things, which are set down in the forenamed places: to wit, shamefacedness, modesty, a quiet spirit, and a meek spirit.

Phil. These be fine suits of apparel, indeed. I would all women would put them on, and never put them off, but wear them continually. For they are the better for wearing, though all other apparel be the worse.

Theol. If women would deck themselves inwardly with these aforesaid virtues, they would be unto them as ornaments of gold, and jewels of pearl. "For the women that feareth the Lord shall be praised," Prov. xxxi. 30.

Phil. But now I pray you, sir, set down your judgment for outward attire.

Theol. This is all that I can say, touching the point, that it must be as the apostle saith: comely, decent, handsome, neat and seemly: not light, not wanton, not lascivious, not immodest, not offensive.

Phil. But who shall judge what is comely, sober, handsome, modest, &c.? For every man and women will say, their apparel is but decent and cleanly, how gallant, brave, and flaunting soever they be.

Theol. Herein the examples of the most godly, wise, grave, and modest men and women are to be followed: for who can better judge what is comely, sober, and modest, than they?

Phil. But we see some, even of the better sort, in this matter are a little infected, run out, and go beyond their bounds.

Theol. The more is the pity. But alas! we see the sway of the time, and the rage of the stream is so violent, that it carrieth before it whatsoever is not settled, and very deep-rooted. And some godly and well-disposed persons, whose hearts are not with these things, but with God, are, notwithstanding, perforce, carried away with the violence of the wind and tide; whose case, though it cannot be well defended, or excused, yet it is much to be pitied and lamented.

Phil. Have you any further directions touching this point.

Theol. There is one thing yet more to be added, to wit, that attire be according to men's places, callings, and degrees. For that is not seemly for one that is seemly for another: that becomes not one man's place that becometh another's: for that is not meet for poor men which is meet for rich men: nor that meet for mean men which is meet for men of note and great place.

Phil. Then you think it lawful for kings, princes, and great personages, to wear pearl, gold, silver, velvet, &c. ?

Theol. Questionless; it is lawful for such in sober manner and measure, to wear the most costly and precious things which the earth can afford: and that, to set out the magnificence, pomp and glory of their places. And therefore such things are in them most comely and decent.

Phil. But now-a-days few will keep within compass, few will know their places: but the most part run beyond their bounds, and leap quite out of their sockets.

Theol. True indeed, for now-a-days, mean gentlewomen, yea, some gentlewomen of their own making, will ruffle it, and brave it out in their attire, like countesses and ladies of honour. Plain folks also, in the country, will flaunt it like courtiers, and like good gentlemen and gentlewomen: and they seem to say in their hearts, fie of this plainness, we will no more of it, we will not take it as we have done. So that now the old proverb is verified "every Jack will be a gentleman, and Joan is as good as my lady." For now we cannot, by their apparel, discern the maid from the mistress; nor the waiting gentlewoman from her lady. And thus we see, in this matter of apparel, how all is out of joint.

Phil. Is there any more ·to be said in this case?

Theol. There is yet another thing to be respected in this matter of attire.

Phil. What is that?

Theol. That it be according to men's abilities. For it is lamentable to consider, how poor men and women, poor hired servants, milk-maids, and such like, go quite beyond their abilities. And more lamentable, to see what wretched and ill-favoured shifts they make to compass these things, so sharp and so eagerly are they set upon them.

Phil. Well sir, now you have sufficiently rolled the stone, and at large satisfied us touching the matter of pride, which is the first sign of condemnation; now proceed to the second, which is whoredom, and unfold unto us out of the scriptures the dangers thereof.

Theol. Solomon in his *Proverbs,* xxii. 14, saith, "That the mouth of a strange woman, or an harlot, is as a deep pit: he, that is a detestation to the Lord, shall fall therein;" wherein he plainly sheweth, that those whom God detesteth, and is exceeding angry with, are given over to this vice. And, in another place, xxiii. 27, he saith, "A whore is as a deep ditch, and as a narrow pit;" noting thereby, that if a man be once fallen in with an harlot, he shall as hardly get out again, as a man that is plunged into a very deep and narrow pit, where he can scarce stir himself. The same Solomon, in the book of Ecclesiastes, vii. 26, yieldeth us the reason hereof; namely, because she is as nets, snares, and bands; wherein if a man be once taken he is fast enough for getting out. " I find," saith he, " more bitter than death, the woman, whose heart is as nets and snares, and her hands as bands. He that is good before God shall be delivered from her; but the sinner shall be taken by her." We do therefore plainly see, in what a labyrinth and a dangerous case they be, that are left of God, and given over to whoredom and harlots. And therefore it is said, Prov. vi. 25, 26, " Desire not her beauty in thine heart; neither let her eyelids catch thee. For, by a whorish woman a man is brought to a morsel of bread: and the adulteress hunteth for life, which is precious." Again he saith, v. 3, 4, "Albeit the lips of an harlot drop as an honeycomb, and the roof of her mouth is softer than oil; yet her latter end is bitter as wormwood, and as sharp as a two-edged sword." All these prudent speeches of the Holy Ghost do most evidently shew unto us, what a fearful thing it is to commit whoredom, and so to fall into the hands of whores and harlots. Therefore Job saith of the wicked, xxxvi. 14, " Their soul dieth in youth, and their life among the whoremongers."

Phil. You have very well shewed, out of God's book, the great danger of whoredom and adultery; and it is greatly to be lamented that men in this age make so light of it as they do, and that it is so common a vice: nay, that some (alas, with grief I speak it) do profess it, live by it, and prostitute themselves wholly unto it.

Theol. Such men and women may justly fear the plaguing hand of God: for the Lord saith, by his prophet, " Though I fed them to the full, yet they committed adultery, and assembled themselves by companies in harlots' houses. They rose up in the morning like fed horses; every man neigheth after his neighbour's wife. Shall I not visit for these things? (saith the Lord) Shall not my soul be avenged on such a nation as this?" Jer. v. 7–9.

Phil. Methinketh, if men were not altogether hardened in this sin, and even past feeling, and past grace, this threatening and thundering of God himself from heaven should terrify them.

Theol. A man would think so indeed: but now we may take up the old complaint of the prophet, Jer. viii. 6, "I hearkened and heard, and lo, no man spake aright: no man repented of his evil, saying, What have I done? Every one turned to their race, as the horse rusheth into the battle."

Antil. Tush, whoredom is but a trick of youth; and we see all men have their imperfections.

Theol. You speak profanely and wickedly; for, shall we count that but a trick of youth for the which the Lord smote three and twenty thousand of his own people in one day? 1 Cor. x. 8. Shall we count that but a trick of youth for the which the Lord threatened David, his own servant, that the sword should never depart from his house? 2 Sam. xii. 10. Shall we count that but a trick of youth, for the which Hamor and Shechem, Gen. xxxiv. 25, the father and the son, and many other, both men, women, and children, were cruelly murdered by Simeon and Levi, the sons of Jacob? Shall we count that but a trick of youth, for which the Lord slew Hophni and Phineas, the two sons of Eli the priest, in the battle of the Philistines? 1 Sam. ii. 22, iv. 11. Shall we thus set all at six and seven, and make light of such horrible villanies? Doth not the severity of the punishment shew the greatness of the sin? Doth not the apostle say, "These things came upon them for our examples, upon whom the ends of the world are come," 1 Cor. x. 11, and yet you pass it over with a tush, and a trick of youth, as if God were to be dallied with? No, no, "be not deceived; God is not mocked" They which will not be moved now in hearing, shall one day be crushed in pieces in feeling. And they which now call whoredom, a trick of youth, shall one day howl and cry, yell and yelp, for such tricks, with woe and alas that ever they were born.

Antil. Oh! Sir, you must bear with youth: youth you know is frail; and youth will be youthful, when you have said all that you can.

Theol. Yes, but God doth allow no more liberty unto youth, than unto age; but bindeth all, upon pain of death, to the obedience of his commandments. The apostle saith, " Let the young men be sober minded," Tit. ii. 6. David saith, " Wherewith shall a young man cleanse his way? In taking heed thereto according to thy word," Ps. cxix. 9. The wise man saith, " Remember thy Creator in the days of thy youth, Eccl. xii. 1. And further addeth, that if they will needs follow their lusts, their pleasures, and their own swing, yet in the end he will bring them to judgment, arraign them, condemn them, and tame them in hell-fire well enough.

Phil. Yet we see, men are so violently carried after their lust, and so desperately bent, that they will have the present sweet and pleasure of sin, come of it what will. Come sickness, come death, come hell, come damnation, they are at a point: they will pay the highest price for their lusts. They will purchase their pleasures with the loss of their souls. Oh, woful purchase! Oh, damnable pleasures!

Theol. Sweet meat will have sour sauce, and a dram of pleasure a pound of sorrow. Such cursed catiffs* shall at last pay a dear shot for their pleasures. Such desperate wretches shall one day know (to their everlasting woe) what it is to pro-

---

* Mean villains.

voke God, and to sin with so high an hand against
him.   They shall well know, in spite of their
hearts, that vengeance is prepared for the wicked,
and that there is a God that judgeth the earth.
Let all men therefore take heed in time, "For
whoremongers and adulterers God will judge,"
Heb. xiii. 4.   And the apostle saith flatly, "That
whoremongers and adulterers shall not inherit
the kingdom of God," 1 Cor. vi. 9.   "Let therefore no fornicator, or unclean person, be found
amongst us, as was Esau," Heb. xii. 16.   "But
let us abstain from fleshly lusts, which fight
against the soul," 1 Pet. ii. 11.   "And let every
one know how to possess his vessel in holiness
and honour, and not in the lust of concupiscence,
as the Gentiles, which know not God," 1 Thess.
iv. 5.   Herein let us consider the wise speech of
an ancient father (Chrysostom), "Sin, while it is
in doing, ministereth some pleasure; but when it
is committed, the short pleasure thereof vanisheth
away, and long sorrow cometh instead of it."
Neither let us here reject the saying of a wise
heathen, "Shun pleasure, for fear of smart."
Sour things follow sweet, and joy heaviness.

Antil. Yet for all this, you shall not make me
believe, that whoredom is so heinous a matter.
You make more of it than it is.

Theol. True indeed.   For you, and such as
you are, will believe nothing against your lusts,
and fleshly delights: and that is the cause why
you are deaf on this ear.   I will therefore add a
word or two more (out of the oracles of God) to
that which hath been spoken.   The wise king
saith, "He that committeth adultery with women, destroyeth his own soul," *Prov.* vi. 32,
and so is accessory to his own death, which is no

small matter. For we used to say, if a man hung himself, drown himself, or any manner of way make away with himself, that he was cursed of God, that God's hand was heavy against him, that the devil owed him a shame, and now he hath paid it him. And all the country rings of such a strange accident, when, and where it falleth out: and the crowner* of the country doth sit upon it.† How much more may all the world wonder at this, that a man should destroy his own soul, and wittingly and willingly cast away himself for ever! Now the Holy Ghost saith, the adulterer doth such an act, giveth such a venture, and willingly murdereth himself. Oh, therefore woe unto him, that ever he was born! For sure it is that great crowner of heaven, that crowns whom he will crown, shall one day sit upon it, and give judgment. Moreover, as the adulterer sinneth against his soul, so also he sinneth against his body after a special manner, as witnesseth the apostle, 1 Cor. vi. 18. Also, he sinneth against his goods and outward estate, as the holy man Job testifieth, saying, "Adultery is a fire, that devoureth to destruction, and it will root out all our increase," Job xxxi. 12. Furthermore, he sinneth against his name, "For the adulterer shall find a wound and dishonour: and his reproach shall never be put away," Prov. vi. 33.—Item, he sinneth against his wife; who is his companion and the wife of his covenant. And God saith, in the same place, "Let none trespass against the wife of his youth; keep yourselves in your spirit, and transgress not." Last of all, he sinneth

---

* Coroner.
† It appears that suicides were rare occurrences in those days. How lamentably frequent are they in these last days!

against his children and posterity: as the Lord said to David, "Because thou hast despised me, and done this, therefore the sword shall never depart from thy house. Behold I will raise up evil against thee, out of thine own house," 2 Sam. xii. 10. Now therefore, to conclude this point, we may see how many deadly wounds men make in themselves, by committing of adultery. They wound themselves in their souls—they wound themselves in their bodies—they wound themselves in their goods—they wound themselves in their names—they wound themselves in their wives and in their children. What man, except he were stark mad, would thrust himself, in so many places, at once? The adulterer, with his own sin of adultery, maketh all these deadly wounds in himself; and it is a hundred to one he will never get them cured, but will die, and bleed to death of them. Lo, thus you see the dangerous quality and condition of this sin. Shall we now therefore make light of it? Shall we say it is but a trick of youth? Shall we smooth over the matter with sweet words, when the Holy Ghost makes it so heinous and capital? Shall we make nothing of that which draweth down God's wrath upon the soul, body, goods, name, wife, and children? That were an intolerable blindness, and most extreme hardness of heart. An ancient writer hath long ago passed sentence upon us, who make so light of this sin: for, saith he, "Adultery is the very book of the devil; whereby he draweth us to destruction." And another godly father saith: that "Adultery is like a furnace, whose mouth is gluttony, the flame pride, the sparks filthy words, the smoke an evil name, the ashes poverty, and the end shame." And so we

plainly see, that howsoever we regard not this sin,
but flatter ourselves in it, yet those, whose eyes
the Lord hath opened, have in all ages condemned
it as most flagitious and horrible: yea, the very
heathen will rise up in judgment against us, who
have spoken and written many things against this
filthy and beastly vice.

Phil. Now indeed you have sufficiently branded
the vice of adultery, and laid out the ugliness
thereof, that all men may behold it stark naked
and abhor it. If any man, notwithstanding all
this, will venture upon it, he may be said to be a
most desperate monster. For what doth he else,
but, as it were, put his finger into the lion's
mouth, and, as it were, take the bear by the
tooth? and they may well know what will follow,
and what they may look for. Let all men therefore in time take heed to themselves, and to their
own souls, as they will answer it at their uttermost peril, at the dreadful day of judgment, when
the secrets of all hearts shall be disclosed. But
now one thing resteth; to wit, that you should
shew us the special roots and causes of adultery.

Theol. There be five special causes of it. The
first is our natural corruption: for the very spawn
and seed of all sin is in our corrupt nature; and
this, of all others, is a most inherent sin, as witnesseth the apostle James, saying, "When lust
hath conceived, it bringeth forth sin; and sin,
when it is perfected, bringeth forth death," i. 15.
—The second is gluttony and fulness of bread: for
when men have filled their bellies, and crammed
their paunches, as full of good cheer, wine, and
strong drink, as their skins can hold, what are
they meet for, or what mind they else, but adultery and uncleanness? And therefore well saith

one, "Great nourishment, and gross food, it is the shop of lust." The heathen poet could skill to say, "*Sine Cicere et Baccho friget Venus*," without meat and drink, lust waxeth cold; and to this effect the wise king saith, "That their eyes shall behold strange women, whose hearts are set upon wine or belly cheer," Prov. xxiii. 3, 33; and therefore he adviseth all men, not to look upon the wine when it appeareth red, when it sheweth his colour in the cup, or stirreth very kindly; and that for fear of this after-clap. An ancient writer saith to the same purpose, "He that delicately pampereth his belly, and yet would overcome the spirit of fornication, is like him that will quench a flame of fire with oil." Therefore to close up this point, sure it is though men pray much, hear and read much, and be otherwise well-disposed; yet except they be abstemious in diet, they will be much troubled with lust.—The third cause of adultery is idleness; for when men are lazy, lurkish, and idle, having nothing to do, they lie wide open to adultery, and lust creepeth into them. Some historiographers write, the crab fish is very desirous to eat oysters; but because she cannot by force open them, she watcheth her time when they open themselves unto the sun after the tide, and then she putteth in her claw, and pulleth out the oyster. Even so Satan watcheth his opportunity against us, that he may infect and breathe into us all filthy lusts, and adulterous desires, when we lie open unto him by idleness. Wisely therefore, to this point, said the Greek poet, "Much rest nourisheth lust;" and another poet saith, "*Quæritur ægistus quare sit factus adulter? In promtu causa est: desidiosus erat*," Slothful laziness is the cause of adultery; and therefore another saith, "Eschew idleness, and cut the sinews of lust."—The fourth cause of adultery, is wanton apparel; which is a minstrelsy, that pipes up a dance into whoredom. But of this enough before.—The fifth and last of adultery, is the hope of impunity, or escaping of punishment. For many being blinded and hardened by Satan, think they shall never be called to an account for it, and because they can blear the eyes of men, and carry this sin so closely under a cloud, that it shall never come to light, they think all is safe, and that God seeth them not; and therefore Job saith, Job xxiv. 15, "The eye of the adulterer waiteth for the twilight, and saith, no eye shall see me;" and in another place, Job xxii. 13, "How shall God know? can he judge through the dark clouds?" But verily, verily, though the adulterer do never so closely and cunningly convey his sin under a canopy, yet the time will come when it shall be disclosed, to his eternal shame. "For God will bring every work to judgment, with every secret thought, whither it be good or evil," Eccles. xii. 14. For he hath set our most secret sins in the light of his countenance," Psalm xc. 8. "And he will lighten the things that are hid in darkness, and make the counsels of the heart manifest," 1 Cor. iv. 5. For this cause Job saith, Job x. 14, "When I sin thou watchest me, and wilt not purge me from my sin."

Phil. Now you have shewed us the causes of adultery, I pray you shew us the remedies.

Theol. There be six remedies for adultery; which no doubt will greatly prevail, if they be well practised.

Phil. Which be they?

Theol. Labour, abstinence, temperance, prayer, restraint of senses, shunning of women's company, and all occasions whatsoever.

COVETOUSNESS.

Phil. Well, sir, now you have waded deep enough in the second sign of damnation: I pray you let us proceed to the third, which is covetousness. And, as you have laid naked the two former, so I pray you, strip this stark naked also, that all men may see what an ugly monster it is, and therefore hate it and abhor it.

Theol. I would willingly satisfy your mind; but on this point I shall never do it sufficiently. For no heart can conceive, or tongue sufficiently utter the loathsomeness of this vice. For covetousness is the foulest fiend, and blackest devil of all the rest. It is even great Beelzebub himself. Therefore I shall never be able fully to describe it unto you; but yet I will do what I can to strip it, and whip it stark naked. And howsoever that men of this earth, and blind worldlings, take it, to be most sweet, beautiful, and amiable, and therefore do embrace it, entertain it, and welcome it, as though there were some happiness in it; yet I hope, when I have shewed them the face thereof in a glass (even the true glass of God's word) they will be no more in such love, but quite out of conceit with it. I will therefore hold out this glass to them. Paul to Timothy brandeth this sin in the forehead, and boreth it in the ear, that all men may know it, and avoid it, when he saith, "Covetousness is the root of all evil," 1 Tim. vi. 10. Our Lord Jesus also giveth us a watch-word to take heed of it, saying, "Take heed and beware of covetousness," Luke xii. 15; as if he should say, touch it not, come not near it, it is the very breath of the devil: it is present death, and the very ratsbane of the soul. The apostle layeth out the great danger of this sin, and doth exceedingly grime the face of it, when he saith, "That the end of all such as mind earthly things, is damnation," Phil. iii. 19. Let all carnal world-lings, and muckish-minded men lay this to heart, and consider well of it, lest they say one day, had I wist.*

Phil. Good, sir, lay open to us the true nature of covetousness, and what it is, that we may more perfectly discern it.

Theol. Covetousness is an immoderate desire of having.

Phil. I hope you do not think frugality, thrif-tiness, and good husbandry to be covetousness.

Theol. Nothing less;† for they be things com-manded; being done in the fear of God, and with a good conscience.

Phil. Do you not think it lawful also for men to do their worldly business, and to use faithful-ness and diligence in their callings, that they may provide for themselves and their families?

Theol. Yes, no doubt. And the rather, if they do these things with calling on God for a bless-ing upon the works of their hands; and use prayer and thanksgiving before and after their labour, taking heed all the day long of the common cor-

* O had I known the consequences.   † Certainly not

ruptions of the world, as swearing, cursing, lying, dissembling, deceiving, greedy getting, &c.

Phil. Wherein I pray you doth covetousness especially consist?

Theol. In the greedy desire of the mind. For we may lawfully do the works of our calling, and play the good husbands and good housewives; but we must take heed that distrustfulness, and inward greediness of the world do not catch our heart: for then are we set on fire, and utterly undone.

Phil. Since covetouness is especially of the heart, how may we know certainly when the heart is infected?

Theol. There be four special signs of the heart's infection.

Phil. Which be they?

Theol. The first is an eager and sharp set desire of getting. Therefore the Holy Ghost saith, "He that hasteth to be rich, shall not be unpunished," Prov. xxviii. 20, 22. And again, "An heritage is hastily gotten at the beginning; but the end thereof shall not be blessed," Prov. xx. 21. The heathen man also saith, "No man can be both justly and hastily rich."—The second is a pinching and niggardly keeping of our own, that is, when men, being able to give, will hardly part with any thing, though it be to never so holy and good use. And when at last with much ado, for shame they give something, it cometh heavily from them, God wot,* and scantily.—The third is, the neglect of holy duties: that is, when men's minds are so taken up with the love of earthly things, that they begin

---

* God knoweth.

to slack and cool in matters of God's worship.—The fourth and last is, a trusting in riches, and staying upon them, as though our lives were maintained by them, or did consist only in them; which thing our Lord Jesus flatly denies, saying, "Though a man have abundance, yet his life consisteth not in the things that he hath," Luke xii. 15.—These then are four evident signs and tokens, whereby we may certainly discern that men's hearts and entrails are infected with covetousness.

Phil. You have very well satisfied us in this point. Now let us understand the original causes of covetousness.

Theol. There be two special causes of covetousness. The one is the ignorance and distrust of God's providence; the other is the want of tasting and feeling of heavenly things: for till men taste better things they will make much of these, till they feel heaven they will love earth, till they be religious they will be covetous. Therefore the cause is soon espied why men are so sharp set upon these outward things, and, do so admire riches, worldly pomp, pleasures, and treasures; because they know no better, they never had taste of feeling of those things which are eternal.

Phil. Now as you have shewed us the causes of covetousness, so let us also hear of the effects.

Theol. If I once enter into this, I shall be entangled and wound up in a maze, where I know not how to get out again. For the evil effects of this vice are so many, and so great, that I know not almost where to begin, or where to end. Notwithstanding, I will enter into it, get out how I can.

Phil. If you do but give us some taste of them it shall suffice.

Theol. Then will I briefly dispatch things in order. And first of all, I reason from the words of the apostle before alleged, that if covetousness, and the love of money, be the root of all evil, then it is the root of idolatry, the root of murder, the root of theft, the root of lying, the root of swearing, the root of simony, the root of bribery, the root of usury, the root of lawing, the root of all contentions in the church, and the root of all brabbling and brawling in the commonwealth. Moreover, it spreadeth far and near; it dwelleth in every house, in every town, in every city; it pryeth into every corner, it creepeth into every heart, it annoyeth our physicians, it infecteth our divines, it choketh our lawyers, it woundeth our farmers, it baneth our gentlemen, it murdereth our tradesmen, it bewitcheth our merchants, it stingeth our mariners. Oh! covetousness, covetousness! it is the poison of all things, the wound of Christianity, the bane of all goodness! For covetousness mars all; it marreth all, everywhere, in all places, in all degrees, amongst all persons. It marreth marriages; for it coupleth young to old, and old to young. It marreth hospitality, it marreth all good housekeeping, it marreth alms-deeds, it marreth religion, it marreth professors, it marreth ministers, it marreth magistrates, it marreth all things. And therefore what sin so grievous, what evil so odious, what vice so enormous as this? For this cause it was prettily said of one, that all other vices are but factors to covetousness, and serve for porters to fetch and bring in her living. She maketh simony her drudge, bribery her drudge, usury her drudge, deceit her drudge, swearing her drudge, lying her drudge.. Oh! what a devil incarnate is this, that setteth so many vices at work, and hath so many factors and underlings to serve her turn! Are they not in a pretty case, think you, that are infected with this sin? Oh! they are in a most miserable case. It had been good they had never been born. For being alive they are dead, dead I mean in their souls; for covetousness is soul's poison, and soul's bane. Covetousness is the strongest poison to the soul that is. It is a confection of all the spiders, toads, snakes, adders, scorpions, basilisks, and all other the most venomous vermin of the whole world. If the devil can get us to take down but one pennyweight of it, it is enough, he desires no more; for presently we fall down stark dead. Therefore the apostle saith, "They that will be rich (he meaneth in all haste, by hook or by crook) fall into temptations and snares, and into many foolish and noisome lusts, which drown men in destruction and perdition," 1 Tim. vi. 9. For as covetousness is rank poison to the soul, so the apostle compareth it to the deep gulf, wherein thousands are drowned; and therefore he addeth, in the same place, v. 11, "But thou, O man of God,. flee these things;" in which words he doth most gravely advise all the ministers of the word of God to take heed of it. For as it is dangerous to all men, so it is most dangerous and offensive in the preachers of the gospel.

Phil. Indeed it must needs be granted that covetousness is a very grievous sin; yea even a monster with seven heads. Yet for all that, we see in this our iron age, how many of all sorts are infected with it; and how few will give any thing to any holy use. Most men now-a-days have nothing to spare for Christ, nothing for his gospel, nothing for his church, nothing for the poor children of God, and needy members of Christ. Christ is a little beholden unto them, for they will do nothing for him, no not so much as speak a good word in his cause, or the cause of his poor saints. Every little thing with them is too much for God, and good men. For when they come to giving unto holy and necessary uses then they will stick at a penny, and scotch at a groat, and every thing is too much. But to bestow upon themselves, nothing is too much. Nothing is too much for lust, for pleasure, for back, belly, and building; for cards and dice, for whores and harlots, for rioting and revelling, for taverns and brothel-houses; hundreds and thousands are little enough, and too little for their expenses this way. It is lamentable to consider, what masses of money are spent and bestowed upon these things. But, alas, alas! how heavy an account are they to make in the day of the Lord, which so spend their lands, livings, and revenues! I quake to think what shall become of them at last. It were well for them, if they might be in no worse case than a crocodile, or a cur dog.

Theol. It is most certain that you say, and we all have great cause to lament it, and to take up the old complaint of the prophet, Jer. vi. 13, saying, " From the least of them even unto the greatest of them, every one is given unto covetousness; and from the prophet even unto the priest, they all deal falsely." *A*nd another prophet saith, "They build up Zion with blood, and Jerusalem with iniquity. The heads thereof judge for rewards, and the priests thereof teach for hire, and the prophets thereof prophesy for money; yet will they lean upon the Lord and say, is not the Lord amongst us? no evil can come unto us," Micah iii. 10, 11. But these holy prophets, and men of God, do fully describe unto us the state of our time; wherein, though all be corrupted, yet we bear ourselves stoutly upon God, we presume of his favour, because of our outward profession, and say in our hearts, no evil can come unto us.

Asun. You say very true, sir. The world was never so set upon covetousness, and men were never so greedily given to the world as now-a-days. And yet, in truth, there is no cause why men should be so sharp set upon this world. For this world is but vanity, and all is but pelf and trash. Fie on this muck!

Phil. Many such men as you are, can skill to give good words, and say, fie on this world; all is but vanity: and yet for all that, in your daily practice you are nevertheless set upon the world, nor never the more seek after God. You hear the word of God no whit the more, you read no whit the more, pray never the more; which evidently sheweth, that all your fair speeches and protestations, are naught else but hypocrisy and leasing. Your heart is not with God, for all this. All is but words: there is no such feeling in the heart. And, therefore, I may justly say to you, as God himself said unto his people, "This people have well said all that they have spoken. Oh! that there were such an heart in them, that they would fear me, and keep all my commandments!" Deut. v. 28, 29.

Theol. His words, indeed, are good, if his

heart were according. For, all things considered, there is no cause why men should be so
given to this world; for they must leave it, when
they have done all that they can. As we say,
"To-day a man, to-morrow none." And as the
apostle saith, "We brought nothing into this
world, and, it is certain, we can carry nothing
out," 1 Tim. vi. 7. We must all die, we know
not how soon: why therefore should men set
their hearts upon such uncertain and deceivable
things? for all things in this world are more
light than a feather, more brittle than glass,
more fleeting than a shadow, more vanishing
than smoke, more inconsistent than the wind.
"Doubtless," saith the prophet David, "man
walketh in a shadow, and disquieteth himself
in vain: he heapeth up riches, and cannot tell
who shall gather them," Ps. xxxix. 6. I wonder, therefore, that these moles and muckworms
of this earth, should so mind these shadowy
things, and so dote on them as they do. If they
were not altogether hardened and blinded by the
devil, they would not be so nearly knit to the
clod and the penny as they are: thinking, and
always imagining, that there is no happiness but
in these things, which are but dung and dross:
and at last they will give us the slip, when we
think ourselves most sure of them. The wise
king, who had the greatest experience of these
things that ever man had, for he enjoyed whatsoever this world could afford, upward and downward, backward and forward, yet could find nothing in them but vanity and vexation of spirit.
Moreover, he flatly avoucheth, that all these
things, riches, wealth, honour, pleasures, and
treasures, will most notably deceive us in the

end, give us the slip and be gone. For he compareth riches, and all the glory of this world, to an eagle or hawk, which a man holdeth upon his fist, stroketh her, maketh much of her, taketh great delight and pleasure in her, and saith he will not take ten pounds for her: yet all on the sudden she taketh her flight, and flieth up into the air, and he never seeth her more, nor she him. The words of the Holy Ghost are these, " Wilt thou cause thine eyes to fly after them? (meaning riches). Thou mayest but they will not be found. For they will make themselves wings like to the eagle, which flieth up to heaven," Prov. xxiii. 5. From thence we may learn, that though we set our hearts never so much on any thing here below, yet at the last it shall be taken from us, or we from it. Therefore, all worldly men do but weave the spider's web, and may fitly be compared to the silly spider, who toileth herself, and laboureth all the week long to finish up her web, that she may lodge herself in it, as in her own house and freehold. But alas, at the week's end, a maid in a moment, with one brush of her broom, dispossesseth her of her inheritance which she had purchased with great labour and much ado. Even so, when the men of this world have, with much care and trouble, purchased great lands and revenues, and gathered all that they can; yet on the sudden, death (with one stroke of his direful dart) will make them give up the ghost; and then where are they? It was prettily, therefore, said of a man in the light of nature, " No man hath ever lived so happily in this life, but in his life-time many things have befallen him, for the which he had wished rather to die than to live." And assuredly I think there was never any man lived any one day upon the face of this earth, but some grief or other either did, or justly might invade his mind ere night; either in the temptations of the world, the flesh or the devil: or in regard of soul, body, goods, or name; in regard of wife, children, friends, or neighbours; in regard of dangers to prince, estate, church, or commonwealth; in regard of casualties and losses by water, by fire, by sea, or by land. What a life therefore is this, that hath not one good day in it? Who would desire to dwell long in it? For it lieth open every day to manifold miseries, dangers, losses, casualties, reproaches, shame, infamy, poverty, sickness, diseases, colics, agues, tooth-ache, head-ache, back-ache, bone-ache, and a thousand calamities.

Phil. You have very well described unto us the vanity of this life, and that no day is free from one sorrow or other, one grief or other; which thing our Lord Jesus ratifieth, in the reason which he bringeth, why men should not distrustfully care for to-morrow. "For (saith he) sufficient unto the day is the evil thereof," Matt. vi. 34; or, as some read it, "The day hath enough with his grief;" wherein he doth plainly shew, that every day hath his sorrow, his evil, his grief, and his thwart. But I pray you proceed further in this point.

Theol. This I say further; that when men have swinked* and sweat, carked and cared, moiled and turmoiled, drudged and droiled,† by night and by day, by sea and by land, with much care and sorrow, much labour and grief, to rake together the

---

* Laboured.   † Slaved.

things of this life; yet at last, all will away again, and we must end where we began. For, as Job said, i. 21, " Naked we came into the world, and naked we must go out." For even as a wind-mill beateth itself, maketh a great noise, whistleth and whisketh about from day to day, all the year long; yet at the year's end standeth still where it began, being not moved one foot backward or forward; so when men have blustered and blown all that they can, and have even run themselves out of breath, to scrape up the commodities of the earth, yet at last they must, spite of their beards, end where they began; end with nothing, as they began with nothing; end with a winding sheet and began with swaddling clouts. For what is become of the greatest monarchs, kings, princes, potentates, and magnificoes, that ever the world had? Where is Cyrus, Darius, Xerxes, Alexander, Cæsar, Pompey, Scipio, and Hannibal? Where are the valiant Henrys, and noble Edwards of England? Are they not all gone down to the house of oblivion? Are they not all returned to their dust, and all their thoughts perished? Though they were as gods, yet have they died as a man, are fallen like others. Who now careth for them? who talketh of them? who feareth them? who regardeth them? Do not beggars tread upon them? Yet, while they lived, they were the lords of the world; they were as terrible as lions; fearful to all men; full of pomp and glory, dignity and majesty. They plowed up all things, they bare all before them, and who but they? But now they have given up the ghost, and are, as Job saith, xxx. 23, " Gone down to the house appointed for all the living." Their pomp is descended with them, and all their glory

F

is buried in the ashes. They are now covered under a clod, cast out into a vault, made companions to toads, and the worms do eat them; and what is become of their souls, is most of all to be feared. Thus we see how all flesh doth but make a vain show for a while upon this theatre of misery, fetcheth a compass about, and is presently gone. For as the poet saith, " *Serius aut citiùs sedem properamus ad unam:*" first, or last, we must all to the grave.

Asun. You have made a very good speech. It doth me good to hear it. I wonder, all these things considered, that men should be so wholly given to this world as they are. I think the devil hath bewitched them. For they shall carry nothing with them when they die, but their good deeds and their ill.

Theol. The grudges and snudges* of this world, may very fitly be compared to a king's sumpter-horse, which goeth laden all the day long, with as much gold and treasure, as he can bear; but at night his treasure is taken from him, he is turned into a sorry dirty stable, and hath nothing left him, but his galled back. Even so the rich cormorants and caterpillars of the earth, which here have treasured and horded up great heaps of gold and silver, with the which they travel laden through this world, shall in the end be stript out of all, let down into their grave, and have nothing left them but their galled conscience, with the which they shall be tumbled down into the dungeon of eternal darkness.

Phil. Wherein doth the sting and strength of the world especially consist?

---

* Misers.

Theol. Even as the great strength of Sampson lay in his hair, so the great strength of the world lieth in her two breasts: the one of pleasure, the other of profit. For she, like a notable strumpet, by laying out these her breasts, doth bewitch the sons of men, and allureth thousands to her lust. For if she cannot win them with the one breast, yet she gaineth them with the other: if not with pleasure, then with profit; if not with profit, then with pleasure. He is an odd man of a thousand that sucketh not of the one breast or the other. But sure it is, whichsoever he sucketh, he shall be poisoned. For she giveth none other milk, but rank poison. The world therefore, is like to an alluring Jael, which sitteth at her door, to entice us to come in and eat of the milk of her pleasures: but when she hath once got us in, she is ready, even while we are eating, with her hammer and nail, to pierce through our brains, Judges iv. 21.

Phil. I see plainly, this world is a very strumpet, a strong bait, and a snarling net, wherein thousands are taken. It is very bird lime, which doth so belime our affections that they cannot ascend upward. It is like the weights of a clock, hanged upon our souls, which draweth them down to the earth: it naileth us fast down to the ground. It mortifieth us into clay: it maketh us abominable unto God. For I remember God made a law, that whatsoever goeth with his breast upon the ground, should be abominable unto us, Levit. xi. How much more these carnal worldlings, which are fast soldered to the earth!

Theol. The apostle James, seeing into the deep wickedness of this world, and knowing right well how odious it maketh us in the sight of God, crieth out against it, terming it adultery, and

all worldlings adulterers; because they forsake
Christ, their true husband, and whorishly give
their hearts to this world, iv. 4, " O ye adulterers
and adulteresses, saith he, know ye not that the
amity of this world, is the enmity of God? Whosoever therefore, will be a friend of this world,
maketh himself the enemy of God." And who
dare stand forth and say, I will be the enemy of
God? Who therefore dare be a worldling? for
every worlding is the enemy of God. What
then will become of you, O ye wicked worldlings?

Phil. It appeareth then plainly by the scriptures, that the excessive love of this world, and
unsatiable desire of having, is a most dangerous
thing; and men do not know what, in seeking
so greedily after it.

Theol. The heathen man, Sophocles, will rise
up in judgment against us: for he saith, " Unsa-
tiableness is the foulest evil amongst mortal men;
but many of our seagulfs and whirlpools make no
conscience of it." They think it is no sin: they
devour and swallow up all; and yet are never
satisfied. They will have all, and more than all,
and the devil and all. The whole world cannot
satisfy their mind: but God must create new
worlds to content them. These men are sick of
the golden dropsy: the more they have, the more
they desire. The love of money increaseth, as
money itself increaseth. But the scripture saith,
" He that loveth silver, shall not be satisfied with
silver," Eccles. v. 10. Oh, therefore, that we
would strive earnestly to get out of this gulf of
hell, and tread the moon, that is, all worldly
things, under our feet, as it is spoken of the
church, and that we would set our affections on
the things that are above, and not on the things

that are beneath: that we would fly an high pitch, and soar aloft as the eagles, looking down at this world, and all things in it, as at our feet, contemning it, and treading the very glory of it under our feet, that it may never have more power over us! Rev. iii. 1.

Phil. O happy and twice happy are they that can do so! And I beseech the Almighty God, give us his Holy Spirit, whereby we may be carried above this world, into the mountains of myrrh, and the mountains of spices, Cant. iv. 6. For how happy a thing is it to have our conversation in heaven, that is, to have an inward conversation with God, by much prayer, reading, meditation, and heavenly affections! This, indeed, is to climb up above the world, and to converse in the chambers of peace. Oh, therefore, that we could seriously and thoroughly conceive and consider of this world as it is, that we would well weigh the vanity of it, and the excellency of that which is to come, that we might loathe the one and, and love the other; despise the one, and embrace the other: love God more than ever we did, and this world less. For what is this world but vanity of vanities?

Asun. You do exceedingly abase that which some make their god. You speak contemptuously of that which most men have in greatest price and admiration. You disgrace that which multitudes would grace. You make light of that which numbers make greatest account of. Let us therefore hear your reasons: shew us more fully what it is; describe it unto us.

Theol. The world is a sea of glass, a pageant of fond delights, a theatre of vanity, a labyrinth of error, a gulf of grief, a sty of filthiness, a vale of misery, a spectacle of woe, a river of tears, a stage of deceit, a cage full of owls, a den of scorpions, a wilderness of wolves, a cabin of bears, a whirlwind of passions, a feigned comedy, a delectable phrenzy; where is false delight, assured grief, certain sorrow, uncertain pleasure, lasting woe, fickle wealth, long heaviness, short joy.

Phil. Now, you have indeed described it to the full, and laid it out, as it were, in orient colours. And a man would think, he were bewitched, or stark mad, which hereafter should set his mind on it. But yet I am desirous to hear a little more of that, which I asked you before, wherein the strength and poison of the world doth especially consist.

Theol. In this lieth a great strength of the world, that it draweth down the stars of heaven and maketh them fall to the earth, as it is said of the dragon's tail, (Rev. xii. 4.) which is ambition, covetousness, and the love of this world. For we may wonder and lament, to see how the love of these things hath wounded and overborn many excellent servants of God, both preachers and professors of the gospel: which thing doth plainly argue the strength of it. For it is the strongest and the very last engine, that Satan useth to impugn us withal, when none other will prevail. For when no temptation could fasten upon Christ, he bringeth forth this last weapon which never faileth; "All these things will I give thee," Matt. iv. 9, shewing him the glory of the whole world. So then he, having the experience of this, that it never faileth, thought to have overcome Christ himself with it. Here, therefore, lieth the very sting and strength of the world and the devil. For whom hath he not taken with "all these things will I give thee?" whom hath he not wounded? whom hath he not deceived? whom hath he not overthrown? With this he enticed Balaam; with this he beguiled Achan; with this he overthrew Judas; with this he bewitched Demas; with this, in these our days, he deceived many of excellent gifts. For assuredly, he is a phoenix* amongst men, which is not overcome with this. He is a wonderment in the world, that is not moved with money.

Phil. I am now fully satisfied with this matter. But one thing cometh often into my mind; to wit, that these miserable wordlings can have no sound comfort in their pleasures and profits: because they have no comfort in God, nor peace in their own consciences.

Theol. You say very true. It is impossible, that men, loving this world, should have any sound comfort in God. For no man can serve two masters, both God and riches. Their case therefore, is very dangerous and fearful, though they never see it, nor feel it: as I will shew you by a plain example. Put a case: one of these great rich wordlings should be clothed in velvet and cloth of gold, in most stately manner, and also should be set at his table, furnished with all the dainties of the world; should be attended and waited upon by many, in most lordly and pompous manner; should sit in his goodly dining-chamber, all glittering like gold; should have his first, second, and third service served in, with minstrels and instruments of music, in most royal sort; he sitteth in his chair, like a

---

* A very rare bird, of which the ancients used to say there was but one at a time in being.

king in his throne: yet for all this, if a dagger
should be held to his heart all this while, ready
to stab him, what pleasure, what joy, what comfort can he have in all the rest? Even so, whatsoever pomp or pleasures wicked wordlings have
here below, yet their guilty and hellish conscience
is, as it were, a dagger, held always hard to their
heart, so as they can have no sound comfort in
any thing. Or let me give it you thus: put this
case, a man hath committed high treason, and
were therefore apprehended, arraigned, and condemned to be hanged, drawn, and quartered: what
then can comfort him in such a case? can mirth,
can music, can gold, can silver, can lands, can
livings? No, no: none of all these can help him,
or give him any comfort. For the continual
thoughts of death do so gripe him at the heart,
that none of all these can do him any good or any
whit mitigate his grief. What then is the thing
that may comfort him in this case? Only a
pardon, sealed with the king's broad seal, and
subscribed with his own hand. For as soon as
he hath got this, his heavy heart reviveth, and
he leaps for joy. This then assuredly is the very
case of all profane atheists and worldlings, who
are not assured of the king of heaven his pardon
for their sin: and then, what joy can they have
either in their meat, drink, goods, cattle, wines,
children, lands, revenues, or any thing whatsoever?
For the dreadful thoughts of hell, do eftsoones*
cross them inwardly, and quite damp and dash all
their mirth. Their own consciences will not be
stilled; but in most terrible manner, rise up and
give evidence against them, telling them flatly

* Speedily.

they shall be damned, how merry and jocund soever they seem to be in this world; setting a good face on the matter. For sure it is, that inwardly they have many a cold pull, and many heart gripes. And all their mirth and jollity, is but a giggling from the teeth outward: they can have no sound comfort within. And therefore the wise king saith, "Even in laughter the heart is sorrowful: and the end of that mirth is heaviness," Prov. xiv. 13. Likewise saith the holy man Job, xxvii. 20, "Terrors of conscience come upon the wicked man like waters: in the night a whirlwind carrieth him away secretly." Eliphaz, the Temanite, avoucheth the same point, saying, "The wicked man is continually as one that travaileth of child; a sound of fear is in his ears," &c. Job xv. 20, 21. Thus then we see, that howsoever many carnal atheists, and ungodly persons, seem outwardly to float aloft in all mirth and jollity, bearing it out, as we say, at the breast: yet inwardly they are pinched with terrors, and most horrible convulsions of conscience.

Antil. You have spoken many things very sharply against covetousness: but in my mind, so long as a man covets nothing but his own, he cannot be said to be covetous.

Theol. Yes, that he may. For not only is he covetous which greedily desireth other men's goods; but even he also which over-niggardly and pinchingly holdeth fast his own, and is such a miser, that he will part with nothing. We see the world is full of such pinch-pennys, that will let nothing go, except it be wrung from them perforce, as a key out of Hercules'* hand. These

---

* A hero of heathen fable of prodigious strength.

gripple* muck-rakers had as leave part with their blood as their goods. They will pinch their own backs and bellies, to get their god into their chests. And when they had once got him in there, will they easily part with him, trow ye? No, no; a man will not part with his god, for no man's pleasure. He will eat pease-bread, and drink small drink, rather than he will diminish his god. Therefore the scripture saith, "Eat not the meat of him that hath an evil eye; and desireth not his dainty dishes. For as he grudgeth his own soul, so he will say unto thee; eat and drink, when his heart is not with thee. Thou shalt vomit thy morsels which thou hast eaten and loose thy pleasant speeches," Prov. xxiii. 6–8. The old saying is, the covetous man wanteth as well that which he hath, as that which he hath not; because he hath no use of that which he hath. So then you see, there is a great strength of covetousness, in the niggardly keeping of our own.

Antil. Yet, for all this, men must follow their worldly business, and lay up to live. For it is an hard world, and goods are not easy to come by. Therefore men must ply their business, or else they may go to beg or starve.

Theol. I deny not, but that you may follow the works of your calling dilligently: so it be in the fear of God, and with a good conscience, as I told you before; but this greediness and gripleness God doth condemn, and also, his excessive love of money.

Phil. Believe me, I know nobody that hateth it; I cannot see but that all men love gold and silver.

* Eager getters.

Theol. It is one thing to use these things, and another thing to love them and set our hearts upon them. For the scripture saith, "If riches increase, set not your heart upon them," Psalm lxii. 10. Saint John also saith, ii. 15, "Love not this world, nor the things that are in this world." He saith not, use not this world; but love not this world. For use it we may; love it we may not. Therefore the apostle saith, "That they which use this world, should be as though they used it not," 1 Cor. vii. 31, where he alloweth a sober and moderate use of the things of this life in the fear of God. We must use this world for necessities' sake, as we use meat and drink. For, no more of this world then needs must, for fear of surfeiting. The Holy Ghost saith, "Let your conversation be without covetousness, and be content with things present," Heb. xiii. 5. Happy is that man therefore, that is well content with his present estate whatsoever it may be, and carrieth himself moderately and comfortably therein. For the Spirit saith, "There is no profit to a man under the sun: but that he eat and drink, and delight his soul with the profit of his labours. I saw also this, that this is of the hand of God," Eccles. ii. 24. In which words, the prudent king saith thus much, in effect, "That this is all the good we can attain unto in this world, even to take sober and comfortable use of the things of this life, which God bestoweth upon us. And further he avoucheth, "That thus to use them aright, and with sound comfort, is a very rare gift of God." For as one saith, Gregorius Nazi, "He is a wise man, that is not grieved for the things which he hath not; but doth rejoice in the things that he hath; using them to

God's glory, and his own comfort." So then, I conclude this point, and return you an answer thus: that we may in sober and godly manner, use gold, silver, and the things of this life; but at no hand to overlove them, or give our hearts unto them.

Antil. Well, yet for all this, I cannot see but that these preachers and professors, these learned men, and precise fellows, are even as eager of the world, and as covetous as any other.

Theol. Now you show your venomous spirit, against better men than yourself: And I have a fourfold answer for you.—First, I answer, that although godly men may be somewhat overtaken this way, and over-spirt* a little, yet they break not so grossly as others.—Secondly, if God leave them sometimes to be overcome of the world, yet he, in his great wisdom and mercy, turneth it to their good. For thereby he first humbleth them and afterward raiseth them up again. "And so all things work together for good, to them that love God," Rom. viii. 28.—Thirdly, I answer, that we live by rules, and not by examples. For even the best of God's people have had their wants and weakness. Therefore we may not frame rules to live by out of the infirmities of the most excellent servants of God. Wicked, therefore, and impious is their allegation, which allege David's adultery, Lot's drunkenness, Peter's fall Abraham's slips, Solomon's sins, &c. for a shelter and defence of themselves in the like sins.—Lastly, I answer that you do greatly wound yourself, in your own speech: so far off are you from mending your market any whit thereby. For if preachers and

* Overtaken.

other godly men, after many prayers and tears, and much means used, cannot escape scot-free, but sometimes are wounded, and almost overthrown, by the world and the devil; what then shall become of you, which use no means at all, nor any gain striving, but willingly give place to the devil? If the devil did over-master David, Lot, Sampson, Solomon, and other such excellent worthies, alas! what shall become of mere worldlings and atheists? If the most valiant men, and chief captains in a battle go down, what shall become of the faint-hearted soldiers? and, as St. Peter saith, 1 Epis. iv. 18, "If the righteous scarce be saved, where shall the wicked and ungodly appear?" So then I take you at the rebound, and return your own weapon upon yourself, that since godly men cannot escape through this world, without blows, what shall become of them which know not what godliness meaneth?

Antil. Yet, I say once again, that men must live, men must lay up for this world: we cannot live by the scriptures. And as for that which you call covetousness, it is but good husbandry.

Theol. I thought, we should have it at last. Now you have paid it home: you are come to the old bias, and as an hare to her old form, and her old covert. For this is the very covert and thicket of the world, wherein they would hide covetousness: but I will do what I can to hunt you out of it, by the scriptures. First, Solomon saith, " He that spareth more than is right, shall surely come to poverty," Prov. xi. 24. So then you see, that covetousness bringeth poverty. Thus .therefore I reason: that which bringeth poverty is no good husbandry: but covetousness, and too much sparing, bringeth poverty; there-

fore it is no good husbandry. The same Solomon
saith, "He that is given to gain, troubleth his
own house."   That is, the covetous man is an
occasion of many evils, in his estate and family.
From this scripture I do thus reason: that which
troubleth a man's house, is no good husbandry;
but covetousness troubleth a man's house: therefore it is no good husbandry.   Last of all, the
old proverb saith, "Covetousuess bringeth nothing
home;" and therefore it is no good husbandry.
For oftentimes we do see, that men, for covetousness of more, lose that which otherwise they
might have had.   One of the wise heathens saith,
(Hesiodus), "Evil gain is as bad as loss."   But
the covetous man doth seek after wicked gain,
and therefore seeketh loss: and consequently is
no good husband.   Another saith, (Phocillides),
"Unjust gain bringeth both loss and misery."
And therefore it is far enough off from virtue,
and all good husbandry.   Thus then, I hope, you
are so hunted both by God and men, that this
covert cannot hide you.   And therefore you must
out of it, and seek some other shelter; for this
will not serve your turn.

Phil. Now I must needs say, you have fully
stopt his mouth, and thoroughly ferreted him out
of his deep burrow.   And it is most certain that
you say, that the wise heathen have condemned
covetousness, and all unjust gains, which we both
practice and defend; and therefore will rise up in
judgment against us.   But now let us leave the
caviller for the present.

REMEDIES AGAINST COVETOUSNESS.

Phil. I must confess, Theologus, that you have fully entered into the matter of covetousness, yet there is one thing remaining wherein I desire to be satisfied.

Theol. What is that?

Phil. I would gladly know which be the special remedies against covetousness.

Theol. There be two special remedies against covetousness; to wit, contentment, and the meditation of God's providence.

Phil. Let us hear somewhat of contentment out of the scriptures.

Theol. The apostle saith, 1 Tim. vi. 7, 8, "Having food and raiment, we must therewith be content; for we brought nothing into this world, and it is certain we shall carry nothing out." The Spirit also saith, "Let your conversation be without covetousness, and be content with your present estate," Heb. xiii. 5. Again, the apostle saith, "He had learned in what estate soever he was, therewith to be content," Phil. iv. 11. Note that he saith, he had learned; for he had it not of himself. For contentment is the singular gift of God: as it is written; "The righteous eateth to the contentment of his soul. but the belly of the wicked shall want," Prov. xiii. 25. An ancient father saith, (Cyril in Joan iv.) "We ought to accustom ourselves to live of a little, and to be content; that we may do no wicked or filthy thing for lucres' sake." Another saith, (Chrysost. homil. li.) "He is not poor that hath nothing; but he that desireth much. Neither is he rich that hath much but he that wanteth nothing; for contentment never wanteth. There is no grief in lacking, but where there is immoderate desire in having. If we will live after nature, we shall never be poor; if after our own appetite, we shall never be rich." Well therefore, said the poet, (Euripedes,) "Wax not rich unjustly, but justly; be content with thine own things; abstain from other men's." Thus then we see, that both God himself, the fountain of all wisdom, and men also, both in the state of nature and grace, do all jointly advise us to strive for contentment; and then shall we have a sovereign remedy against covetousness.

Phil. Let us hear somewhat of the second remedy against covetousness.

Theol. An earnest thinking upon the providence of God, is a present remedy against the most foolish and pining carefulness of men for this life. For if we would seriously weigh and deeply consider the provident care that God hath had for his children in all ages, touching food and raiment; and how strangely he hath provided for them, it might suffice to correct this evil in us, and minister unto us a notable preservative against covetousness.—We read how wonderfully the Lord did provide for his prophet Elijah, in the time of the great dearth and drought, that was in Israel. Did not the Lord command the ravens to feed him, by the river Cherith? did not the ravens bring him bread and flesh in the morning, and bread and flesh in the evening, and he drank of the river? 1 Kings xvii. What should I speak

how miraculously God provided for Hagar and
her infant, when they were both cast out of
Abraham's house, and brought to great extremity!
even both of them ready to give up the ghost for
want of food, Gen. xxi. 15–21. Did not God
help at a pinch, as his manner hath always been?
did not he send his angel unto them, and both
comfort them, and provide for them? What
should I speak how strangely God provided for
his church in the wilderness? Exod. xvi. 4. Did
he not feed them with manna from heaven, and
gave them water to drink out of the rock? Exod.
xvii. 6. Hath not our heavenly father made many
royal and large promises, that he will provide
necessaries for his children? Psalm lxxviii. Shall
we not think that he will be as good as his word?
Doth he not say, Psalm xxxiv. 10, "The lions
lack, and suffer hunger; but they which seek him,
shall want nothing that is good?" Doth he not
say, v. 9, "Fear him all ye saints; for nothing
is wanting to them that fear him?" Doth he not
say, Psalm lxxxiv. 11, "No good thing shall be
withheld from them that walk uprightly? Doth
he not say, Matt. vi. 23, "Our heavenly Father
knoweth that we have need of these things; and
that all these things shall be cast upon us, if we
earnestly seek his kingdom?" Doth he not bid
us cast all our care upon him? 1 Pet. v. 7,
"for he careth for all." Doth he not bid us,
"Take no thought what we shall eat, or what we
shall drink, or wherewithal we shall be clothed?"
Luke xii. 29, meaning thereby, no distracting
or distrustful thought. Doth he not say, he
will not leave us, nor forsake us? Heb. xii. 5.
Doth he not say, "The Lord is at hand: in
nothing be careful?" Phil. iv. 5, 6. Are not these

G

large promises sufficient to stay up our faith in
God's providence? shall we think God jesteth
with us? shall we think he meaneth no such matter? shall we imagine he will not keep truth?
Oh, it were blasphemy once to think it? for God
is true, and all men liars. He is faithful that
hath promised. His word is more than the faith
of a prince: more than ten thousand obligations.
Why then do we not rest upon it? why go we
any further? why do we not take his word? why
do we not depend wholly upon him? why are we
still covetous? why are we still distrustful? why
do we dissemble and deceive? Oh we of little
faith! Our Lord Jesus, knowing right well the
distrustfulness of our nature, and the deep root it
hath in us, is not only content to make these
large and royal promises unto us which were
enough; but also strengtheneth and backeth us
with many strong reasons, to support our weakness in this behalf. He therefore bringeth us
back, to a due consideration of things. " Consider
(saith he) the ravens; consider the fowls of the
heavens: for they neither sow nor reap, nor carry
into barns; and yet God feedeth them; they want
nothing. Consider the lilies how they grow;
they neither labour, nor spin; yet Solomon in all
his royalty, was not clothed like one of these,"
Luke xii. 22–30. Oh, therefore, that we would
consider these considers! Oh that we would consider that our life is more worth than meat, and
our bodies than raiment! Oh that we would consider, that with all our carking and caring, we
can do no good at all; no, not so much as add
one cubit to our stature!* Truly, truly, if we

* "Stature." The original Greek signifies "age." See John ix. 23,
as well as stature. All our distrustful care cannot prolong our life one

would deeply ponder these reasons of our Saviour, and apply them to ourselves, they might serve for a bulwark and sure defence against covetousness. If men would consider how that great King of heaven, who hath his way in the whirlwind, and the clouds are the dust of his feet, careth for the little wren, and silly sparrow; how he looketh to them, how he tendereth them, how he provideth for them every day, both breakfast, dinner, and supper: it might serve to correct our distrustfulness. For who ever saw these, or any other soul starve for hunger? so good a father, and so good a nurse have they. And are not we much better than they? hath not God more care of us, than of them? yes, verily, a thousand times. For he loveth them, but for our sakes: how much more then doth he love ourselves? Therefore I say again and again, if we would consider these things, and lay them to heart, they would nip covetousness on the head, and drive it quite out of our hearts. Let us consider, therefore, that God provided for man before man was: then how much more will he provide for man, now that he is? Is he our Father, and will he not provide for us? Is he our King, and will he not regard us? Is he our Shepherd, and will he not look to us? Hath he provided heaven for us, and will he not give us earth? Hath he given us his Son Christ, and shall he not with him give us all things? Doth he provide for his enemies, and will he not provide for his friends? Doth he provide for whoremongers, and will he neglect his chosen? Doth he send his rain, and cause his

hour, Job vii. 1. Why heap up treasure for uncertain life? Trust God in well-doing—cast all anxious care upon him—and be ever waiting for his coming.

sun to shine upon the unjust, and shall he not
upon the just?   Doth he provide for them which
are not of the family, and will he not provide for
his own family?   Will a man feed his hogs, and
not care for his servants? or will he care for
his servants, and not regard his own children?
Oh, then, let us consider these reasons: let us remember, that our heavenly Father hath as great
care for the preservation of his creatures, as once
he had for their creation.   Let us therefore remember that our life consisteth not in these
things; but in the providence of God.   Let us
remember that he which giveth the day, will
provide for the things of the day.   Let us remember that God always giveth for sustenance, though
not for satiety.   Let us remember that God will
not famish the souls of the righteous, Prov. x. 3.
Let us remember how God never failed his.   For
who ever trusted in the Lord and was confounded?

Phil. What then is the cause that many do
want outward things?

Theol. The cause is in themselves, because
they want faith.   For if we had faith, we could
want nothing. " For faith feareth no famine," as
saith an ancient father.   And another saith, for
as much as all things are God's, he that hath
God can want nothing : if he himself be not
wanting unto God.   Therefore to have God is to
have all things.   For if we have him our friend
we have enough, we need go no further.   For he
will make men our friends : yea, he will make
angels, and all creatures to be serviceable unto
us : he will give them a special charge to look to
us, to guard us, and to do continual homage unto
us.   Therefore, let us make God our friend, and

then have we done all at once that may concern
our good, both for this life and a better. But if
he stand not our friend; if we have not him on
our side; if he back us not, then all other things
whatsoever can do us no good: all is not worth a
button. For *quid prodest, si omnia habes, eum
tamen, qui omnia dedit, non habere?* What is a
man the better though he have all things, and be
without him which is the author of all things?

Phil. Herein you speak very truly, no doubt.
For we see, many have great plenty of outward
things; but because they have not God, they can
have no true comfort in them, or blessing with
them.

Theol. True, indeed; "For man liveth not by
bread only, (saith our Lord Jesus) but by every
word that proceedeth out of the mouth of God,"
Matt. iv. 4. And again he saith, "Though a man
have abundance, yet his life consisteth not in the
things that he hath," Luke xii. 15. For without
God's blessing there can be no sound comfort in
any thing. We see, by daily experience, how
the Lord curseth the wicked, though they have
abundance. For some, having abundance, yet
are visited with continual sicknesses. Some,
having abundance, pine away with consumptions.
Others, having abundance, die of surfeiting.
Others are snatched away by untimely death, in
the midst of their jollity. Others are visited
with great losses, both by sea and by land.
Others are vexed with cursed wives and disobedient children. Some, again, commit murders,
and treasons, and so lose all at once. Others
are wasted and consumed by the secret curse of
God; no man knoweth how. Some having great
riches are given over to the murderer, some to

the thief, some to the poisoner. Therefore the
wise king saith, " There is an evil sickness under
the sun; riches reserved to the owners thereof,
for their evil," Eccles. v. 13.   Zophar, also, the
Naamathite, saith, " When the wicked shall
have sufficient and enough, he shall be brought
into straits," Job xx. 22, 23: the hand of every
troublesome man shall be upon him.   When he
should fill his belly, God will send upon him
his fierce wrath, which he shall rain upon him
instead of his meat.   Thus, then, it is clear that
man's life and good estate dependeth not upon
the abundance of outward things, but only upon
the blessing and providence of God.   For, " His
blessing only maketh rich, and it doth bring no
sorrow with it," Prov. x. 4.   For, " Better is a
little unto the just, than great abundance to
many of the wicked," Psalm xxxvii. 16. " Better
is a little with righteousness, than great revenues
without equity," Prov. v. 16, and xvi. 18.   Thus,
then, I conclude this point: man liveth not by
bread, but by a blessing upon bread; not by
outward means, but by a blessing upon means.
For how can bread, being a dead thing, and
having no life in itself, give life to others?

Phil. I do not well understand the meaning
of these words: " By every word that proceedeth
out of the mouth of God."

Theol. Thereby is meant, the decree, ordinance,
and providence of God, which upholdeth all
things, even the whole order of nature; for the
scriptures saith, "He spake and it was done: he
commanded and they were created, Psalm xxxiii.
9. In words which we plainly see, that God doth
but speak, and it is done; he doth command, and
all creatures are preserved. For God doth all

things with a word. He created all with his word; he preserveth all with his word; he speaketh, and it is done. His words are words of power and authority. Whatsoever he saith, whatsoever he calleth for, it must be done presently, without any delay, there is no withstanding of him. He calleth for famine, and behold famine. He calleth for plenty, and behold plenty. He calleth for pestilence, and behold pestilence. He calleth for the sword, and behold the sword. All angels, all men, all beasts, all fishes, all fowls, all creatures whatsoever must obey him, and be at his beck. He is the greatest commander; his word commandeth heaven and earth and the sea. All creatures must be obedient to his will, and subject to his ordinance. This is the cause why all things, both in heaven, earth, and the sea, do keep their immutable and invariable courses, times and seasons, even because he hath charged them so to do. And they must of necessity always, at all times and for ever, obey; for the creatures must obey the Creator. This act of parliament was made the first week of the world, and never since was or can be repealed.

Phil. But, to call you back again to the point we had in hand, resolve me, I pray you, of this: whether many of the dear children of God do not in this life sometimes want outward things, and are brought into great distress?

Theol. Yes, certainly. For Elijah did want, and was in distress. Paul did want, and was in many distresses. The holy Christians, mentioned in the Hebrews, did want, and were in marvellous distresses. Many of God's dear ones have in all ages wanted, and at this day also do want, and are greatly distressed. But this is a most infallible truth, that howsoever God's children may want, and be low brought, yet they are never utterly forsaken, but are holpen even in greatest extremities; yea, when all things are desperate, and brought even to the last cast.—To this point, most notably speaketh the apostle, saying, "We are afflicted on every side, but yet we despair not; we are persecuted, but not forsaken; cast down, but we perish not," 2 Cor. iv. 7, 8. The prophet Jeremiah also saith, "The Lord will not forsake for ever: but though he send affliction, yet will he have compassion, according to the multitude of his mercies. For he doth not punish willingly, or from his heart, nor afflict the children of men," Lam. iii. The kingly prophet saith, "Surely the Lord will not fail his people, neither will he forsake his inheritance," Psalm xciv. 14. The Lord himself saith, "For a moment in mine anger, I hid my face from thee; but with everlasting mercy have I had compassion on thee," Isa. liv. 7, 8. So then we may fully assure ourselves, and even write of it, as a most undoubted and sealed truth, that God's children shall never be utterly forsaken in their troubles.

Phil. Since the care and providence of God is so great for his children, as you have largely declared, what then I pray you is the cause, why God suffereth his to be brought into so many troubles and necessities?

Theol. Their profit and benefit is the cause, and not their hurt. For he loveth them, when he smiteth them. He favoureth them, when he seemeth to be most against them. He aimeth at their good, when he seemeth to be most angry with them. He woundeth them, that he may heal them. He presseth them, that he may ease them.

He maketh them cry, that afterward they may laugh. He always meaneth well unto them, he never meaneth hurt. He is most constant in his love towards them. If he bring them into necessities, it is but for the trial of their faith, love, patience, and diligence in prayer. — If he cast them into the fire, it is not to consume them, but to purge and refine them. If he bring them into great dangers, it is but to make them call upon him more earnestly, for help and deliverance.— He presseth us, that we might cry; we cry, that we may be heard; we are heard, that we might be delivered. So that there is no hurt done; we are worse scared than hurt. Even as a mother, when her child is wayward, threateneth to throw it to the wolf, or scareth it with some poker or bull-beggar, to make it cling more unto her and be quiet; so the Lord oftentimes sheweth us the terrible faces of troubles and dangers to make us cleave and cling faster unto him; and also to teach us to esteem better of his gifts when we enjoy them, and to be more thankful for them; as health, wealth, peace, liberty, safety, &c. So then, still we see, here is nothing meant on God's part, but good; as it is written, "All things work together for good, to them that love God." For even the afflictions of God's children are so sanctified unto them by the Spirit, that thereby they are made partakers of God's holiness. Thereby they enjoy the quiet fruit of righteousness. Thereby they attain unto a greater measure of joy in the Holy Ghost. Thereby the world is crucified to them, and they to the world. Thereby they are made conformable to Christ's death. Thereby they are kept from the condemnation of the world. Thereby they learn experience, patience, hope, &c. So that, all things considered, God's children are no losers by their afflictions, but gainers. It is better for them to have them, than to be without them; they are very good for them. For when God's children are chastised, it is as it should be. For to them, the cross is mercy, and loss is gain. Afflictions are their schooling, and adversity their best university. "It is good for me, saith the holy man of God, that I have been afflicted, that I might learn thy statutes" By his afflictions thereby, he learned much, and became a good scholar in God's book, and well seen in his statutes and laws. He grew to great wisdom and judgment by his chastisements. All things turned about, in God's merciful providence, to his everlasting comfort. For I say again, and again, that all things tend to the good of God's chosen people. And therefore, that estate, which God will have his children to be in, is always best for them. Because he, who can best discern what is best, seeth it to be best for them: whether be it sickness or health, poverty or plenty, prison or liberty, prosperity or adversity. For sometimes sickness is better for us than health, and poverty than plenty. Are therefore the children of God sick? it is best for them. Are they poor? it is best for them. Are they in any trouble? it is best for them; because their good Father will turn it to the best. He will oftentimes cut us short of our lusts and desires; because he seeth we will bane ourselves with them. He, in fatherly care, will take the knife from us; because he seeth we will hurt ourselves with it. He will keep us short of health and wealth, because he knoweth we will be the worse for them. He will not give us too much ease and prosperity in this world; for he knoweth it will poison us. He will not allow us continual rest, like standing ponds; for then he knoweth we will gather scum and filth. He dealeth fatherly and mercifully with us in all things, even then seeking our greatest good, when we think he doth us most harm. And, to speak all in a word, he bringeth us into troubles and straits, to this end especially, that he may hear of us. For he right well knoweth our nature; he is well acquainted with our disposition. He knoweth we will not come at him, but when we stand in need of him: we care not for him so long as all goeth well with us. But if we come into distress, or want any thing that we would fain have, then he is sure to hear of us. As he saith by the prophet, " In their affliction, they will seek me early," Hosea v. 15. And another prophet saith, " Lord, in trouble have they visited thee. They poured out a prayer, when thy chastisement was upon them," Isa. xxvi. 16. So then now, I hope, you do plainly see the cause why the Lord bringeth his children into so many troubles and necessities.

Phil. I do see it indeed; and I am very well satisfied in it. But let me ask you one thing further. Are God's children always sure to be delivered out of their troubles?

Theol. Yes, verily; and, out of doubt, so far forth, as God seeth it good for them. For it is written, "Great are the trouble of the righteous; but the Lord delivereth them out of all," Psalm xxxiv. 19. St. Peter saith, 2 Epis. ii. 9, " The Lord knoweth how to deliver the godly out of temptation." As if he should say, he is beaten

in it, and well seen and experienced in it: so as he
can do it easily, and without any trouble at all.
It is said of Joseph, being in prison, Psalm cv.
19, 20, that, "When his appointed time was
come, and the counsel of the Lord had tried him,
the king sent and loosed him, the ruler of the people
delivered him;" and again the scripture saith,
"The righteous cry, and the Lord heareth them,
and delivereth them out of all their troubles.
The angel of the Lord tarrieth round about them
that fear him, and delivereth them," Psalm xxxiv.
7, 17.   And, in another place, the Lord himself
saith, concerning the righteous man, Psalm
xci. 14, 15, "Because he hath loved me, therefore I will deliver him.   I will exalt him, because
he hath known my name.   He shall call upon me
in trouble, and I will hear him; I will be with
him in trouble; I will deliver him, and glorify
him."   So also saith Eliphaz the Temanite, Job
v. 19, "He shall deliver thee in six troubles; and in
the seventh, the evil shall not touch thee."   "Come
my people, saith the Lord, enter thou into thy
chambers, and shut thy doors after thee; hide
thyself for a very little while, until the indignation pass over," Isa. xxvi. 20.   And the prophet
saith, Obad. 17, "Upon Mount Zion shall be deliverance, and it shall be holy; and the house of
Jacob shall possess their hereditary possessions."
Almost innumerable places of the scriptures might
be alleged, to this purpose; but these may suffice.
Therefore let us know for a certainty, that so
sure as trouble and affliction are to the children
of God, so sure also is deliverance out of the same.
As we may write of the one, and make reckoning
of it as sure as the coat of our back: so may we
also, in God's good time, write of the other, and

make full account of it, as sure as the Lord is true. Abraham was in trouble, but delivered. Job in trouble, but delivered. David in great troubles, but delivered. The three children in the furnace, but delivered. Daniel in the lion's den, but delivered. Jonah in the whale's belly, but delivered. Paul in innumerable troubles, but delivered out of all.

Phil. All this being true, that you say, it followeth that God's children are chastised only for their good, and evermore sure of deliverance in his appointed time. Which thing being so, methinketh there is no cause at all why they should be over heavy, or too much cast down in their afflictions.

Theol. Assuredly there is no cause at all; but rather cause why they should rejoice, clap their hands, and sing care away. For can a father forsake his children? a king his subjects? a master his servants? or a shepherd his sheep? Doth not Jehovah say, "I will not leave thee nor forsake thee?" Heb. xiii. 5. Doth not our heavenly Father know, we have need of these things? Hath not God given us his word, that we shall not want outward things. Hath he not said, they shall be cast upon us? Why then should we be dismayed? Why should we hang down our heads? Why do we not pluck up our hearts, and be of good cheer? God is our dear Father; he is our best friend: he is our daily benefactor: he keepeth us at his own costs and charges: he grudgeth us nothing: he thinketh nothing too much for us. He loveth us most dearly: he is most chary and tender over us: he cannot endure the wind should blow upon us: he will have us want nothing that is good for us. If

we will eat gold, we shall have it. He hath
given us his faithful promise that, as long as we
live, we shall never want. Let us therefore rejoice and be merry: for heaven is ours, earth is
ours, God is ours, Christ is ours, all is ours:
as the apostle saith, "All is your's, and you are
Christ's, and Christ is God's." The world clap
their hands, and crow long before it be day, saying, all is theirs: but the children of God may
say, and say truly, all is ours. For they have a
true title and proper interest, through Christ, in
all the creatures. Many are their privileges;
great are their prerogatives. They are free of
of heaven, and free of earth. They are the only
free denizens of the world. Christ hath purchased for them their freedom. Christ hath
made them free, and therefore they are free indeed. They are free from sin, free from hell, free
from damnation. They are at peace with God,
men, and angels. They are peace with themselves. They are at peace with all creatures.
They are young princes, angels' fellows, descended
of the highest house, of the blood royal of heaven,
states of paradise, and heirs apparent to the immortal crown. Therefore God hath commanded
his angels to guard them, being such young
princes as they are: yea, he hath given a very
straight charge to all his creatures, to look to
them, to see to them, that they want nothing,
that they take no hurt; so zealous, so chary, so
tender is he of them. The angels must comfort
Jacob. The whale must rescue Jonah. The
ravens must feed Elias. The sun and moon
must stay for Joshua. The sea must divide
itself, that Moses and his people may pass
through. The fire must not burn the three

children. The lions may not devour Daniel. All the creatures must change their nature, rather than God's children should not be holpen and delivered. Oh, therefore, how great is the happiness of God's chosen! Who can express it? who can utter it? They know not their own happiness: it is hid from them. Afflictions do cloud it, troubles do overshadow it, crosses do dim it; and there is an interposition of the earth, between their sight and it. But this is most certain and sure, that the best is behind with the children of God: all the sweet is to come. Their happiness doth not appear in this world, "Their life is hid with Christ in God. When Christ shall appear, then shall they also appear, with him in glory," Col. iii. 3, 4. "It doth not yet appear, what they shall be: but when he cometh, they shall be made like unto him," 1 John iii. 2. Their names are already taken, and entered into the book of life: and one day, they shall be crowned. One day it shall be said unto them, "Come ye blessed," &c. One day they shall enjoy "his presence, where is fulness of joy; and at whose right hand, there is pleasure for evermore," Psalm xvi. Therefore let all God's secret ones rejoice, sing and be merry. For howsoever in this world they be contemned, trodden under the foot, made nobodies, and walk as shadows; being counted as the very rags of the earth, and the abjects of the world: yet the time will come, when their happiness and felicity shall be such, as never entered into the heart of man: it is endless, unspeakable, and inconceivable.

Phil. I do now plainly see, that there is no cause why God's people should be too heavy and dumpish in their afflictions. I see, that though they be not free from all afflictions, yet they are free from all hurtful afflictions. For no rod, no cross, no chastisement is hurtful unto them: but all, in the conclusion, cometh to a blessed issue.

Theol. You have uttered a great, and a most certain truth. For there is no affliction or trial, which God imposeth upon his children, but if they endure it quietly, trust in his mercy firmly, and tarry his good pleasure obediently, it hath a blessed and comfortable end. Therefore the people of God may well be merry in the midst of their sorrows. They may, with patience and comfort, submit themselves to their Father's corrections; taking them patiently, and even kissing his holy rod, and saying in themselves, since my Father will have it so, I am content; seeing it is his mind, I am willing withal. As old Eli said, "It is the Lord, let him do what he will," 1 Sam. iii. 18. And as David, in like submission, said in a certain case, "Behold, here am I; let him do to me, as it seemeth good in his own eyes," 2 Sam. xv. 26. And in another place he saith, "I was dumb, and opened not my mouth: because thou, Lord, hast done it," Psalm xxxix. 9. Behold, here, then the patience of God's saints, and their humble submission unto his most holy will. They know all shall end well; and that maketh them glad to think of it.—I conclude then, that the children of God are happy, in what state soever they are: happy in trouble, happy out of trouble, happy in poverty, happy in plenty, blessed in sickness, blessed in health, blessed at home likewise, and abroad, and every way blessed. But on the contrary, the wicked are cursed, in what state soever they are: cursed in sickness, cursed in health, cursed in plenty, cursed in poverty, cursed in prosperity, cursed in adversity, cursed in honour, cursed in dishonour. For all things work together for their destruction. Nothing doth them any good. They are not anything the better, either for God's mercies or judgments. All weathers are alike unto them. They are always the same, in prosperity and adversity: they are no changelings. And, as we say, "a good year doth not mend them; nor an ill year pare them."

CONTEMPT OF THE GOSPEL.

Phil. You have long insisted upon the point of covetousness. Now proceed to the fourth sign of a man's damnation; which is the contempt of the gospel; and lay open both the greatness of the sin, and the danger of it.

Theol. This sin is of another nature than the former. It is a sin against the first table. It toucheth the person of God himself. For to contemn the gospel is to contemn God himself; whose gospel it is. If to contemn the ministers of the gospel be to contemn God and Christ, as our Lord Jesus avoucheth, Luke x. 16, how much more, then, to contemn the gospel itself? Therefore, it is dangerous meddling in this sin. It is to meddle with edged tools, to meddle with princes' matters—to touch the ark, to come near the holy mountain : which all were things full of great peril and danger. Yea, it is to spill the sacrament. It is *noli me tangere.** It is to rail

* A sin too horrible to be touched.

H

at a king. It is to spit God in the face. It is
high treason against the King of Glory. Therefore this sin, of all other, can never be endured;
and may, at no hand, be borne withal. For can
a mortal king endure the contempt of his laws?
can he put up with the contempt of his own
person? Can he abide any to spit at his sceptre,
or to throw a stone at it? No, surely, he will
not: therefore, the Holy Ghost saith, "He that
despiseth Moses' laws, dieth without mercy,
under two or three witnesses. Of how much
sorer punish, suppose ye, shall he be worthy
which treadeth under foot the Son of God, and
counteth the blood of the Testament as an
unholy thing (wherewith he was sanctified), and
doth despite unto the Spirit of grace," Heb.
x. 28, 29. And, again, "If they were punished
which obeyed not the word spoken by angels,
how shall we escape if we neglect so great
salvation?" Heb. ii. 2, 3. "If they escaped not
which refused him that spake on earth, how
shall we escape if we turn away from him that
speaketh from heaven?" Heb. xii. 25. Therefore,.
our Saviour Christ saith, "That it shall be easier
for Sodom in the day of judgment, than for the
contemners of the gospel," Luke x. 12. Moreover, he saith, "The queen of the south shall
rise up in judgment against all froward despisers
of his word," Matt. xii. 42. For she came from
the uttermost parts of the earth to hear the
wisdom of Solomon; and behold a greater than
Solomon is here." For Christ is greater than
Solomon—his doctrine and wisdom far more
excellent; and therefore their sin is the greater
which contemn it. They shall never be able to
answer it; for the Spirit saith, "He that

despiseth the word shall be destroyed," Prov.
xiii. 13. St. Peter also telleth us that the old
world, and men of the first age, are now in
hell-fire, because they both despised and were
disobedient to the doctrine of Christ, which—
though not personally, yet in his divine Spirit—
he spake by Noah," 1 Pet. iii. 19; 2 Pet. ii. 5.
So, then, we see clearly God will never take it at
our hands that his glorious gospel should be so
universally and openly contemned as it is.

Phil. You have spoken most truly, and also
shewed it out of the scriptures, that the contempt
of the gospel is a most heinous sin; yet for all
that, it is most lamentable to consider how little
men esteem it, and how light they make of it.
Many regard it no more than an egg-shell; they
think it is not worth a gally* halfpenny; they
will not go to the door to hear it; they take it
to be but a breath from us, and a sound to them;
and so the matter is ended. They esteem it but
as a noise, or empty sound, in the air; or as a
voice afar off, which a man understandeth not:
they never felt the power of it in their hearts.
Therefore they prefer their sheep, their farms,
their oxen, their profits, their pleasure, yea,
everything, before it; they know it not to be
any such a precious jewel as it is. Although our
Lord Jesus himself compare it to a hid treasure,
and a most precious pearl; yet these filthy swine
of the world tread it under foot: for they know
not the price of it, though Solomon the wise
saith, Prov. iii. " All the merchandize of gold and
silver, pearls and precious stones, are not to be
compared unto it;" yet these beasts, these dogs

* A bad or French halfpenny, not passable.

and hogs of the world contemn it. They esteem
a cow more than Christ's most glorious gospel.
They are like Æsop's cock, which made more
account of a barley-corn than all the precious
stones in the world; they are like little children,
that esteem their rattles more than a bag of
gold; they are like the Gadarenes, which esteemed
their hogs more than Christ and his gospel;
they make nothing of it. They think it not
worth the while. Many of them sit idle in the
streets even upon the Sabbaths. While the
gospel is preached in their churches, many are at
cards, and tables, in ale-houses. Many, upon the
Sabbaths, sleep upon their beds, all the sermon
while, in the afternoon. Many will hear a sermon
in the forenoon; and they take that to be as
much as God can require at their hand, and that
he is somewhat beholden unto them for it; but
as for the afternoon, they will hear none; then
they will to bowls or tables. These men serve
God in the forenoon, and the devil in the afternoon; some run after whores and harlots on
the Sabbaths; some run to dancing and bear-
baitings; some sit upon their stalls; some sit
in their shops; some by the fire-side; some sit
idly in the streets; some go to the stool-ball,
and others look on, O miserable wretches! O
cursed caitiffs! O monstrous hell-hounds, which
so grossly and openly contemn the gospel of
Christ! What will become of them in the end?
Assuredly their damnation sleepeth not. A
thousand deaths wait for them : they lie open
on all sides to the wrath of God. And we may
wonder at his marvellous patience, that he doth
not throw down balls of fire from heaven, to
consume and burn up, both them, their shops,

and houses, and even make them spectacles of his vengeance, for so notorious contempt of such sacred, holy, and high things.

Theol. You have spoken very truly, zealously, and religiously; and I do greatly commend you for it. And I must needs affirm the same things. For they cannot be denied. And for mine own part, I think the gospel was never so openly contemned in any age—of a people living under the profession of it, and under a godly and Christian prince—as it is in this age. For howsoever some make a shew of religion, yet they have denied the power thereof. " They turn the the grace of God into wantonness," as St. Jude saith, ver. 4. They make the gospel a cloak for their sins. They receive it and embrace it, as it will best stand with their profits and pleasures, their lusts and likings, their credit and policies, and not a jot further. They will practise it at their leisure. " These men profess they know God; but by their works they deny him, and are abominable, disobedient, and to every good work reprobate," Tit. i. 16. This age is full of such carnal Protestants.

Phil. This age, indeed, aboundeth with many hollow-hearted hypocrites, dissemblers, and time-servers; which howsoever they make a face, and bear a countenance as though they loved the gospel, yet their heart is not with it. Their heart is with atheism; their heart is with popery. They have a pope in their belly; they be church papists. Howsoever, now and then, they come to the church, and hear a sermon, and shew a good countenance to the preacher; yet their heart goeth after covetousness. The Lord complaineth of this, by his prophet Ezekiel, saying, Ezekiel

xxxiii. 31-32, "This people will sit before thee
and hear thy words; but they will not do them.
For, with their mouths they make jests; and
their heart goeth after covetousness." God complaineth of this also, by his prophet Jeremiah,
Jer. vii. 9-11, "Will you steal, murder, and
commit adultery, and swear falsely, and stand
before me in this house, whereupon my name is
called, and say we are delivered, though we have
done all these abominations? Is this house become a den of thieves, whereupon my name is
called?" Where we see how the Lord doth chide
his people, and sharply reprove them for abusing
of his temple, worship, and sacrifices; making
them a cloak for their sins, and making his house
a den of thieves, which should be an assembly of
saints. Now all this is a lively description of our
time; wherein many use the exercises of the word,
prayer, and sacraments, not to kill and mortify
sin, but to nourish and shelter their sins. For
they blindly imagine, that if they come to the
church and pray, and hear the sermon, they are
discharged of their sins, though they leave them
not. They imagine they have given God his full
due; and that, therefore, they may be the more
bold to sin afterward. These kind of hypocrites
are like rogues, which use medicines, not to cure
sores, but to make sores. These are like the papists, which think if they hear mass in the morning, they may do what they list all the day after.

Theol. I see now, you have very well profited
in the knowledge of God, and true religion. You
have spoken soundly, and like a man of knowledge in God's matters. For the common sort of
people think indeed, that all religion consisteth
in the outward service of God, though their hearts

be far from him: to whom God may justly say, "This people draweth near me with their lips, but their hearts are far from me," Matt. xv. 8. Of whom also God may justly take up all his just complaints of his people Israel and Judah; which are so frequent in all the prophets: to wit, that he did abhor their sacrifices, loathe their oblations, detest their incense, despise their new moons, disdain their rams, lambs, and goats; accounting them all but as man's blood, dog's blood, swine's blood; and all, because their hands were full of blood; because they executed not justice and judgment in the gate; because they were not obedient to his will; because their hearts were not with him; because they used or rather abused all these things, as shelters for their sins, Isa. lxvi. 3.

Phil. The great contempt of the ministers of the gospel in this age, doth strongly argue the contempt of the gospel itself. For a man cannot love the gospel, and hate the faithful ministers thereof. But we see, by lamentable experience, that the most grave, godly, and learned ministers are had in derision of very base and vile persons. And as Job saith, ch. xxx. 1, "They whose fathers I have refused to set with the dogs of my flock;" they were the children of fools, and the children of villains, which were more vile than the earth, for now every rascal dares scoff and scorn at the grave and ancient fathers and pastors of the church, dares flout them as they walk in the streets, and as they ride by the highways. And though the Holy Ghost giveth them glorious and lofty titles, as the stewards of God's own house, disposers of his secrets, disbursers of his treasure, keepers of the broad seal, keepers of

the keys of heaven, God's secretaries, God's ambassadors, angels; yea, the very glory of Christ,"
Tit. i. 7; 1 Cor. iv. 1; Matt. xvi. 19; 2 Cor. v. 20;
Rev. iii. 7; 2 Cor. viii. 23; and all this, to express the excellency of their calling, yet these
vile varlets and venomous vermin of the earth,
dare call them proud prelates, pild* parsons, pelt-
ing† priests. O monstrous and intolerable impiety! Now it is come to pass, that this most
sacred function, which is glorious in the sight of
God, and his angels, and in itself most honourable
is had in greatest contempt of all callings. For
now the earth is full of rank atheists, and mock
gods, which scoff at the gospel, and blare out
their tongues at all religion. These kind of fellows never dissemble for the matter. They make
no shew at all, they are no hypocrites, they hide
not their sins, but declare them openly, like Sodom.
They care not if they never come to the church:
they are too full of it. They live like brute beasts.
They think the scriptures are but fables. They
rail at the ministers and preachers. They make
flat opposition against them, and are notorious
mockers and past-graces.

Theol. Of such the apostle St. Peter foretold
"that in the last days should come mockers, and
such as would live after their own lusts," &c.
2 Pet. iii. 3.—Of such a godly writer, Calvin
saith, *Verbum Dei securè contemnitur, promis-
siones inanes esse creduntur, minæ pro fabulis
habentur;* that is, the word of God is carelessly
contemned, his promises are counted vain, and

---

* Bald, alluding to the shaven crowns of the Catholic priests.

† From pelt, a sheep's skin. Shepherds loving to shear or skin their
flocks, rather than to feed them.

his threatenings fables.   Of such the poet saith,

"Heu vivunt homines, tanquam mors nulla sequatur·
Aut velut infernus fabula vana foret."

"Alas, men live, as they should never die:
Or as though all speech of hell were a stark lie."

Now is also the time wherein the world swarmeth
with papists and atheists; and most men live as
if there were no God.   For now religion is hated,
true godliness despised, zeal abhorred, sincerity
scoffed at, uprightness loathed, preachers contemned, professors disdained, and almost all good
men had in derision.   For now we may justly
complain with the prophet, Isa. lix. 14, "Judgment is turned backward, and justice standeth far
off.   Truth is fallen in the streets, and equity cannot enter.   Yea, truth faileth; and he that re-
fraineth from evil, maketh himself a prey."   The
prophet Micah bewaileth the times, saying, Micah
vii. 2, "The good man is perished out of the earth,
and there is none righteous among men.   They
all lie in wait for blood: every man hunteth his
neighbour with a net."   The prophet Jeremiah
complaineth of the same evil in his time; namely,
that the people were come to be past shame in
sinning, Jer. viii. 12, "Were they ashamed,
saith he, when they had committed abomination?
Nay, they were not ashamed, neither could they
blush."   This is a lively picture, and a very coun-
terpane of our time.   For now we have put on
a brow of brass: we are become impudent in sin.
We cannot blush: we cannot be ashamed.   We
are almost past shame, and past grace.   O Lord,
what will this gear grow to in the end!

Phil. We may justly fear some great judgment
of God to be near us; yea, even to hang over our

heads. For the Lord will never leave the contempt of his gospel and his ministry unpunished.

Theol. You ·have spoken a truth. And we
have heard before how the old world was plagued
for it. And we read how grievously the Jews
were afflicted by the Romans for this sin: as our
Lord Jesus did plainly foretell. We read also,
that after the Lord had broached the gospel himself, and spread it abroad by his apostles, con-
quering the world thereby (which thing was
signified by the white horse, his rider, his bow,
and his crown, Rev. vi. 2), and yet shortly after
saw that the same began to be contemned in the
world and made light of; then he did in most
fearful manner plague the earth with wars, blood-
sheddings, tumults, dearth, famine, and pestilence:
which all are signified by the red horse, the black
horse, and the pale horse, which did appear at the
opening of the second, third, and fourth seal. So
likewise undoubtedly, God will severely punish
all injuries, wrongs, and contempts, done to his
faithful ambassadors, as appeareth, Rev. xi. 5;
where it is set down, that if any would hurt the
two witnesses with their two olives, and two can-
dlesticks, (whereby is signified the faithful preachers of the gospel, with all their spiritual treasures
and heavenly light) fire should proceed out of
their mouths, and devour their adversaries. That
is, that the fire of God's wrath should consume
all that had oppressed them, either by mocks,
flouts, railings, slanders, imprisonment, or any
other kind of indignity. Of this we have a plain
example or two in the scripture. First, we read
how fire came down from heaven, and consumed
the contemptuous captain and his fifty, at the
threatening and calling for of Elijah," 2 Kings

i. 10. Secondly, how two bears came from out of the forest, and tore in pieces forty-two younkers which mocked Elisha the prophet of God; calling him bald-head, bald-pate, 2 Kings ii. 23. So then, by these examples, it is manifest that howsoever the Lord may wink at these things for a time, and make as though he saw them not; yet the time will come, when he will rain fire and brimstone upon all the scoffers of his faithful ministers, and contemners of his gospel. All this is plainly declared in the first chapter of the Proverbs: where is shewed how the wisdom of God, even Jesus Christ the highest wisdom, doth cry aloud all abroad in the world, and manifest himself in the open streets; but yet is contemned of wicked worldlings and scoffing fools. Therefore, saith Christ, verse 24–28, "Because I have called, and ye refused, I have stretched out my hand, but none would regard: ye have hated knowledge, and despised all my counsel; therefore will I laugh at your destruction, and mock when your fear cometh upon you like sudden desolation, and your destruction like a whirlwind. Then shall they call upon me, but I will not answer; they shall seek me early, but they shall not find me." Here, then, we see is terrible wrath and vengeance threatened from heaven, against all profane contemners of Christ, and his everlasting gospel, or any of the faithful publishers and proclaimers thereof. Behold therefore, ye despisers, and wonder: consider well what will become of you in the end. Do not think, that the most just God will always put it up at your hands, that ye should so manifestly contemn both his word and the most zealous preachers and professors thereof. No, no; assure yourselves he will be even with you at last. He will smite you both sidelings and overthwart: he will dog you and pursue you with his judgments, and never leave following the chase with you till he have destroyed you, and consumed you from off the face of the earth. For remember, I pray you, what he saith in Deut. xxxii, "If I whet my glittering sword, and my hand take hold of judgment, I will execute vengeance on mine enemies, and I will reward them that hate me; I will make mine arrows drunk with blood, and my sword shall eat the flesh of mine adversaries."

Phil. Truly, sir, you may justly fear, that for our great contempt for the gospel, and general coldness both in the possession and practice thereof, God will take it from us, and give it to a people that will bring forth the fruit thereof.

Theol. We may well fear indeed, lest for our sins, especially our loathing of the heavenly manna, the Lord will remove our candlestick, take away our silver trumpets, let us no more hear the sweet bells of Aaron, cause all vision to fail, and our Sabbaths to cease, and bring upon us that most grievous and sore famine of not hearing the word of the Lord, spoken of by Amos the prophet, viii. 8. Then, shall all our halcyon days, and golden years, be turned into weeping, mourning, and lamentation. God, for his infinite mercy's sake, turn it away from us!

Phil. Amen, amen; and let us all pray earnestly, night and day, that those fearful judgments may, according to God's infinite mercies, be held back, which our sins do continually cry for; and that his most glorious gospel may be continued to us and our posterity, even yet with greater success.

Asun. No doubt, it is a very great sin to despise the word of God; and I think there is none so bad that will do it: for we ought to love God's word; God forbid else. He that loveth not God's word, it is a pity he liveth.

Theol. These are but words of course. It is an easy matter to speak good words; and very many will say as you say; but both you, and they, in your practice, do plainly shew that you make no reckoning of it: you esteem it no more than a dish-clout. I think, if the matter were well tried, you have scarce a bible in your house. But though you have one, it is manifest that you seldom read therein, with any care or conscience; and as seldom hear the word preached. How else could you be so ignorant as you are?

Asun. I grant that I and some others are somewhat negligent in the hearing and reading of the word of God; but you cannot say therefore we do contemn it.

Theol. Yes, verily. Your continual negligence, and carelessness, doth argue a plain contempt. Sure it is, you have no appetite nor stomach to the holy word of God. You had rather do any thing, than either read or meditate in it. It is irksome unto you. You read not two chapters in a week. All holy exercises of religion are most bitter and tedious unto you. They are as vinegar to your teeth, and smoke in your eyes. The immoderate love of this world, and of vanity, hath taken away your appetite from all heavenly things. And, whereas you shift it off with negligence, as though that would excuse you, the apostle hits you home when he saith, "How shall we escape, if we neglect so great salvation?" Heb. ii. 3. Mark that he saith, "if we neglect."

Antil. Belike you think men have nothing else to do but read the scriptures, and hear sermons?

Theol. I do not say so. I do not say ye should do nothing else. For God doth allow you, with a good conscience, and in his fear, to follow the works of your calling: as hath been said before. But this I condemn in you, and many others, that you will give no time to private prayers, reading, and meditation in God's word; neither morning nor evening, neither before your business nor after. And, although you have often vacant time enough, yet you will rather bestow it in vanity, and idle prattling, and gossipping, than in any good exercise of religion. Which doth plainly shew, that you neither delight in holy things; neither is there any true fear of God before your eyes.

Antil. I tell you plainly, we must attend our business; we may go beg else; we cannot live by the scriptures. If we follow sermons we shall never thrive. What, do you think every man is bound to read the scriptures? Have we not our five wits? Do we not know what we have to do? You would make fools of us belike. But we are neither drunk nor mad.

Theol. That every man, of what condition soever, is bound in conscience to hear and read the word of God, hath been shewed, and proved in the beginning of our conference. But as for your five wits, they will not serve your turn in these matters; though you had fifteen wits. For all the wit, reason, and understanding of natural men, in God's matters, is but blindness, and mere foolishness. The apostle saith, "That the wisdom of the most wise in this world, is not only foolishness with God; but indeed very en-

mity against God," 1 Cor. iii. 19 ; Rom. viii. 7.
And again, he saith, that "The natural man (with
all his five wits,) understandeth not the things of
the Spirit of God; because they are spiritually
discerned," 1 Cor. ii. 14. Most prudently to this
point speaketh Elihu, saying, " There is a spirit
in man; but the inspiration of the Almighty
giveth understanding," Job xxxii. 8.

Antil. I understand not these scriptures which
you do allege; they do not sink into my head.

Theol. I think so, indeed. For the Holy Ghost
saith, "Wisdom is too high for a fool," Prov.
xxiv. 7.

Antil. What, do you call me a fool? I am no
more a fool than yourself.

Theol. I call you not a fool; but tell you what
the scripture saith; which calleth all men, though
otherwise never so wise, polite, and learned, very
fools, till they be truly lightened, and inwardly
sanctified by the Spirit of God; as appeareth,
Titus iii. 3, where the apostle affirmeth that both
Titus and himself, before they received the
illuminating Spirit of God's grace, were very
fools, without wit, and without all sense in God's
matters.

Phil. I pray you, good Mr. Theologus, let
him alone; for he will never have done cavilling.
I see he is a notable caviller. Let us therefore
proceed to speak of the fifth sign of condemnation, which is swearing.

Theol. Swearing may well, indeed, be called a sign of condemnation. For I think it more than a sign; it is indeed an evident demonstration of a reprobate. For I never wist any man, truly fearing God in his heart, that was an usual and a common swearer.

Phil. I am flat of your mind for that. For it cannot be that the true fear of God, and ordinary swearing should dwell together in one man, since swearing is a thing forbidden by flat statute. And God addeth a sore threat to his law, that "he will not hold him guiltless that taketh his name in vain;" but will most sharply and severely punish that man.

Theol. You say true. And God saith, moreover, that if we do not fear and dread his glorious and fearful name Jehovah, he will make our plagues wonderful. He sayeth also by his prophet, Malachi iii. 5, that he will "be a swift witness against swearers." The prophet Zechariah saith, v. 3, 4, that the flying book of God's curse and vengeance shall enter into the house of the swearer, and he shall be cut off. Therefore let all swearers take heed and look to themselves in time; for we see there is a rod in pickle laid up in store for them.

Phil. These threatenings being so great and grievous, and that from the God of heaven himself, one would think should cause men's hearts to quake and tremble, and make them afraid to rap out such oaths as they do; if they were not altogether hardened, past feeling, and past grace.

Theol. True, indeed: but yet we see, by lamentable experience, how men are given over both to swear, and forswear. For at this day there is no sin more common amongst us than swearing. For many there be which cannot speak ten words, but one shall be an oath. And numbers have got such a wicked custom of swearing that they can by no means leave it: no more than a black can change his skin, or a leopard his spots. For it is made natural unto them, through custom; and they have got the habit of it. I do verily think, if it were high treason to swear, yet some could not leave swearing. And sure I am, as light as we make of it, that it is high treason against the crown of heaven. Yea, it is a sin immediately against God: even against his own person; and therefore he hath forbidden it, in the first table of his law.

Phil. Questionless, this vice of swearing is of all other sins most rife in this land. For you shall hear little boys and children in the streets rap out oaths in most fearful manner. It would make a man's heart quake to hear them. We may think, they have sucked them out of their mother's breasts; but sure we are, they have learned them from the evil example of their parents. And now-a-days we cannot almost talk with a man, but, in ordinary speech, he will belch out one oath or another.

Theol. I will tell you a strange thing, and with great grief I speak it: I do verily think there are sworn in this land an hundred thousand oaths every day in the year.

Phil. No doubt, sir, you are within compass. For now almost so many men, so many oaths; excepting some few in comparison. Nay, I know divers of mine own experience, which, if they may be kept in talk, will swear every day in the year an hundred oaths for their parts.

Theol. Oh, what a lamentable thing is it! We may well take up the old complaint of the prophet Jeremiah, who saith, that in his time, "The land did mourn because of oaths." And we may well wonder, that the land sinketh not because of oaths: For, if God were not a God of infinite patience, how could he endure his most sacred and glorious name to be so many thousand times blasphemed in one day, and, that, by such miserable wretches as we be?

Phil. We may indeed admire and wonder at the patience and long-suffering of God, that he spareth us so long, and giveth us so large a time of repentance; but sure it is that the prophet saith, that howsoever "the Lord is slow to anger, yet he is great in power, and will not clear the wicked," Nah. i. 3. Though he may wink at their monstrous oaths for a time, yet he forgeteth them never a whit, but scoreth them up, and registereth them in his book of accounts, so as they stand in record against them; and, when the great day of reckoning shall come, he will set them all in order before them, and lay them to their charge. Let not wicked swearers and blasphemers therefore think that they shall always escape scot-free, because God letteth them alone for a while, and deferreth their punishment. For the longer God deferreth, the more terrible will his strokes be when they come. The longer an arrow is held in the bow, the stronger will be the shot when it cometh forth. Though God have leaden feet, and cometh slowly to execute wrath, yet hath he an iron hand, and will strike deadly

when he cometh. " Though God giveth the
wicked security for a time (saith Job, xxiv. 23)
yet his eyes are fixed upon all their ways."
And in another place he saith, xxi. 30, " The
wicked is reserved unto the day of destruction,
and they shall be brought forth unto the day of
wrath." So then the holy man, Job, plainly
affirmeth, that the state and condition of all the
rich and wealthy worldlings is, as the condition of
an ox that is fatted up against the day of slaughter; for, in the same chapter, he saith, ver. 13,
" They spend their days in wealth, and suddenly
go down to hell." But now I pray you nominate the oaths which are so rife and common
amongst us.

Theol. There be six oaths, which are, of all
other, most rife and common in every man's
mouth; and they be these:—by my faith—by
my troth—by our Lady—by St. Mary—by God
—as God shall judge me. For you cannot lightly
talk with a man, but he will flush out some of
these in his ordinary speech.

Asun. Do you count it so great a matter for a
man to swear by his faith or his troth?*

Theol. Yes, indeed do I; for our faith and our
troth are the most precious jewels we have.
Shall we then lay them to gage, for every word
we speak? It sheweth we are of small credit;
nay, very bankrupts. For who but a bankrupt
will lay the best jewel in his house to pledge for
every small trifle?

Asun. I know a man that will never swear
but by cock, or pie, or mouse-foot.† I hope you

* Truth.
† Reliques of the superstition of the dark ages, when birds and
herbs were often thought sacred to some saint. See Matt. v. 34-37.

will not say they be oaths; for he is as honest a man as ever brake bread. You shall not hear an oath come out of his mouth.

Theol. I do not think he is so honest a man as you make him; for it is no small sin to swear by creatures. The Lord saith by his prophet, Jeremiah v. 7, "They have forsaken me, and sworn by them that are no gods." So then, to swear by creatures, is to forsake God; and I trow you will not say he is an honest man which forsaketh God.

Asun. I do not believe that to swear by small things is a forsaking of God.

Theol. You, and such as you are, will believe no more of the word of God than will stand with your fancy. But whatsoever you believe, or believe not, the word of God standeth sure; and no jot of it shall ever be proved false. But this I will say unto you, because you think it so small a matter to swear by creatures, that the more base and vile the thing is which you swear by, the greater is the oath; because you ascribe that unto a base creature, which is only proper to God: namely, to know our hearts, and to be a discerner of secret things. For whatsoever a man sweareth by, he calleth it as a witness unto his conscience that he speaketh the truth, and lieth not; which thing only belongeth unto God. And, therefore, in swearing by creatures, we do rob God of his honour. Therefore, to swear by the cross of the money, or by bread, or a mouse-foot, or the fire which they call God's angel, or any such like, is a robbing of God of his honour, and an ascribing of that to the creature which is proper only to the Creator.

Asun. What say you then to them which swear by the mass* and by the rood?†

Theol. Their sin is as great as the other; for it is an heinous thing to swear by idols: as St. Mary, our Lady, by the mass, by the rood, &c. The prophet Amos saith, viii. 14, "They that swear by the sin of Samaria, and that say, thy God, O Dan, liveth; even they shall fall, and never rise up again." To swear by the sin of Samaria is to swear by idols; for Samaria was full of idols. Moreover, the Lord threateneth by the prophet Zephaniah, i. 5, that he "will cut off them that swear by the Lord, and by Malchom," or by their king. For the idolators called their idol Moloch, their king.

Asun. Seeing you condemn both swearing by creatures, and swearing by idols, what then must we swear by? You would have us swear by nothing belike.

Theol. In our ordinary communication we must not swear at all, either by one thing or another; but, as our Lord teacheth us, "our communications must be yea, yea; nay, nay. For whatsoever is more than these, cometh of evil," Matt. v. 37. And St. James saith, v. 12, "Before all things, my brethren, swear not: neither by heaven, nor by earth, nor by any other oath; but let your yea be yea, and your nay, nay; least you fall into condemnation."

Antil. It seemeth you are an anabaptist. You condemn all swearing; you will have no swearing at all.

Theol. Not so; for though I condemn swearing by creatures, swearing by idols, and all other

---

* The chief ordinance of the Romish worship
† The image of Christ on the cross.

swearing, yet do I allow swearing before a magistrate, and privately also, in matters of weight and importance, for the further bolting out of the truth. This is warranted from God's own mouth, where he saith, "Thou shalt swear, the Lord living, in truth, in judgment, and in righteousness," Jer. iv. 2. And in these cases only, the name of God is to be sworn by; as it is written, Deut. x. 20, "Thou shalt fear the Lord thy God, and thou shalt serve him, and shalt cleave unto him, and shalt swear by his name."

Asun. May we not swear by God in our common talk?

Theol. At no hand; for that is to take the name of God in vain, which you know is forbidden. And one of the wise heathens could say thus, "When an oath is laid upon thee, undertake it for two causes; either to deliver thyself from some grievous crime and accusation, or else to preserve thy friends from danger." So then, that heathen man in common talk will not allow any oath, much less to swear by God. Another saith, "Avoid an oath, though thou swear truly." So then we see vain swearing condemned even by heathens.

Asun. Yea, but for all that we must swear; men will not believe us else.

Theol. Neither yet will they believe you any whit the more for your swearing. For it doth manifestly appear, that thousands make no conscience at all of it. They make no more conscience of it than of cracking nuts; and therefore what wise man will believe them, though they swear never so much? But if you would make conscience always to speak the truth, from your heart, without any oaths at all, you should be better believed of all honest and wise men, than otherwise with a thousand oaths.

Antil. It is the custom to swear.

Theol. But a wicked and devilish custom.

Antil. I hope, sir, we may swear as long as we swear truly, and swear by nothing but that which is good.

Theol. It hath been answered before, that in vain matters you may not swear at all.

Antil. As long as we do no worse than that, I hope God will hold us excused.

Theol. God will not hold you excused when you break his commandments, and continue so doing.

Antil. What say you then, to them, that swear wounds and blood,* and such like, in a bravery, thinking that it setteth out their speech very well?

Theol. Hell gapeth for them. And they shall know one day what it is to blaspheme God.

Antil. What may we think of such as swear by God's life, God's soul, God's body, God's heart?

Theol. That their cause is most woful and dangerous: and I quake at the naming of them. They are most horrible, monstrous, and outrageous blasphemies : enough to make the stones in the street to crack, and the clouds to fall upon our heads. And we may think, that all the devils in hell are in a readiness to carry such blasphemous villains headlong into that lake which burneth with fire and brimstone for ever.

Antil. Do you find in the scriptures that God will so severely punish swearers ?

---

* That is, by Christ's wounds and blood.

Theol. Yes, verily. For besides that which hath been spoken before, we have divers other examples: first, of Senacherib, the king of Ashur,* who, for his outrageous blasphemies against the God of heaven, was in most fearful and tragical manner slain by his own sons, Adramelech and Sharezer, 2 Kings xix. 35; and that in the temple, when he was worshipping his idol god, Nisroch. And yet, behold a more fearful example of God's wrath, against blasphemers, in 1 Kings xx. 29, 30, where we read that an hundred thousand of the Aramites† were slain by the Israelites, in one day, for blaspheming of God; and seven and twenty thousand being left, and flying into the city of Aphek for refuge, were all slain, by the fall of an huge great wall. What should I here speak how the seven sons of Saul, the king of Israel, were hanged up before the Lord in Mount Gibeah, for the breach of the oath made to the Gibeonites long before? 2 Sam. xxi. In these examples we may plainly see that the just God, even in this life, sometimes will be revenged of blasphemers, and oath - breakers; and, therefore, the very heathen in all ages have been very careful for the performing of oaths; as Pharaoh, king of Egypt, willed Joseph to go up into the land of Canaan, to bury his father, according to his oath made to his father.

Phil. Methinketh these so terrible and fearful examples of God's vengeance, against swearers and blasphemers, should strike some terror into the hearts of our blasphemers.

Theol. One would think so indeed, if any thing could do it. But, alas! they are so hardened in it,

---

* Assyria.   † Syrians.

and in all other sin, that nothing can move them; except, peradventure, there were a law made that every swearer and blasphemer should hold his hand a quarter of an hour in boiling lead. This, or some such like severe law, might peradventure curb them a little, and make them bite in their oaths. But otherwise, they will never fear any thing till they be in hell-fire, when it will be too late to repent.

Phil. What may be the cause of this so often and great swearing? for surely it is no inherent and inbred sin in our nature, as some of the other sins be.

Theol. No, verily. But these three I judge to be the cause of it: custom, want of admonition, want of punishment.

Phil. What then are the remedies for it?

Theol. The remedies are these: disuse, prayer, friendly admonition, some sharp law.

LYING.

Phil. Well, sir, we have heard enough of swearing, I pray you proceed to the next sign of damnation, which is lying.

Theol. Swearing and lying be of very near kindred; for he that is a common swearer is for the most part a common liar also. For he that maketh no conscience of swearing, will make no conscience of lying. And as the Lord hateth the one, so also he hateth the other. And as he punisheth the one, so he will punish the other. Therefore Solomon saith, " Lying lips are an abomination unto the Lord," Prov. xii. 22. St. John saith, "Without shall be dogs, enchanters, whoremongers, murderers, and whosoever loveth or maketh lies," Rev. xxii. 15. Again, the same holy man of God saith, "That liars shall have their part and portion in the lake which burneth with fire and brimstone: which is the second death," Rev. xxi. 8.

Phil. These scriptures, which you allege, do manifestly declare that God abhorreth liars, and hath reserved great torments for them. Therefor, the princely prophet David saith that he would banish all liars out of his house. "He that telleth lies (saith he) shall not remain in my sight," Psalm ci. 7. A lying tongue is one of the six things which God doth hate and his soul abhor, Prov. vi. 17. Yet for all this we see the lamentable experience, how many have even taught their tongues to lie, (as the prophet saith, Jer. ix.) and there is no truth in their lips. This vice is almost as common as swearing. For it is hard to find a man that will speak the truth, the whole truth, and nothing but the truth from his heart, in simplicity and plainness, at all times, in all places, and amongst all persons, without all glossing or dissembling, either for fear, gain, flattery, men-pleasing, hiding of faults, or any sinister respect whatsoever. Where, I say, is this man to be found? I would fain see him. I would fain look upon such a man. It would do my heart good to behold him. I would rejoice to set mine eyes upon such a man.

Theol. Such a man as you speak of is hardly to be found among the sons of men. They be black swans in the earth; they be white crows; they be rare birds. For there be very few that will speak the truth from their heart: yet some such I hope there be. But, for the most part, and amongst the greater sort, lying, dissembling, and fraud, do bear all the sway. There is no truth, no honesty, no conscience, no simplicity, no plain dealing, amongst men in these most corrupt times. Faith and truth are parted clean away. And as the kingly prophet saith, "The faithful are failed from among the children of men. They speak deceitfully every one with his neighbour; flattering with their lips, and speak with a double heart," Psalm xii. Men now-a-days study the art of lying, flattering, fawning, glossing, and dissembling: they have a heart and a heart.* They have honey in their mouth, and gall in their heart. Their tongues are as soft as butter and oil; but their hearts are full of bitterness, poison, and wormwood. They are full of outward courtesy and civility, full of court holy water, when there is no truth nor plainness in their inward affection. They will speak you fair when they would cut your throats. They will shew you a good countenance, when they would eat your heart with garlic. In outward show, they will carry themselves plausibly, when their hearts are full of venom and malice. This viperous brood do but watch their times and opportunities till they can get a man upon the hip; and then they will sting him, and work their malice upon him. These fawning curs will not bark till they bite. They will lurk and lie close till they spy their vantage, and then they will shew themselves in their kind: then they will hoist a man, and turn

---

* A Hebrew speech for a deceitful heart. See the margin of our Bibles.

him over the perk* if they can.   These men are
like the waters, which are most deep, when they
are most calm; like a dangerous rock, hid under
a calm sea; or, as the heathen say, "like the
Syren's song, which is the sailor's wreck;" like
the fowler's whistle, which is the bird's death;
like the hid bait, which is the fishes' bane; like
the harpies,† which have virgin's faces, and vul-
ture's talons; or like the hyena, which speaketh
like a friend, and devoureth like a foe; or, as the
scripture saith, like Joab, (2 Sam. xx. 10,) the
captain of the host, which spake kindly to Amasa,
another captain, and kissed him, when presently
he stabbed him; or like unto the Herodians, and
Pharisees' servants, which came to our Lord
Jesus with many fawning insinuations, calling
him good master, and telling him that he was the
plain truth, that he taught the way of God truly,
he regarded no man's person, and many " good
morrows," and all this gear, when as, in very deed,
their purpose was to entangle him in his words,
and to entrap him, that they might catch advantage against him, and so cut his throat, and give
him pap with a hatchet.‡   This it is which the
wise man saith, Prov. xxix. 5, " A man that flattereth his neighbour, spreadeth a net for his feet."
And again, " As silver dross, overlaid upon an
earthen pot: so are fawning lips, and an evil
heart."   And in another place he saith, "He
that beareth hatred, will counterfeit with his lips:
but he layeth up deceit in his heart.   When he
speaks fair, trust him not.   For there are seven
abominations in his heart.   He will cover hatred

---

* Probably off the perch, a treacherous and dangerous fall.
† Fabulous beasts.
‡ Pretend to feed him tenderly, and knock him on the head.

by deceit: but his malice shall be discovered in the congregation," Prov. xxvi. 23–26. In another place he pronounceth a curse on all these hollow-hearted hypocrites, and meally-mouthed flatterers; for saith he, "unto him that blesseth his friend, with a loud voice, betimes in the morning, rising up early, a curse shall be imputed," Prov. xxvii. 14.

Phil. You have very well described the conditions of the men of this age, which have faces, countenances, and tongues, but no hearts; which profess lying and dissembling; which say, he cannot live that cannot dissemble; which have fair faces, and false hearts; which have forgotten that plain honesty is the best policy.

Theol. The Holy Ghost, often in the Proverbs of Solomon, calleth all unregenerate men fools; or, as it is in the Hebrew, men without hearts; because they have no heart to God, no heart to his word, no heart to his children, no heart to godliness, no heart to any thing that is good. They are without an honest heart, an upright heart, a plain heart. They are all in words; nothing in deeds. They promise mountains, and perform mole-hills. They will speak well of religion, and practise nothing. They will give fair words to their friends, and do just nothing for them.

Phil. The world is full of these masked counterfeits; and lying and dissembling did never more abound.

Theol. It is too true that lying and dissembling are most rife, and over-common vices amongst all sorts of men; but, especially, it doth overflow and superabound in shopkeepers and servants. For both these make a trade and occupation of it; they can do no other but lie. It cleaveth unto them as the nail to the door.

Phil. I do certainly know some shopkeepers which (to utter their bad wares, and to blind the eyes of the simple) do trade in lying, all the day long, from sun to sun; from the opening of the shop and windows, to the shutting of the same. And what is their life, if customers come in apace, but swearing, lying, dissembling, and deceiving? They will lie as fast as a dog will trot, as we say. It is a wonder, that their shops and all their wares do not fire over their heads, for their so common, so lewd, and so abominable lying; and that against their own knowledge, against their conscience, against God, against their neighbour, against heaven and earth, men and angels.

Theol. True it is, we may marvel at the long-suffering of God in this behalf. But this is to be noted, that God doth not immediately punish all notorious sinners in this life; but reserveth thousands to the judgment of the great day. In this life he only culleth out some few, whom he smiteth for the example of others, that they might fear and tremble, and learn by other men's harms to beware. Therefore, even in this life, we see before our eyes, some liars, some drunkards, some whoremongers, some swearers, some misers of the world, some ruffians, and cut-throats, striken down by the revenging hand of God. But whereas God smiteth one of these, in this life he letteth an hundred escape. For if he should punish all offenders in this life, to what purpose should the judgment to come serve? If he should punish none, then we should think there were no God, or that he were shut up idle in heaven, and would do neither good nor evil, nor once meddle in the

matters of the earth, as some epicures have dreamed. Therefore, to avoid both these extremities,
God in his heavenly wisdom hath thought good
to mete with some even in this world.

Phil. I am of this mind, that the goods which
men get by swearing, lying and deceit, will never
prosper long.

Theol. You are not therein deceived; for God
will blow upon all such kind of evil-gotten goods,
and they shall put it in a bottomless purse, as the
prophet saith, Hag. i. 6. The Holy Ghost, in the
Book of Proverbs, hath many excellent sayings
to this effect: as chap. xiii. 11, "The riches of
vanity shall be diminished. but he which laboureth with the hand shall increase them." Again,
"He that dealeth with a deceitful hand shall become poor: but the hand of the diligent maketh
rich." Prov. x. 4. In another place he saith,
"The deceitful man roasteth not that which he
hath caught in hunting," Prov. xii. 27. That
is, he shall not long enjoy or taste the prey which
he hath gotten by fraud; for either one trouble
or other will come upon him, that he shall not be
able to possess, or take delight in the spoil.
Therefore it is said, "The bread of deceit is
sweet to a man; but afterwards his mouth shall
be filled with gravel," Prov. xx. 17. That is, in
the end the crafty person shall meet with many
troubles; for either his conscience will upbraid
him and check him, or vengeance will plague
him for his deceit. The fears, cares, and sorrows,
which he shall have, shall be as it were so many
sharp stones, to set his teeth on edge, and to vex
him. Wherefore, instead of meat, he shall feed
on gravel; and instead of wheat, on pebble-
stones. Small pleasure is taken in the end in

goods ill-gotten, or livings unlawfully come by. For the Holy Ghost hath passed sentence upon them that they shall never prosper.

Phil. It sometimes falleth out that they prosper for a time; but as we say, the third heir shall never enjoy them. For God will curse them in our posterity; and our children's children shall feel the smart of our sins. Therefore, the holy man Job saith, xxviii. 14, " The offspring of the wicked shall not be satisfied with bread." For out of doubt, God will bless that only which is got with a good conscience in the works of our calling; and it shall remain blessed to us and our posterity. Therefore, the Spirit saith, "The just man that walketh in his uprightness is blessed, and blessed shall his children be after him," Prov. xx. 7. But God will not bless, but curse that which is got with an evil conscience; as swearing, lying, dissembling, deceiving, &c.

Theol. Some ancient writers have spoken very prudently to this point; for one saith, (Jerom.) " *Injusta lucra breves habent voluptates : longos autem dolores.*" That is, unjust gain hath long sorrow and short joy. Another saith, (August.) "*Eligas damnum, potius quàm turpe lucrum illud: enim semel tantùm te dolere afficiet; hoc verò semper.*" That is, choose loss rather than filthy lucre. For the one will grieve thee but once; the other, for ever. A third saith, (Bernard.) " *Melius est honeste pauperem esse, quàm turpiter divitem. Hoc enim commiserationem, illud verò reprehensionem adfert.*" It is better to be honestly poor, than wickedly rich. For the one moveth pity, the other reproof. One of the wise heathen also saith, "We may not wax rich unjustly;" but live of just things; which he calleth holy things.

Phil. Have we not examples in the scriptures of such as have been punished for lying?

Theol. Yes. For we read how the Gibeonites, for their lying and dissembling, were made drudges and slaves to the Israelites. Josh. ix. 23. Gehazi, also, the servant of Elisha the prophet, for his lying and covetousness together, was smitten with a most grievous leprosy, 2 Kings, v. Ananias and Sapphira his wife, for their lying and dissembling, were stricken down stark dead, by the immediate hand of God, at the rebuke of Peter, Acts v. 5. Zophar, one of Job's friends, speaking of these kind of men, saith, "They shall suck the gall of asps, and the viper's tongue shall slay them. They shall flee from the iron weapons, and a bow of steel shall strike them through," Job xx. 16, 24. Now then, by all these examples, we may plainly see how greatly God abhorreth lying and dissembling.

Phil. Oh, therefore, that we could follow the counsel of the apostle, who saith, Col. iii. 9, "Lie not one to another: seeing that ye have put off the old man, with his works." And again, Eph. iv. 25, "Cast away lying, and speak every one the truth to his neighbour." The manner of speech which the apostle useth is very forcible, implying this much, that we should in a kind of disdain or detestation, cast it away, and throw it from us, as a filthy, stinking and bewrayed clout, hanging about a man's neck; which he doth suddenly snatch away, and hurleth into the fire, as being ashamed that ever it should be seen or known. Would to God, therefore, that we were come to such a detestation and loathing of lying, that we would even spattle at it, and cry fie upon it, and all that use it! Oh that we could hate it as the

devil, which is the father of it; and as hell-fire,
which is the reward of it!   Oh that we were come
but so far as the heathen man who saith, (Homer,
Iliad iii.) " I hate him as the gates of hell who
hath one thing in his tongue, and another in his
heart!"

Antil. Yet for all this we find in the scriptures that even some of the godly have been
taken tardy in lying, and yet have not sinned in
so doing; as Abraham, Jacob, Rahab, the mid-
wives of Egypt; and, therefore, why may we not
do so too?

Theol. I told you before that you may not
make the infirmities of God's people rules for you
to live by; and further, I answer that all these
did offend in their lying.   Some of them, indeed,
I grant, are commended for their love to the
church, and charitable affections to God's people,
but none of them simply for lying; which is a
thing condemned even of the heathen; for saith
one of them, " Lying doth corrupt the life of
many;" and every wise and godly man doth hate
lying.

Antil. But may we not live now and then for
advantage?

Theol. No, verily: neither is there any good
advantage to be got that way; for when you have
made up your accounts, all charges deducted, and
all expenses defrayed, your clear gains will be
very small.   For by your wilful and customary
lying you gain inward grief, and lose true joy;
you gain short pleasure, and lose perpetual glory;
you gain hell, and lose heaven; you make the
devil your friend, and God your enemy.   Now
then, reckon your gain.

Phil. I pray you, let us grow towards a conelusion of this point, and show us briefly the chief causes of lying.

Theol. The chief causes of lying are these: custom, fear, covetousness, the devil.

Phil. What be the remedies?

Theol. The remedies be these: disuse, godly boldness, contentment, earnest prayer.

———

DRUNKENNESS.

Phil. You have spoken enough of the vice of lying to cause all such to abhor it and forsake it, as have any drop of grace, or spark of God's fear in them; but as for them that are filthy, let them be more filthy. Now, I pray you, speak your judgment of the seventh sign of condemnation, which is drunkenness.

Theol. It is so brutish and beastly a sin that a man would think it should not need to be spoken against; but that all reasonable men should even abhor it, and quake to think of it; for it is a most swinish thing: it maketh of a man a beast; it taketh away the heart of man from all goodness, as witnesseth the prophet Hosea, iv. 11, "Whoredom, wine, and new wine, take away their heart." For what heart, what stomach, what appetite can whoremongers and drunkards have to any thing that is good? either to hear or read the word of God, or to pray or to meditate in the same? Alas! they are far from it; far from God; and far from all grace and goodness. Therefore the prophet Joel saith, i. 5, "Awake ye drunkards; weep and howl ye drinkers of wine."

Yea, the mighty God of heaven doth pronounce a woe against them, saying, Isa. v. 11, " Woe unto them that rise up early to follow drunkenness; and to them that continue until night, till the wine do inflame them."   Our Lord Jesus himself giveth us a caveat to take heed of it, Luke xxi. 34, " Take heed, saith he, that your hearts be not overcome with surfeiting and drunkenness, and the cares of this life; and so that day come upon you unawares."   Thus you hear how both Christ himself, and sundry of the prophets, do thunder down from heaven against this gross beastliness which now aboundeth and reigneth amongst the sons of men.

Phil. True indeed; but yet nothing will make men leave it, for it is a most rife and over-common vice   We see many that think themselves somebodies, and as we say no small fools, which yet will be overtaken with it; and thereby lose all their credit and reputation with all wise men: yea, do prove themselves to be but swine and brute beasts, as the Holy Ghost avoucheth, saying, "Wine is a mocker, and strong drink is raging; whosoever is deceived therein is not wise," Prov. xx. 1.

Theol. The wise king, in the same book, doth most notably and fully describe unto us the inconveniences and mischiefs which do accompany drunkenness, and follow drunkards at the heels, "To whom is woe? to whom is sorrow? to whom is strife? to whom is babbling? to whom are wounds without cause? to whom is the redness of the eyes?   Even to them that tarry long at the wine: to them that go and seek out mixed wine," Prov. xxiii. 29.   In the same chapter he saith, ver. 20, 21, " Be not of the number of them which are bibbers of wine, nor of them which glut themselves with flesh; for the drinker and the feaster shall become poor: and the sleeper shall be clothed with rags." Moreover he saith, ver. 33, "Their eyes shall behold strange women:" and that "they shall be like him that lieth in the midst of the sea, and sleepeth on the top of the mast." In all these speeches, the Holy Ghost doth, in most lively manner, describe unto us the properties of drunkards; even their staggering, their reeling, their snorting, their senseless sensuality. Behold, then, what be the cursed fruits and events of drunkenness, even these which follow: woe, alas! grief, misery, beggary, poverty, shame, lusts, strife, babbling, brawling, fighting, quarrelling, surfeiting, sickness, diseases, swinish sleeping, security, and sensuality. So then, I conclude that drunkenness is a vice more beseeming a hog than any reasonable man; and, as one saith, "It is the metropolitan city of all the province of vices." Well, therefore, saith the heathen writer (Demosthenes), "When the wine is in, a man is as a running coach without a coachman."

Phil. Let us hear what executions have been done upon drunkards in former ages, that now men may learn to take heed by their examples.

Theol. Ammon, one of David's ungracious children, being drunk, was slain by his brother Absalom. Benhadad, king of Syria, being drunk, was discomfitted by Ahab, king of Israel. Elah, king of Israel, being drunk, was slain by Zimri his servant, and captain of his chariots; who also succeeded him in the kingdom. Lot, being drunk, committed incest with his own daughters; and therefore was punished in his

posterity. Thus we see, what executions have
been done, even upon kings, for this kind of sin.
Therefore, let man learn, once at last, to shun
vice, and embrace virtue; and as the apostle saith,
to make an end of their salvation in fear and
trembling. For all our shifts and starting holes
will serve us to no purpose in the end: but when
we have fisked* hither and thither, never so much,
yet at the last we must be fain to be shut up in
God's wrath.

Antil. What I pray you, do you make it so
great a matter if a man be a little overtaken with
drink, now and then? There is no man but he
hath his faults: and the best of us all may be
amended. If neighbours meet together, now and
then, at the ale-house, and play a game at maw,
for a pot of ale, meaning no hurt, I take it to be
good fellowship, and a good means to increase
love amongst neighbours, and not so heinous a
thing as you make it.

Theol. I see you would fain make fair weather
of it, and smooth over the matter with sweet
words, as though there were no such great evil
in it; but howsoever you mince it, and blanch
it over, yet the apostle saith flatly, "That drunkards shall not inherit the kingdom of God,"
1 Cor. vi. 10. I think this one sentence is enough
to amaze and strike through the hearts of all
drunkards in the world: for it is as much in effect,
as if the apostle had said, all drunkards are notorious reprobates, and hell-hounds branded of
Satan, and devoted to perpetual destruction and
damnation; but you say you mean no hurt. I
answer, whatsoever you mean, your actions are

---

* Run about carelessly, here and there.

naught, and your fellowship as bad; for what good meaning can you have? or what good fellowship call you it, for poor labouring men, artificers, and such like, to sit idly all the day long in taverns and ale-houses, mis-spending their time and their money in gaming, rioting, swearing, staring, swilling, embezzling, bibbing, brawling, and brabbling? There is no true fellowship in it: it is mere impiety; if we may call it impiety, for poor men to live idly, dissolutely, neglecting their callings, while their poor wives and children sit crying at home for bread, being ready to starve, to beg, or to steal. I pray you speak your conscience, what good fellowship is there in this?

Antil. Yet, for all that, there be some which abstain from ale-houses, and yet are as bad as any other; for they will backbite and slander their neighbours: they will do them a shrewd turn as soon as any other: they are envious, they censure us, and disdain our company: yet we think ourselves as good as they, for all their shews of holiness.

Theol. You speak more than you know, or can justify, against some better than yourself; but, if it were so, you should but justify one sin by another—a lesser by a greater; which is to no purpose.

Antil. Will you then condemn all good fellowship?

Theol. No, no; I do greatly allow godly and Christian fellowship; and acknowledge it to be one of the chiefest comforts we have in the world. I know we are commanded to love brotherly fellowship; but as for your pot-companionship, I hate it, and abhor it; for it is written, " He that followeth the idle shall be filled with poverty." And again, "He that keepeth company with banqueters shameth his father." And in another place, "He that loveth pastime shall be a poor man: and he that loveth wine and oil shall not be rich."

Phil. Good Mr. Theologus, talk no more with him: but let us draw near unto the wind-up of this matter; and tell us, in a word, which be the chief causes of drunkenness.

Theol. The causes are these: ill company, ale-houses, idleness, a wicked humour.

Phil. Which be the true remedies?

Theol. The remedies are these: avoiding of ill company, shunning of ale-houses, labour in our callings, a good course of life.

Phil. Well sir, you have waded far enough in this point: let us now come to the eighth sign of condemnation, which is idleness.

IDLENESS.

Theol. Concerning idleness, this I say briefly, that it is the mother of all vice, and the stepdame of all virtue: yea, it is the very beldame* of all enormities: it is the mother of whoredom; the mother of pride, the mother of theft, the mother of drunkenness, the mother of ignorance, the mother of error, the mother of poverty, the mother of slandering and backbiting, prattling and gossiping, brawling, scolding, quarreling, and what not? Idleness was one of the principle sins of

* Chief mother.

Sodom, as the prophet Ezekiel testifieth, xvi. 49, "Pride, fulness of bread, and abundance of idleness was in her, and in her daughters." Solomon is very plentiful in this matter; for, saith he, "The sluggard lusteth and hath not," Prov. xiii. 4. And again, "The sluggard is wiser in his own conceit, than seven men that can give a sensible reason," xxvi. 16. That is, he taketh himself the wisest of many, because he spareth his body, when others take pains, he saith, "Yet a little sleep, yet a little slumber, yet a folding of the hands: and his poverty cometh like a traveller (that is unawares), and his necessity like an armed man" (that is strongly). Then he foldeth his hands together, and eateth his own flesh, Eccles. iv. 5. For, he hideth his hand in his bosom; and it wearieth him to put it to his mouth again, Prov. xxvi. 15. In another place the Holy Ghost saith, "The slothful man will not plough, because of winter: therefore he shall beg in summer, and have nothing," xx. 4. Again, "The slothful man is brother to him that is a great waster," xviii. 9. Moreover, it is said, that "The sluggard turneth himself upon his bed, as the door doth upon the hinges," xxvi. 14; that is, he keepeth his bed, as if he were fastened to it. And, because the spirit will abound in this point, it is further written of the slothful man that he saith, v. 13, "An huge lion is in the way: I shall be slain in the streets." That is, when any good matter is in hand, as preaching, praying, reading, giving to the poor, &c. then he draweth back, he shrinketh into the shell, he findeth one let* or other, one excuse or other. Then profit and pleasure, business and

* Hindrance.

idleness, matters at home and matters abroad, company, and a thousand occasions will lie in his way, as so many lions, to let and hinder him. So then, we see how lively and plentifully the holy scriptures do paint out the lazy lubbers of this world, and sons of idleness, which are as hardly drawn to any good thing as a bear to the stake. As for the duties of religion, they go as lively and as cheerful about them as a thief goeth up the ladder, to be executed for his theft.

Phil. I do plainly see that this sin of idleness is a very gross evil, and the root of many vices: yet, for all that, there be a great number which think they were born to live idly, as many young gentlemen, and such like, which imagine they came into the world for no other purpose but to hunt and hawk, card and dice, riot and revel, and to spend their days in pleasure and vanity. Again, there be many lazy lozels,* and luskish† youths, both in towns and villages, which do nothing all the day long but walk in the streets, sit upon the stalls, and frequent taverns and ale-houses. Many rich citizens, especially women, do ordinarily lie in bed till nine of the o'clock, and then, forsooth, rise and make themselves ready to go to dinner; and, after they have well dined, they spend the rest of the day, and a good part of the night also, in playing, prattling, babbling, cackling, prating, and gossipping. Fie of this idle life! Many profane serving men also do falsely suppose that they were born only to game, riot, swear, whore, ruffle it, and roist it out, and to spend their time in mere idleness. But of all these, well said the heathen philosopher

* Idle lubbers, or clowns.   † Lazy.

(Aristotle), "*Illi pariter indignantur et dis et homines quisquis otiossus*"—both God and man do hate the idle person.

Theol. It is a lamentable thing to see so many men and women live so idly and so unprofitably as they do. For, alas! there be too many which follow no honest calling, live to no use, nobody is the better for them. They do no good, neither to the church or commonwealth. They are like drone bees : they are unprofitable burthens of the earth. God hath no use of them; the church no good, the commonwealth no benefit, their neighbours no profit, the poor no relief. They imagine they came into the world to do nothing but eat and drink, and sleep, and rise up to play. They think they should spend their time in dicing and dancing, in whoredom and bravery, in gluttony and belly-cheer; in masting themselves, like hogs of Epicurus* herd; in pampering their paunches, and cramming their bellies; in fatting themselves like boars in a frank,† till they be well brawned; and, as Job saith, till their bones run full of marrow, their faces strout with fatness, and they have collops in their flank. Oh, what a beastly life is this ! Fie upon it; fie upon it. It is more meet for epicures than Christians ; for swine, than for men ; for Sardanapalus,‡ and Heliogabalus,§ and such like belly-gods, than for the professors of the gospel. But of all such, Job saith enough, " They spend their days in pleasure, and suddenly go down to hell."

Phil. But may it not be allowed unto lords

* An ancient philosopher, who taught that ease and pleasure were the chief good.
† A swine stye.
‡ A luxurious king of Assyria, burned to death in his palace.
§ A gluttonous Roman Emperor.

and ladies, gentlemen and gentlewomen, and other great ones, to live idly, since they have wherewithal to maintain it.

Theol. God doth allow none to live idly, but all, great and small, are to be employed one way or other, either for the benefit of the church or commonwealth, or for the good government of their own households, or for the good of towns and parishes, and those amongst whom they do converse, or for the succour and relief of the poor, or for the furtherance of the gospel, and the maintaining of the ministry, or for one good use or other. To these ends, our wits, our learning, our reading, our skill, our policy, our wealth, our health, our wisdom, and authority, are to be referred; knowing this, that one day, we shall come to give an account of our bail-wick,* and to be reckoned with, for the employment of our talents. For this cause, Job saith, v. 7, "That man is born to travail as the sparks fly upward." And God hath laid this upon Adam, and all his posterity, "In the sweat of thy brow, thou shalt eat thy bread." Some do set down four causes, why every man should labour diligently in his calling:—First, to bear the yoke laid upon all mankind; by the Lord; secondly, to get the necessaries of this life; thirdly, to live unto the profit of human society; lastly, to avoid evil thoughts and actions. St. Paul findeth great fault with some in the church of Thessalonica, 2. Epis. iii. because they walked inordinately, that is, idly, and out of lawful calling: and therefore concluded, that such as would not labour should not eat. So then, we do plainly see

* Stewardship.

that God alloweth idleness in none. For when
we are idle, as hath been shewed before, we lie
open to the devil and his temptations; and he
getteth within us and prevaileth against us.
While David tarried idly at home in the beginning of the year, when kings used to go forth to
the battle, he was soon overtaken with those two
foul sins of adultery and man-slaughter. So
long as Sampson warred with the Philistines he
could never be taken or overcome; but after he
gave himself to idleness and pleasure, he not
only committed fornication with the strumpet
Delilah, but also was taken of his enemies, and
his eyes miserably put out. These examples
do shew what a dangerous sin idleness is; therefore, the Holy Ghost sends us to school, to the
little creature, the ant, to learn of her both to
avoid idleness, and also to use wisdom and prudence in our actions, "Go to the ant, O sluggard, behold her ways, and be wise: for she
having no guide, task-master, nor ruler, pre-
pareth her meat in the summer, and gathereth
her food in harvest," Prov. vi. 6. And in good
sooth it is wonderful to observe, what infinite pains
and unwearied labour, that silly creature taketh
in summer that she may be well provided for
against winter. Let us, therefore, learn wisdom
from her example; and let us set before our eyes
the looking-glass of all creatures. Let us consider how the birds fly, the fishes swim, the
worms creep, the heavens turn, the elements
move, the sea ebbeth and floweth incessantly:
yea, the earth itself, which is the most heavy and
unwieldy creature of all other, yet never ceaseth
his working, bringing forth his burden in summer, and labouring inwardly all the winter, in

concocting and digesting his nourishment for the next spring. Thus we see how all creatures are diligently and painfully exercised in their kinds; and therefore it is a great shame for us to live idly, carelessly, and dissolutely. Let us therefore learn, once at last, to fly sloth, and every one to live faithfully, diligently, and industriously in our several callings. So shall we both keep Satan at the staves' end, and also much sin out of our souls which, otherwise, idleness will force in upon us.

Phil. I must needs confess that idleness is a gross vice in whomsoever it is found. But specially, in my judgment, it is most odious in magistrates and ministers.

Theol. That is so in truth; for they ought to be the guides, governors, shepherds, and watchmen over the people of God. And therefore, for them to neglect their duties and charges is a most horrible thing, since it concerneth the hurt of many. Therefore, well saith the heathen poet (Homer, Iliad ii.), "A magistrate or a minister may not be lazy and slothful, to whom the nursing of the people is given in charge, and of whom many things are to be cared for." What a lamentable thing, therefore, is it when magistrates are profane, irreligious, popish, vicious, and negligent in the duties of their calling? And how much more lamentable is it when ministers neglect their studies, slack preaching and prayer, and give up themselves, some to covetousness, some to pride, some to husbandry, some to other worldly affairs, and some to spend their time idly in taverns, ale-houses, gaming, rioting, and lewd company? Would to God, therefore, that both these kinds of public persons would cast off idleness and sloth; and with diligence, faithfulness, care, and conscience, perform the duties of their places. For it is an excellent thing for any to be a good man in his place: as a good magistrate that ruleth well, that governeth wisely, which favoureth good men and good causes, and defendeth them; which also setteth himself against bad men and bad causes, and punisheth them sharply and severely; which, moreover, maintaineth virtue, even of a very love he beareth unto it in his heart; and punisheth vice of a very zeal and hatred against it; and not for his credit only, or to please some, or because he must needs do it, and can do no less, or for any such sinister respect; but even of a love to God, a care of his glory, a conscience of duty, and a fervent zeal against sin. So, likewise, it is a notable thing for a minister to be a good man in his place; to be studious in the law of God; diligent and painful in preaching; and that of a love to God, a zeal of his glory, deep pity and compassion towards the souls of the people, seeking by all means possible to win them unto God; carrying himself in all his actions amongst them wisely, religiously, unblameably, and inoffensively. So again, it is a worthy thing to be a good rich man, which doth much good with his riches, which keepeth a good house, relieveth the poor, ministereth to the necessity of the saints, and giveth cheerfully, and with discretion, where need is. So also, it is a commendable thing to be a good neighbour, or a good townsman; by whom a man may live quietly, peaceably, joyfully and comfortably. And lastly, to be a good poor man: that is, humble, lowly, dutiful, painful, ready to help, and ready to please. Oh, I say this is a most excellent and glorious thing, when every man keepeth his standing, his range, and his rank; when all men, with care and conscience, perform the duties of their places; when the husband does the duty of an husband, and the wife of a wife; when the father doth the duty of a father, and the child of a child; when the master doth the duty of a master, and the servant of a servant; when every man setteth God before his eyes in doing those things which especially belong unto him. For herein consisteth the honour of God, the glory of the prince, the crown of the church, the fortress of the commonwealth, the safety of cities, the strength of kingdoms, and the very preservation of all things.

Antil. You have said well in some things. But yet I do not see, but that rich men and women may live idly, since they have enough wherewithal to maintain it; for may not a man do with his own what he list?

Theol. No, verily. For you may not take your own knife, and cut your own throat with it: neither may you take your own axe, and kill your own child with it. Therefore, that reason is naught. Albeit therefore wealthy men and women have great plenty of all things, so as they need not to labour; yet let them be profitably employed some other way. Let them exercise themselves in one good thing or other. If they can find nothing to do, let them give themselves much to private prayers and reading of the scriptures, that they may be able to instruct and exhort others. Or else let ladies and gentlewomen do as that good woman Dorcas did: that is, buy cloth, cut it out, work it, make shirts, shifts, coats, and garments, and give them to the poor, when they have so done. For it is said of Dorcas, that she was a woman full of good works and alms-deeds, which she did. She was a merciful and tender-hearted woman; she was the poor man's friend; she clothed the poor and naked; she knew it was a sacrifice acceptable to God. Oh that the wealthy women of our land would follow the example of Dorcas! But, alas! these days bring forth few Dorcasses, Acts ix. 36–39.

Phil. As you have shewed us the causes of the former evils; so now, I pray you, shew the causes of this also.

Theol. The causes of idleness are: evil examples, bad education, living out of calling.

Phil. Shew us also the remedies.

Theol. The remedies are: good education, labour in youth, good examples, diligence in a lawful calling.

OPPRESSION.

Phil. Now, then, let us come to the last sign of condemnation, which is oppression; and I beseech you, good sir, speak your mind of it out of the scriptures.

Theol. It is so infinite a matter that I know not where to begin, or where to make an end of it; it is a bottomless sink of most grievous enormities. I shall enter into a labyrinth where I shall not know how to get out again; but since you are desirous to hear something of it, this I say, that it is a most cruel monster, a bloody vice,

a most ugly and hideous fiend of hell. The
scriptures, in very many places, do cry out upon
it, arraigning it, adjudging it, and condemning it
down to hell. They do also thunder and lighten
upon all those which are stained and corrupted
with this vice, calling them by such names and
giving them such titles as are taken from the
effects of this sin, and most fit for oppressors;
as namely, "That they grind the faces of the
poor; that they pluck off their skin from them,
and their flesh from their bones; that they eat
them up as they eat bread," Isa. iii. 15 ; Amos
viii. 6 ; Micah iii. 2; Psalm xiv. 4. These are
they which strive to devour all, like savage
beasts, and to get the whole earth into their
hands either by hook or by crook, by right or
by wrong, by oppression, fraud, and violence.
These caterpillars and cormorants of the earth
are like unto the whale fish, which swalloweth up
quick other little fishes; they are like the lion,
that devoureth other beasts; they are like the
falcon, which seizeth, plumeth, and preyeth upon
other fowls. These greedy wolves devour all,
and swallow up the poor of the land; therefore,
the prophets of God do thunder out many great
woes against them. First, the prophet Isaiah
saith, v. 8, "Woe unto them that join house to
house, and field to field, till there be no place
for the poor to dwell in ; that they may be placed
by themselves in the midst of the earth." Secondly, the prophet Jeremiah saith, xxii. 13,
"Woe unto him that buildeth his house by un-
righteousness, and his chambers without equity,"
&c. Thirdly, the prophet Micah saith, ii. 2,
"Woe unto them that covet fields, and take
them by violence; and so oppress a man and his

house, even a man and his heritage." Fourthly, the prophet Habbakuk, ii. 12, crieth out, saying, " Woe unto him that buildeth a town with blood, and erecteth a city by iniquity." St. James also most terribly threateneth these kind of men, saying, v. 1–3, " Go to now, you rich men, weep and howl for your miseries that shall come upon you. Your gold and silver is cankered, and the rust of them shall be a witness against you; and shall eat your flesh as it were fire." Lastly; St. Paul saith flatly, 1 Cor. vi. 10, " That extortioners shall not inherit the kingdom of God." Thus we see how many fearful woes and threats are denounced from heaven against these pestilent cut-throats of the earth.

Phil. And all little enough; for they are steeped in their sin, and the stain of it is so soaked into them, as it will hardly ever be washed out. True it is, that you said, that these cruel oppressing blood-suckers are the most pernicious and pestilent vermin that creepeth upon the face of the earth; and yet, I think, there were never more of them than in these days. For now the wicked world is full of such as do sundry ways bite, pinch, and nip the poor, as we see by every day's lamentable experience; but you can speak more of it than I; therefore, I pray you, lay open the sundry kinds of oppression used in these days.

Theol. There is oppression by usury, by bribery, by racking of rents, by taking excessive fines; oppression in bargaining, in letting of leases, in letting of houses, in letting of grounds, in binding poor men to unreasonable covenants, in thrusting poor men out of their houses, in hiring poor men's houses over their heads, in taking of fees; oppression by lawyers, by church officers, by engrossers, by forestallers; oppression of the church, of the ministry, of the poor; oppression of widows, oppression of orphans; and thus we see how all swarm with oppressions, and nothing but oppressions, oppressions.*

Phil. In truth, this is a most cruel and oppressing age wherein we live; yea, a very iron age. It seemeth that the great ones mind nothing else: they are altogether set upon oppression; they dote and dream of it, they find sweet in it, and therefore they are mad of it; as Solomon saith, Eccles. vii. 7, "Oppression maketh a wise man mad." It seemeth therefore, that this vice is of such marvellous force, that it can bereave men of their wits, and make men stark mad of getting goods by hook or by crook, they care not how, nor from whom; so they have it. Yet, no doubt, the wise God hath enacted many good laws for the suppressing of this evil, and doth threaten the execution of them in his own person; and especially his law doth provide for the safety of the poor, the fatherless, the widow, and the stranger. But you, Mr. Theologus, can repeat the statutes better than I, because you are a professed divine; therefore, I pray you, let us hear them from you.

Theol. In the twenty-second chapter of Exodus, God made this law following · " You shall not trouble an widow or fatherless child; if thou vex or trouble such, and so he call and cry unto me, I will surely hear his cry. Then shall my wrath be kindled, and I will kill you with the sword, and your wives shall be widows, and your children fatherless," Exodus xxii. Again, he

---

* The word oppression occurs twenty-three times in the old Editions.

saith, Deut. xxiv. 14, 15, "Thou shalt not
oppress an hired servant that is needy and poor,
but thou shalt give him his hire for his day;
neither shall the sun go down upon it, for he is
poor, and therewith sustaineth his life, lest he
cry against thee unto the Lord, and it be sin unto
thee." Moreover, the Lord saith, "Thou shalt
do no injury to a stranger, for ye were strangers
in the land of Egypt." And God himself threateneth that he will be "a swift witness against
those which keep back the hireling's wages, and
vex the widow and the fatherless," Mal. iii. 5.
The apostle saith, "Let no man oppress or defraud
his brother in any matters; for the Lord is an
avenger of all such things," 1 Thes. iv. 6. Solomon also saith, "If in a country thou seest the
oppression of the poor, and the defrauding of
justice and judgment, be not astonished at the
matter, for he that is higher than the highest
regardeth; and there be higher than they,"
Eccles. v. 8. All these holy statutes and laws,
enacted and provided against oppressors, do
plainly shew what care the Lord hath for his
poor, distressed, and desolate people.

Phil. But these oppressing hell-hounds are such
as care for nothing. No law of the Almighty
can bridle them; nothing can fear them; nothing
can restrain them. They have made a covenant
with hell and death. They are frozen in the
dregs; they are past feeling; and, as Job saith,
"These are they that abhor the light, they know
not the ways thereof, neither continue in the paths
thereof." Their hearts are as hard as the adamant.
Nothing can move them; nothing can work upon
them. There is a great crying out everywhere of
the stone in the reins, which indeed is a great

torment to the body (but their is no complaining
of the stone in the heart; I mean, a stony heart;
which is the sorest disease that possibly can fall
into the soul of man) and yet in these times it
groweth very rife. For men's hearts are as hard
as brass, and as the nether millstone, as the scripture speaketh. For many, especially of these unmerciful and oppressing tyrants, say in their
hearts, " God will do neither good nor evil," Zeph.
i. 12. Therefore they put the evil day far from
them, and approach unto the seat of iniquity.
They are at ease in Zion; they lie upon beds of
ivory, and stretch themselves upon their beds;
and eat the lambs of the flock, and the calves out
of the stall. They sing to the sound of the viol;
they invent instruments of music, like David.
They drink wine in bowls, and no man is sorry
for the affliction of Joseph" (Amos vi. 3–6); that
is, the troubles of God's people. The prophet
Isaiah, v. 12, also complaineth of these kind of
men, saying, " They regard not the work of the
Lord, neither consider the work of his hands."
And another prophet saith, " They say in their
hearts God hath forgotten; he hideth away his
face, and will never see. They are so proud, that
they seek not for God. They think always, there
is no God; his judgments are far out of their
sight. Their ways always prosper; and therefore
they say in their hearts, tush, we shall never be
moved, nor come in danger."

Theol. You have spoken very well, touching
the steeliness and hardness of these men's hearts,
who are so unmerciful to their poor neighbours,
that almost none can live by them. They do so
disturb and disquiet all things, that poor men can
dwell in no rest by them. Therefore truly saith

the wise king, "A mighty man molesteth all, and both hireth the fool, and hireth those that pass by." But the poor man speaketh with prayers; that is, by the way of entreaty and supplications. For the poor are afraid of them. They quake when they see them; as the beasts quake at the roaring of the lion. Many poor farmers, poor husbandmen, poor herdsmen, poor labourers, poor widows, and hirelings, do quake and tremble, when these greedy wolves come abroad. And, as Job speaketh, xxiv. 4, "The poor of the earth hide themselves together." For, alas! in their hearts they cannot abide the sight of them; they had as leave meet the .devil as meet them, for fear of one displeasure or another. For either they fear that they will warn them out of their houses, or parley about more rent and and straighter covenants, or beg away their best kine, or borrow their horses, or command their carts, or require a week's work of them, and never pay them for it, or a twelve months' pasture for a couple of geldings, or that they will make one quarrel or another unto them, or one mischief or another. So that these poor souls cannot tell what to do, nor which way to turn them, for fear of these cruel termagants. They are even weary of their lives; for they have no remedy for these things, but even to bear it off with head and shoulders. Therefore, they often wish they were out of the world, and that they were buried quick. They say, if any will knock them on the head, they will forgive him. Oh most piteous case! Oh lamentable hearing! These poor silly creatures are fain to drudge and moil all the year long, in winter and summer, in frost and snow, in heat and cold, to provide their rents that they may be able to pay their cruel landlord at his day: for else, how shall they be able to look him in the face? Yet, their rent is so racked, that all that they can do, is little enough to pay it. And when that is paid, alas! the poor man, and his wife, and his children, have little left to take to, or to maintain themselves withal; they are fain to gnaw of a crust, to fare hardly, and to go thinly clad. Sometimes they have victuals, and sometimes none. The poor children cry for bread. Poor widows, also, and poor fatherless children, are found weeping and mourning in their houses, and in their streets. So that now we may with Solomon, "Turn and consider all the oppressions that are wrought under the sun," Eccles. iv. 1. We may behold the tears of the oppressed, and none comforteth them. For the mighty ones do wrong the weaker; even as the stronger beasts do push and harm the feebler. These griping oppressors do pinch the poor even to the quick. They pluck away from the fatherless and widows that little which they have. If there be but a cow, or a few sheep left, they will have them. If there be a little commodity of house or land, oh what devices they have to wind it in, and to wring it away! These tyrants will go as nigh as the bed they lie upon. They know well enough the poor men are not able to wage law with them: and therefore they may do what wrong they will, and shew what cruelty they list. Hence cometh the tears of the oppressed; hence cometh the weeping and wailing of the poor. But, alas! poor souls, they may well weep to ease their hearts a little; but there is none to comfort them: remedy they can have none. But yet assuredly the ever-lasting God doth look upon them, and will be revenged. For the cries of the poor, the fatherless, and the widows, have entered into the ears of the Lord of Hosts, who is an avenger of all such things, yea, a strong revenger, as Solomon saith, "Enter not into the field of the fatherless; for their revenger is strong. He himself will plead their cause against thee," Prov. xxiii. 10, 11. And again he saith, "Rob not the poor, because he is poor; neither tread down the afflicted in the gate: for the Lord pleadeth their cause, and will spoil their soul that spoil them," Prov. xxii. 22. We see then, that the most just God will be revenged on these unmerciful tyrants. He will not always put up these wrongs and injuries done to the poor. In the eighth chapter of the prophet Amos, he sweareth by the excellency of Jacob, that he will never forget any of their works. And again, he saith, by his prophet Jeremiah, "Shall I not be avenged on such a nation as this?" Surely he will set his face against them, to root them out of the earth. For indeed they are not worthy to crawl upon the face of the earth, or to draw breath amongst the sons of men. It is written in the book of Psalms, xxi. 12, that God will set their fellows opposite against him, as a butt to shoot at—that he will put them apart— and the strings of his bow shall he make ready against their faces. Be astonished at this, O ye heavens; and tremble, O thou earth. Hear this, O ye cruel landlords, unmerciful oppressors, and blood-suckers of the earth. You may well be called blood-suckers: for you suck the blood of many poor men, women, and children: you eat it, you drink it, you have it served in at your sumptuous tables every day, you swallow it up, and live by it; and, as Job saith, xxiv. 5, "The wil-

derness giveth you and your children food;" that
is, you live by robbing and murdering. But woe,
woe! unto you that ever you were born. For the
blood of the oppressed, which you have eaten
and drunken, shall one day cry for speedy vengeance against you; as the blood of Abel cried
against Cain. Their blood shall witness against
you in the day of judgment; and the tears of
many poor starved children, orphans, and widows shall cry out against you. Was the Lord
revenged of Ahab, for his cruel and unjust dealing with poor Naboth, and shall he not be revenged of you? Did the dogs lap the blood of
Ahab, and shall you escape? No, no; you
shall not escape. "The Lord will be a swift witness against you:" as he saith in Malachi. Was
the Lord angry with the rich of his people, for
oppressing the poor (so as the cry of the people
and of their wives, against their oppressors, was
heard of the Almighty) and do you think, you
shall escape scot-free? Doth not the like cause
bring forth the like effect? the like sin, the like
punishment? Know therefore for a certainty,
that the Lord hath coffers full of vengeance
against you, and one day he will unlock them,
and bring them forth in the sight of all men.
Know also, that the timber of your houses, and
the stones of your walls, which you have built
by oppression and blood, shall cry against you in
the day of the Lord's wrath, as the prophet
Habakkuk, ii. 11, telleth you, " The stone (saith
he) shall cry out of the wall; and the beam out
of the timber shall answer it." Where the prophet telleth you, that the walls of your houses
built in blood shall cry out loud and shrill, and
play the choristers in that behalf; so as they shall

answer one another on either side. The one side singeth, behold blood: the other, behold murder. The one side behold deceit: the other, behold cruelty. The one behold piling and poling: the other, behold covetousness. The one, behold robbery: the other, behold penury. And thus you see how the stones and timber of your houses shall descant upon you. And howsoever you put on your brazen brows, and harden your hearts against these threatenings of the most terrible God and Lord of Hosts; yet one day, you shall (spite of your hearts) will ye, nill ye, be brought forth unto judgment; you shall once come to your reckoning, you shall at last be apprehended, convented, and arraigned at the bar of God's tribunal-seat before the great Judge of all the world. Then sentence shall pass against you; even that most dreadful sentence, " Go ye cursed into hell-fire, there to be tormented with the devil and his angels for ever." Oh then, woe, woe unto you! "For what shall it profit a man to win the whole world, and lose his own soul?" saith our Lord Jesus. Surely even as much, as if one should win a farthing, and lose an hundred thousand pounds: For, if he shall be cast into hell-fire, which hath not given of his own goods righteously gotten, as our Saviour avoucheth; where then shall he be cast that hath stolen other men's goods? And if he shall be damned that hath not clothed the naked, what shall become of him that hath made naked them that were clothed? Oh, therefore, repent in time, O ye cruel oppressors; seek the Lord whilst he may be found; call upon him while he is near; lay aside your savage cruelty; visit the fatherless and widow in their distress; deal your bread to the hungry;

help them to their right which suffer wrong; deal
mercifully with your tenants; rack not your rents
any more: pinch not the poor souls, for whom
Christ died; pity them I say, but pinch them not;
deal kindly and friendly with them; remember
your great accounts; consider the shortness of
your days, and the vanity of your life: rend your
hearts, and not your clothes. Turn unto the Lord
with all your heart, with weeping, fasting, and
mourning: prevent God's wrath with a sacrifice
of tears; pacify his anger with the calves of your
lips and with a contrite spirit; be grieved for
that which is past, and amend that which is to
come. Stand it out no more at the sword's point
against God; for it will not boot you to strive:
he is too strong for you. Your only wisdom is to
come in. Come in, therefore, come in ye rebellious generation; submit yourselves to the great
King, humble yourselves under his mighty hand;
cast down your swords and targets; yield unto
your God. So shall you escape the vengeance to
come; so shall God accept you, have mercy upon
you, receive you to favour, grant you a general
pardon for all your rebellions, and admit you into
the number of his faithful and loyal subjects.

Phil. I do conceive, by divers speeches which
you have alleged, that goods gotten by oppression
and cruelty, will never prosper long. For oppressors coin their money upon their neighbour's skins.
How then can it be blessed?

Theol. You have spoken a truth. For, as it
hath been shewed before, that those goods which
are gotten by swearing and lying are cursed: so
all these that are gotten by oppression and
violence are more cursed. Therefore the Lord
saith by his prophet Jeremiah, xvii. 11, " As the

partridge gathereth the young which she hath not brought forth, so he that gathereth riches, and not by right, shall leave them in the midst of his days: and at his end shall be a fool, and his name shall be written in the earth."

Phil. Would to God our magistrates and governors would take speedy order for the remedying of these things; and for the redressing of such grievous enormities as are amongst us; or that they themselves would step in, and deliver the oppressed from the hand of the oppressor.

Theol. Job was an excellent man for such matters. For it is said of him, xxix. 17, "That he brake the jaws of the unrighteous man, and plucked the prey out of his teeth;" where we see, how Job was the means to deliver the innocent, and to pull the lamb out of the lion's claws. Moreover, it is written of him in the same chapter, that " The blessing of him that was ready to perish came upon him, and that he caused the widow's heart to rejoice: that he was eyes to the blind, feet to the lame, and the father to the poor; and when he knew not the cause, he sought it out diligently." Oh, what a notable man was this! Oh, that we had many Jobs in these days! Wise Solomon doth most gravely advise us all to follow Job's example in this behalf. " Deliver (saith he) them that are oppressed and drawn to death. For shouldest thou withdraw thyself from them which go down to the slaughter?" ·Prov. xxiv. 11, 12. Would to God that this holy counsel were well weighed and practised amongst us!

Phil. I marvel much, with what face these cruel oppressors can come before God in his holy temple, to pray, and offer up their sacrifices unto him. For we see, many of them though they have such foul hands and foul hearts, as we have heard; yet for all that, will most impudently presume to come to the Church and pray; or at least, when they are laid in their beds at nights, and half asleep, then will they tumble over their prayers, or be pattering some paternosters.*

Theol. Alas, alas! poor souls; all that they do in matters of God's worship is but hypocrisy, and dissimulation; for in truth, they care not for God, they love him but from the teeth outward; their mouths are with him, but their heart goeth after covetousness, and their hands are full of blood. And therefore God doth both abhor them and their prayers; for he saith, "Though they stretch out their hands, yet will I hide mine eyes from them; and though they make many prayers, yet will I not hear them. For their hands are full of blood," Isa. i. 15. Moreover the Holy Ghost saith, "He that turneth away his ear from hearing the law, even his prayer is abominable," *Prov.* xxviii. 9. David saith, "If I regard wickedness in my heart, God will not hear my prayer," *Psalm* lxvi. 18. It is also affirmed, John ix. 31, that, "God heareth not sinners:" that is, stubborn and careless sinners. So then, we may clearly see, by all these testimonies of holy writ, what account God maketh of the prayers of oppressors, and all other profane and ungodly men; namely, that he doth hate them, and abhor them, as most loathsome and odious in his sight.

Phil. Now in conclusion, shew us the causes of oppression.

Theol. The causes are these: cruelty, covet-

* "Our Father," a name for the Lord's Prayer.

ousness, hard-heartedness, an evil conscience, the devil.

Phil. Let us hear also the remedies.

Theol. The remedies are these: pity, contentment, tender affections, a good conscience, much prayer.

THE DREADFUL EFFECTS OF SIN ON INDIVIDUALS AND UPON NATIONS.

Phil. Now, sir, as you have at large uttered your mind, concerning these gross corruptions of the world, and have plainly and evidently proved them to be the deadly poison of the soul, so also, I pray you, satisfy us in this, whether they be not hurtful also to the body, goods, and name.

Theol. I have dwelt the longer in these common vices of the world, because almost all sorts of men are stained with one or other of them; and therefore they can never be enough spoken against. "For the whole world lieth in them," as St. John testifieth, 1 Epis. v. 19. If men therefore, could be recovered of these diseases, no doubt there would be a ready passage made for the abundance of grace; and we should have a most flourishing church and commonwealth; but as long as these do lie in the way, there is small hope of greater mercies and blessings to be poured upon us; or that ever we shall come to have an inward conversation with God. For these vices blind our eyes, burden our hearts, and as the prophet Jeremiah saith, v. 25, " hinder many things from us." But touching

your petition, I must needs grant, that as these
vices are the very bane of the soul, and most
certain signs of condemnation, so are they very
dangerous to the body, goods, and name; yea,
and to the whole land, both church and commonwealth.

Phil. Shew us out of the scriptures what
danger they bring to the body?

Theol. The Lord our God saith, "That if we
will not obey him nor keep his commandments,
but break his covenant, he will appoint over us
hasty plagues, consumptions, and the burning
ague, to consume the eyes, and to make the
heart heavy," Lev. xxvi. So also he saith,
"That if we will not obey his voice, to observe
all his commandments and ordinances, that then
he will make the pestilence cleave to us, until
he have consumed us; that he will smite us with
fever, with the botch of Egypt, with the eme-
rods, with the scab, and with the itch, that also
he will smite us with madness, and with blindness, and with astonishment of heart," Deut.
xxviii. So then, you see what great evils the
Lord threateneth to inflict upon our bodies in
this life, for these and such like sins. But on the
contrary the Holy Ghost saith, "Fear God, and
depart from evil: so health shall be unto thy
navel, and moisture unto thy bones," *Prov.* iii.
7, 8.

Phil. What evil do these fore-named sins bring
upon us in our goods and outward estate?

Theol. They cause God to curse us all in that
we set our hand unto, as plentifully appeareth in
the fore-named chapters, where the Lord saith
thus, "If thou wilt not obey the commandments
of the Lord thy God, cursed shalt thou be in the

town, cursed also in the field, cursed shall be thy basket and thy store, cursed shall be the fruit of thy body, and the fruit of thy land, and the increase of thy kine, and the flocks of thy sheep; cursed shalt thou be when thou comest in, and cursed also when thou goest out. The Lord shall send upon thee cursing, trouble, and shame, in all that thou settest thy hand unto; and further he saith, "That he will break the staff of their bread; that ten women shall bake their bread in one oven, and they shall deliver their bread again by weight; and shall eat and not be satisfied." You do, therefore, apparently see that these sins will draw down God's wrath upon us and all that we have.

Phil. What hurt do these sins to our good name?

Theol. They bring reproach, shame, and infamy upon us, and cause us to be abhorred and contemned of all good men; they do utterly blot out our good name. For as virtue maketh men honourable and reverend, so vice maketh men vile and contemptible. This is set down where the Lord threateneth Israel, that for their sins and disobedience he will make them a proverb and common talk; yea, a reproach and astonishment amongst all people. In sundry other places of the prophets, he threateneth for their sins to make them a reproach, a shame, an hissing, and nodding of the head to all nations.

Phil. I do verily thus think, that as sin generally doth stain every man's good name, which all are chary and tender of, so especially it doth blot those which are in high places, and of special note, for learning, wisdom, and godliness.

Theol. You have spoken most truly, and

M

agreeable to the scriptures; for the scriptures saith, "As a dead fly causeth the apothecary's ointment to stink, so doth a little folly him that is in reputation for wisdom and honour." Where Solomon sheweth, that if a fly get into the apothecary's box of ointment, and die, and putrify in it, she marreth it, though it be never so precious; even so, if a little sin get into the heart, and break out in the forehead of a man of great fame for some singular gifts, it will blear him, though he be never so excellent.

Phil. Shew this, I pray you, more plainly.

Theol. We observe this in all experience, that if a nobleman be a good man, and have many excellent parts in him of courtesy, patience, humility, and love of religion; yet if he be covetous, the common people will have their eye altogether upon that; and they will say, such a nobleman is a very good man, but for one thing: he is exceedingly covetous, oppresseth the poor men, and dealeth hardly with his tenants, keepeth no house, doth little good in the country where he dwelleth; and this is it that marreth all. Moreover, let a judge, a justice, or a magistrate, be endued with excellent gifts of prudence, policy, temperance, liberality, and knowledge in the law, yet if they be given to anger, or taking of bribes, oh, how it will grieve them amongst the people! for they will say, he is a worthy man indeed, but there is one thing in him that marreth all: he is an exceedingly angry and furious man; he is as angry as a wasp; he will be in a pelting chafe* for every trifle; he will fret and fume if you do but blow upon him;

* A raging passion, so as to pursue and pelt you.

and beside this, he is a very corrupt man; he is a great taker of bribes; he loveth well to be bribed; he will do any thing for bribes. Furthermore, if any preacher be a man of great gifts, the common people will say of him, oh! he is a worthy man indeed, an excellent scholar, a profound divine, a singular man in a pulpit; but yet for all that he hath a shrewd touch which marreth all; he is an exceedingly proud man; he is as proud as Lucifer; he hath very great gifts indeed, but I warrant you he knoweth it well enough; for he carrieth his crest very high, and looketh very sternly and disdainfully upon all other men. He is unmeasurably puffed up with overweening,* and thinketh that he toucheth the clouds with his head. Thus, therefore, we see how the dead flies mar all, and how some one sin doth disgrace a man that otherwise doth excel.

Phil. What is the cause why some one sin doth so blot and smite the most excellent men?

Theol. The reason hereof is, because such men are a candle, set upon a candlestick, or rather upon a scaffold or mountain, for all men to behold and look upon; and sure it is, they have a thousand eyes upon them every day; and that not only gazing upon them, but also prying very narrowly into them, to spy out the least mote that they may make a mountain of it. For, as in a clean white paper, one little spot is soon espied, but in a piece of brown paper twenty great blurs scarce discerned; even so in noblemen, judges, magistrates, justices, preachers, and professors, the least spot or speck is soon seen into;

---

* High conceits of himself.

but amongst the baser sort, and most gross livers, almost nothing is espied or regarded.

Phil. Since the eyes of all men are bent and fixed upon men as are of some note, therefore, they had need very heedfully to look to their steps, that they may take away all advantage from them that seeth advantage.

Theol. Yes, verily. And furthermore, they had need to pray with David always, "Direct my steps, O Lord, in thy word; and let none iniquity have dominion over me;" and again, "Order my doings, that my footsteps slip not: uphold me in mine integrity;" for if such be never so little given to swearing, to lying, to drink, or to women, it is espied by and by; and therewith their credit is cracked, their fame overcast, their glory eclipsed, and the date of their good name presently expired.

Phil. Now as you have shewed what great hurt these sins do bring upon our souls, bodies, goods, and names; so also, I pray you, shew what danger they do bring upon the whole land.

Theol. Questionless they do pull down the wrath of God upon us all, and give him just cause to break all in pieces, and utterly to subvert and overthrow the good estate both of church and commonwealth; yea, to make a final consumption and desolation of all; for they be the very firebrands of God's wrath, and as it were touchwood, to kindle his anger and indignation upon us. For the apostle saith, "For such things cometh the wrath of God upon the children of disobedience," Col. iii. 6.

Phil. Declare unto us, out of the scriptures, how the Lord in former times hath punished whole nations and kingdoms for these and such like sins.

Theol. In the fourth of Hosea, the Lord telleth his people, that he hath a controversy with the inhabitants of the land, and the reason is added, because there was no truth, nor mercy, nor knowledge of God in the land. By swearing, lying, killing, stealing, and whoring, they break out, and blood toucheth blood. Therefore shall the land mourn; and every one that dwelleth therein shall be cut off. Here then we see what it is will incense God against us, and cause us all to mourn. So likewise the Lord threateneth, by his prophet Amos, viii. 4–8, " That for cruelty and oppression of the poor, he would plague the whole land. Shall not the land tremble for this, and every one mourn that dwelleth therein?" Again, the Lord saith by his prophet Jeremiah, vii. 19, 20, "Do they provoke me to anger, and not themselves, to the confusion of their own faces? Therefore thus saith the Lord, behold mine anger and my wrath shall be poured upon this place, upon man, and beast, upon the tree of the field, and upon the fruit of the ground; and it shall burn, and not be quenched." Again the Lord saith, " If ye will not hear these words, I swear by myself, saith the Lord, that this house shall be waste, and I will prepare destroyers against thee, every one with his weapons, and they shall cut down thy chief cedar trees, and cast them in the fire." Likewise the Lord threateneth, by his prophet Ezekiel, v. 7, " Because ye have not walked in my statutes, nor kept my judgments; therefore behold, I, even I, come against thee, and will execute judgment in the midst of thee, even in the sight of nations; and I will do in thee that I never did before, neither will I do any more the like because of all thine abominations. For, in the midst of thee, the fathers shall eat their sons, and the sons shall eat their fathers." Again, by the same prophet, the Lord saith, vii. 23–27, " The land is full of the judgment of blood, and the city full of cruelty. Wherefore, I will bring the most wicked of the heathen, and they will possess their houses. I will also make the pomp of the mighty to cease, and the holy places shall be defiled. When destruction cometh, they shall seek peace, and not have it. Calamity shall come upon calamity, and rumour upon rumour. Then shall they seek a vision of the prophet, but the law shall perish from the priests, and counsel from the ancient. The king shall mourn, and the prince shall be clothed with desolation, and the hands of the people in the land shall be troubled. I will do unto them according to their ways, and according to their judgments will I judge them; and they shall know that I am the Lord." Last of all, the Lord saith by his prophet, "Hear, O earth! behold, I will cause a plague to come upon this people, even the fruit of their own imaginations, because they have not taken heed to my words, nor to my law; but cast it off." Almost innumerable places to this purpose are to be found in the writings of the prophets; but these may suffice to prove the main point: to wit, that the just God doth punish whole nations and kingdoms for the sins and rebellions thereof.

Phil. Since all these sins (for the which the Lord did execute such universal punishments upon his own people) do abound and overflow in this land, may we not justly fear some great plague to fall upon us? and the rather, because our transgressions do increase daily, and grow to a full height and ripeness; so as it seemeth the harvest of God's vengeance draweth near, and approacheth.

Theol. We may indeed justly fear and tremble. For if God spared not the angels that sinned, how shall he spare us? If he spared not his own people, what can we look for? If he spared not the natural branches, how shall he spare us which are wild by nature? Are we better than they? Can we look to be spared, when they were punished? Are not our sins as many and as great as theirs? Doth not the same cause bring forth the same effect? Is the arm of the Lord shortened? or is not God the same just God, to punish sin now, that he was then? Yes, yes, assuredly. And therefore we have great cause to mourn and lament, to quake and tremble; because there is a naked sword of vengeance hanging over our heads. Thus did Jeremiah, iv. 19, thus did Amos, v. 6, thus did Habakkuk, iii. 16, when they plainly saw the imminent wrath of God approaching upon the people of Israel and Judah.

Phil. I think we may the rather doubt and fear because the punishment of these forenamed vices is neglected by the magistate. For commonly, when they that bear the sword of justice, do not draw it out to punish notorious offenders and malefactors, the Lord himself will take the matter into his own hands, and be revenged in his own person, which is most dreadful and dangerous; "for it is a fearful thing to fall into the hands of the living God," Heb. x. 31.

Theol. You have spoken a truth: for if those which are God's deputies and vicegerents in the earth, do their duties faithfully in punishing vice and maintaining virtue, in smiting the wicked and favouring the godly, then assuredly evil shall be taken out of Israel, God's wrath prevented, and his judgments intercepted; as it is written, Ps. cvi. 30, "Phineas stood up and executed judgment, and the plague was stayed." But if they (for fear, favour, affection, gain, flattery, bribery, or any other sinister respect) will be too sparing and remiss in punishing of gross offenders, and be rather ready to smite the righteous; then do they exceedingly provoke God's wrath against the land, and against themselves.

Phil. One thing I do greatly lament, that there be either none at all, or very slender censures, either by the civil or ecclesiastical authority, for divers of these forenamed vices: as pride, covetousness, oppression, lying, idleness, swearing, &c.

Theol. It is a thing to be lamented indeed. For where do we see a proud man punished, a covetous man punished, an oppressor punished, a swearer punished, a liar punished, an idle person punished? Now, because they know they cannot or shall not be punished, therefore they are altogether hardened, and emboldened in their sins; as the wise man saith, Eccl. viii. 11, "Because sentence against an evil work is not executed speedily, therefore the hearts of the children of men are fully set in them to do evil."

Phil. One thing I do much muse at, wherein also I desire to be further satisfied, to wit what is the cause that under so godly a prince, so many good laws, and so much good preaching and teaching, there should notwithstanding be such an excess and overflowing of sin, in all estates.

Theol. The causes hereof are divers and manifold. But I will nominate four especial ones in my judgment:—The first is man's natural corruption, which is so strong as almost nothing can bridle it; the second is ill-precedents and external provocations to evil; the third is the want of teaching in many congregations of the land, by reason whereof many know not sin to be sin; the last reason is the corruption and negligence of some such as are in authority.

Phil. Doth not this inundation and overflowing of sin, with the impunity of the same, prognosticate great wrath against us?

Theol. Yes, undoubtedly, as hath in part been shewed before. And there be divers other presages of wrath, though not of the same kind, which are these:—Unthankfulness for the gospel—the abuse of our long peace—our general security—our secret idolatries—our ripeness in all sin—our abuse of all God's mercies—our abuse of his long patience—the coldness of professors—our not profiting by former judgments; as pestilence, famine, death, and the shaking of the sword.

Phil. This last I take to be a special token of approaching vengeance, that we have not profited by former warnings.

Theol. True indeed: for it is an ordinary thing with God, when men will not profit by mild corrections, and common punishments, then to lay greater upon them; and when a former trouble doth us no good, we are to fear a final consuming trouble. For so we read in the prophecy of Hosea, v. 12, 14; that at the first, God was to Ephraim as a moth, and to Judah as rottenness, but afterwards, when as they profited not by it, he was to Ephraim as a lion, and to Judah as a lion's whelp. So the Lord saith, in another place, that if they will not come in and yield obedience at the first call of his wrath, then he will punish them seven times more, Lev. xxvi. 18. But if they continue in their stubbornness, then he threateneth to bring seven times more plagues upon them, according to their sins. If by all these they would not be reformed, but walk stubbornly against him, then he threateneth yet seven times more for their sins; and the fourth time, yet seven times more, ver. 21, 24, 28. The proof hereof we have in the book of the Judges, where we read, how the people of Israel, for their sins, were in subjection to the king of Aram, Naharim, eight years; afterward, because they profited nothing by it, but returned to their old sins, therefore they served Eglon, king of Moab, eighteen years. After that again, for their new sins and provocations, the Lord gave them up into the hands of Midian seven years. After all this, for the renewing of their sins, the Lord sold them into the hands of the Philistines and the Ammonites, which did grievously vex and oppress them, for the space of eighteen years. Last of all, we read that when neither famine nor pestilence could cause them to return unto him, then he delivered them up to the sword of their enemies, and held them in bondage and captivity threescore and ten years. After all this, when they were delivered out of captivity and returned home safely to their own nation, and enjoyed some good time of peace and rest, yet at last they fell to renewing of their sins, and therefore the Lord plagued them most grievously by the divided Greek empire, even by Magog, and Egypt, Seleucidæ, and Lagidæ,* and that by the space almost of three hundred years. And this is it that the prophet Hosea did foretell, iii. 4, "That the children of

---

* Names of the enemies of Israel. See 1st Maccabees.

Israel should remain many days without a king, and without a prince, without an offering, and without an image, without an ephod, and without teraphim."

Phil. You have very largely laid open this last token of vengeance; to wit, that God at the first doth but beat us upon the coat, but if we continue in sin he will whip us on the bare skin, and if men will not yield at the first gentle stroke, then he will strike harder and harder, till he have broken our stout stomachs and made our great hearts come down. Therefore it is good yielding at the first, for we shall get nothing by our sturdiness against him. We do but cause him to double his strokes, and strike us both sidelings and overthwart: for he cannot endure that we should gruntle* against him with stubborn sullenness. But now to the point: since there are so many presages and fore-signs of God's wrath, I pray you show what it is that stayeth the execution and very downfall of the same.

Theol. The prayers and tears of the faithful are the special mean that stay the hand of God from striking of us; for the prayers of the righteons are of great force with him, even able to do all things. St. James saith, v. 16, " The prayer of a righteous man availeth much, if it be fervent," and bringeth the example of Elias to prove it; for, saith he, " Though Elias was a man subject to the like passions that we be, yet was he able by his prayers both to open and shut the heavens." Abraham, likewise, prevails so far with God, by his prayers for Sodom, that if there had been but ten just men found in it, it had been

---

* Murmur and grudge.

spared. The Almighty God saith, in the 15th
chap. of Jeremiah, " Though Moses and Samuel
stood before me, yet mine affection could not be
towards this people;" which doth plainly show
that Moses and Samuel might have done much
with him, had he not been so fully bent against
his people for their sins, as he was. So likewise
he saith in the prophecy of Ezekiel, xiv. 14,
" Though these three men, Noah, Daniel, and
Job were amongst them, they should deliver but
their own souls by their righteousness;" which
also sheweth, that if there had been any possible
entreating of him for the land, these three men
might have done it; but now he was resolutely
determined to the contrary. In respect therefore, that the zealous preachers, and true professors of the gospel do so much prevail with God
by their prayers, they are said to be the defence
and strength of kingdoms and countries, of
churches and commonwealths; as it is said of
Elijah, that he was the chariot of Israel and the
horseman thereof. Elisha also was environed
with a mountain full of horses and chariots of fire.
And sure it is that Elijah and Elisha are not only
the chariots and horsemen of Israel, but also by
their prayers they do cause God himself to be a
wall of fire round about it; as the prophet saith,
Ezekiel xx. 30, " The Lord God saith, I sought
for a man among them, that should make up the
hedge and stand in the gap before me for the
land; that I might not destroy it, but I found
none." Which sheweth that if there had been
but some few to have stood in the breach, he
would have spared the whole land. This also
appeareth more plainly in the prophecy of Jeremiah, v. 1, where the Lord saith, " Run to and

fro by the streets of Jerusalem, behold and en-
quire in the open places thereof, if ye can find a
man, or if there be any that executeth judgment
and seeketh the truth, and I will spare it." Oh
then, mark and consider what a man may do; yea,
what one man may do, what an Abraham may do,
what a Moses may do, what an Elijah may do,
what a Daniel, what a Samuel, what a Job, what
a Noah may do. Some one man, by reason of
his high favour with the Eternal, is able sometimes to do more for a land, by his prayers and
tears, than many prudent men by their counsel,
or valiant men by their swords. Yea, it doth
evidently appear, in the sacred volume of the Holy
Ghost, that some one poor preacher, being full of
the spirit and power of Elijah, doth more in his
study (either for offence or defence; either for
the turning away of wrath, or the procuring for
mercy) than a camp-royal, even forty thousand
strong; or as the Spirit speaketh, Cant. iii. 7,
" Though they all have their swords girded to
their thighs, and be of the most valiant men in
Israel." All this is clearly proved in one verse of
the book of the Psalms, cvi. 23, where the prophet,
having reckoned up the sins of the people, addeth,
" Therefore the Lord minded to destroy them,
had not Moses (his chosen) stood in the breach
to turn away his wrath, lest he should destroy
them." See, therefore, what one man may do
with God. Some one man doth so bind the
hands of God, that when he should strike, he hath
no power to do it, as it is said of Lot, Gen. xix.
22, " I can do nothing till thou be come out."
See how the Lord saith he can do nothing, because he will do nothing. He doth wittingly and
willingly suffer his hands to be manacled and

bound behind him, for some few's sake, which he doth make more account of than all the world besides; so precious and dear are they in his sight. Likewise it is written, that the Lord was exceedingly incensed against the Israelites for their idolatrous calf, which they made in Horeb; yet he could do nothing because Moses would not let him ; and therefore he falleth to entreating of Moses, Exod. xxvii. that Moses would let him alone, and entreat no more for them. Oh, (saith the Lord to Moses) "Let me alone that my wrath may wax hot against this people, and that I may consume them." Thus we see that except Lot go out of the city, and Moses let him alone, he can do nothing. Oh the profoundness and altitude of God's mercy towards mankind! Oh the heighth and depth, length and breadth of his love towards some! Oh that the most glorious and invisible God should so greatly respect the sons of men! " For what is man, that he should be mindful of him? Or the son of man that he should regard him?" Let us, therefore, that are the Lord's remembrancers, give him no rest, nor let him alone until we have some security, and good assurance from him, that he will turn away from us the wrath which we most justly have deserved; that he will spare us and be merciful unto us. Yea, and as the prophet saith, Isa. lxii. 7, "Let us never leave him, nor give him over, till he repair and set up Jerusalem, the praise of the world:" lest for default hereof, that be charged upon us, which was charged upon the head of some of the prophets in Israel, that they were like the foxes in the waste places, that they had not risen up in the gaps, neither made up the hedge for the house of Israel. For now-a-days, alas! we have many hedge-breakers—few hedge-makers; many openers of gaps—few stoppers; many breakers of breaches to let in the floods of God's wrath upon us; but very few that, by true repentance, go about to make up the breach, and to let down the sluices, that the gushing streams of God's vengeance may be stopped and stayed.

Phil. I do now plainly see that there be some in high favour with God, and, as we say, greatly in his books; since his love is so great unto them, that for their sakes he spareth thousands.

Theol. It is written in the *Proverbs* of Solomon, that the righteous in a land are the establishment of the king's throne; and the wicked the overthrowing of the same. The words are these, xxv. 4, "Take away the dross from the silver, and there will proceed a vessel for the finer. Take away the wicked from the king, and his throne shall be established in righteousness." Likewise, in another place the wise man affirmeth, that the righteous are the strength and bulwark of cities, towns, and corporations, but the wicked are the weakening and undoing of all, xxix. 8, "Scornful men," saith he, "set a city on fire, but the wise turn away wrath." To this purpose, most excellent is that saying of Eliphaz, in Job xxii. 30, "The innocent shall deliver the land, and it shall be preserved by the pureness of their hands." We read in the book of Chronicles, that when the Levites and the priests were cast out by Jeroboam, they came to Jerusalem, and all such as set their hearts to seek the Lord God of Israel came with them. And then, afterward, it is said, they strengthened the kingdom of Judah, and made Rehoboam the son of Solomon mighty. By all these testimonies, it is evident that princes, kingdoms, cities, towns, and villages, are fortified by the righteous therein; and for their sakes also great plagues are kept back. Which thing one of the heathen did well see into, as appeareth by his words, which are these: " When God meaneth well unto a city, and will do good unto it, then he raiseth up good men; but when he meaneth to punish a city or country, and do ill unto it, then he taketh away the good men from it."

Theol. It is very manifest by all that you have alleged, that the wicked fare the better every day in the year, for the righteous that dwell amongst them.

Theol. All experience doth teach it, and the scriptures do plentifully avouch it; for did not churlish Laban fare the better for Jacob his kinsman? Doth he not acknowledge that the Lord had blessed him for his sake? Did not Potiphar fare the better for godly Joseph? Doth not the scripture say, that the Lord blessed the Egyptian's house for Joseph his sake? And that the Lord made all that he did to prosper in his hands? Did not Obededom fare the better for the ark ? Did not the seventy-and-six souls that were in the ship with Paul, speed all the better for his sake? Did not the angel of God tell him in the night that God had given unto him all that sailed with him ? for, otherwise, a thousand to one, they had been all drowned. Therefore, the children of God may very fitly be compared to a great piece of cork, which, though it be cast into the sea, having many nails fastened in it, yet it beareth them all up from sinking, which otherwise, would sink of themselves. What shall we say then, or what shall we conclude, but that the ungodly are more beholden to the righteous than they are aware of?

Phil. I do think if it were not for God's children, it would go hard with the wicked. For, if they were sorted and shoaled out from amongst them, and placed by themselves, what could they look for, but wrath upon wrath, and plague upon plague—till the Lord had made a final consumption of them, and swept them like dung from the face of the earth.

Theol. Sure it is, all creatures would frown upon them. The sun would unwillingly shine upon them, or the moon give them any light. The stars would not be seen of them, and the planets would hide themselves. The beasts would devour them, the fowls would pick out their eyes. The fishes would make war against them, and all creatures in heaven and earth would rise up in arms against them. Yea, the Lord himself from heaven would rain down fire and brimstone upon them.

Phil. Yet for all this, it is a wonder to consider how deadly the wicked hate the righteous, and almost in every thing oppose themselves against them, and that in most virulent and spiteful manner. They rail and slander, scoff and scorn, mock and mow at them, as though they were not worthy to live upon the earth. They esteem every pelting rascal, and prefer every vile varlet before them. And though they have their lives and liberty, their breath and safety, and all that they have else by them, yet, for all that, they could be content to eat their hearts with garlic; so great, so fiery, so burning and hissing hot is their fury and malice against them.

Theol. They may very fitly be compared to a moth that fretteth in pieces the same cloth

N

wherein she is bred; or to a certain worm or canker, that corrodeth and eateth through the heart of the tree that nourisheth her; or unto a man that standeth upon a bough in the top of a tree where there is no more, and yet, with an axe choppeth it off, and there withal falleth down with it and breaketh his neck. Even so the fools of this world do what they can to chop asunder the bough that upholds them, but they may easily know what will follow.

Phil. I see plainly they be much their own foes, and stand in their own light, and indeed know not what they do. For the benefit which they receive by such is exceeding great, and therefore by their mangling of them, they do but hold the stirrup to their own destruction.

Theol. Now to apply these things to ourselves, and to return to the first question of this argument, may we not marvel that our nation is so long spared, considering that the sins thereof are so horrible and outrageous as they be?

Phil. We may justly marvel at the wonderful patience of God. And we may well think that there be some in the land which stand in the breach, being in no small favour with his Highness, since they do so much prevail.

Theol. The merciful preservation of our most gracious king, who is the breath of our nostrils— the long continuance of our peace, and of the gospel—the keeping back of the sword out of the land, which our sins pull upon us—the frustrating of many plots and subtle devices which have been often intended against our state—yea, and the life of his Majesty's most royal person—make me to think that there be some strong pleaders with God, for the public good of us all.

Phil. You may well think so, indeed; for, by our sins, we have forfeited, and daily do forfeit, into God's hands, both our king, our country, our peace, our gospel, our lives, our goods, our lands, our livings, our wives, our children, and all that we have: but only the righteous (which are so near about the king, and in so high favour) do step in, and earnestly entreat for us, that the forfeitures may be released, and that we may have a lease, in parley, of them all again; or at least a grant of further time. But I pray you, sir, are not we to attribute something, concerning our good estate, to the policy of the land, the laws established, and the wisdom and counsel of our prudent governors?

Theol. Yes, assuredly, very much; as the ordinary and outward means, which God useth for our safety. For though the apostle *P*aul had a grant from God for the safety of his own life, and all that were with him in the ship, yet he said, Acts xxvii. 31, "Except the mariners abide in the ship, we cannot be safe;" shewing thereby, that unto faith, and prayers, the best and wisest means must be joined. We are therefore, upon our knees every day, to give thanks unto God for such good means of our safety, as he hath given us.

Phil. Well then, as the prayers of the righteous have been hitherto great means, both for the averting and turning away of wrath and the continuance of favour; so shew, I pray you, what is the best course to be taken, and what in sound wisdom is to be done, both to prevent future dangers, and to continue God's favours and mercies still upon us.

Theol. The best and surest course, that I can consider or conceive of, is, to repent heartily for sins past, and to reform our lives in time to come, to seek the Lord while he may be found, and to call upon him while he is near: to forsake our own ways, and our own imaginations, and to turn unto him with all our hearts, with weeping, with fasting, and with mourning; as the prophet Joel adviseth, "For our God is gracious and merciful, slow to anger, and of great kindness, and repenteth him of the evil." All the prophets do counsel us to follow this course, and do plainly teach, that if we all (from the highest to the lowest) do meet the Lord with unfeigned repentance, and offer him the sacrifice of a contrite spirit, undoubtedly he will be pacified towards us, and be merciful to our transgressions. This is most plainly set down in the 7th of Jeremiah, where the Lord saith thus to his people, "If you amend and redress your ways, and your works: if you execute judgment betwixt a man and his neighbour, and oppress not the stranger, the fatherless, and the widow, and shed no innocent blood in this place, neither walk after other gods to your destruction; then will I let you dwell in this place; even in the land which I gave unto your fathers, for ever and ever." So likewise he saith by the same prophet, xxii. 3, "Execute ye judgment and righteousness, and deliver the oppressed from the hand of the oppressor, and vex not the fatherless, the widow or the strangers; do no violence, nor shed innocent blood in this place; for if you do this thing, then shall the kings sitting upon the throne of David, enter in by the gates of this house, and ride upon chariots and upon horses, both he, and his servants, and his people;" and again, iii. 22, "O ye disobedient children, return, and I will heal your rebellion."

The Lord also saith by his prophet, Isaiah i. 19, "If ye consent and obey ye shall eat the good things of the land; but if ye refuse and be rebellious, ye shall be devoured with the sword; for the mouth of the Lord hath spoken it." The prophet Hosea, vi. 1, saith, "Come, let us return to the Lord, for he hath spoiled, and he will heal us; he hath wounded us, and he will bind us up; and again, xiv. 1, "O Israel, return unto the Lord, for thou hast fallen by thine iniquity, and I will heal thy rebellion, and will love thee freely; for mine anger is turned away from thee: I will be as the dew unto Israel, he shall grow as the lily, and fasten his root as the tree of Lebanon; his branches shall spread, and his beauty shall be as the olive tree; and his smell as Lebanon." The prophet Micah, vi. 8, telleth us what is good for us, and what is our best course, and what the Lord requireth at our hands; namely, these four things: to do justly, to love mercy, to humble ourselves, and to walk with our God. The prophet Amos, v. 14, giveth the same counsel, saying, "Seek the Lord, and ye shall live; seek good, and not evil; hate the evil, and love the good, and establish judgment in the gate; it may be, that the Lord of Hosts will be merciful unto the remnant of Joseph;" also, the Lord himself saith, "If this nation, against whom I have pronounced, turn from their wickedness, I will repent of the plague I thought to bring upon them," Jeremiah xviii. 8. Thus we do plainly see what advice and counsel the prophets and holy men of God do give unto us. The sum of all is this, that if we do truly repent and turn unto him with all our hearts, studying to obey him, and walk in his ways, then he will grant us any favour that we will require at his hands; for, even as woolpacks, and other soft matter beateth back, and dampeth the force of all shot; so penitent, melting, and soft hearts, do heat back the shot of God's wrath, and turn away his vengeance from us.   Moreover, we may observe in all experience, that when potentates are offended, or any great man hath conceived a displeasure against a poor man, that then he must run and ride, send presents, use his friends, break his sleeps, and never be quiet till he have pacified him.   Even so must we deal with our God, seeing he hath taken a displeasure against us.   Oh, therefore, that we would speedily use all possible means to pacify his wrath!   Oh that we would, with one heart and voice, every one of us, from the highest to the lowest, humble ourselves before our God, forsake our former evil ways, be grieved for that we have done, and purpose never to do the like again!   Oh that it might go to the hearts of us, that we have so often and so grievously offended so loving a God, and so merciful a Father!   Oh that we would awake once at last, and rouse up our drowsy hearts, and ransack our sleepy consciences, crying out against our sins, that our sins might never cry out against us!   Oh that we would judge ourselves, accuse ourselves, indict ourselves, and condemn ourselves; so should we never be adjudged, accused, indicted, or condemned of the Lord!   Oh that all hearts might sob, all souls might sigh, all loins might be smitten with sorrow, all faces gather blackness, and every man smite himself on the thigh, saying, what have I done?   Oh that both magistracy, ministery, and commonalty, would purpose and vow, and even take a bond of themselves, that from

henceforth, and from this day forward, they would
set their hearts to seek the Lord; and that they
would wholly give up themselves to his obedience!
Oh that all men, women, and children, would fear
God and keep his commandments; would eschew
evil, and do good; would study to please God in
all things, and to be fruitful in all good works;
making conscience to perform the duties of their
general callings, and duties of their special callings; duties of the first table, and duties of the
second table; that so God might be sincerely
worshipped, his name truly reverenced, his Sabbaths religiously observed; and that every man
would deal kindly, mercifully, justly, and uprightly with his neighbour; that there might be
no complaining, no crying in our streets! Oh! I
say again and again, that if all of us, of what
estate, degree, or condition soever, would walk in
the paths of our God, then doubtless we should
live and see good days; all future dangers should
be prevented, our peace prolonged, our state
established, our king preserved, and the gospel
continued. Then should we still enjoy our lives,
our goods, our lands, our livings, our wives, our
children, our houses and tenements, our orchards
and gardens; yea, as the prophet saith, we should
eat the good things of the land, spending our
days in much comfort, peace, and tranquility;
and leave great blessings unto our children and
posterity, from age to age, from generation to
generation.

Phil. You have fully answered my question,
and well satisfied me therein, out of the scriptures:
yet I pray you give me leave to add one thing
unto that, which you have at large set down.
The Lord saith by the prophet Amos, iv. 6–11,

that for their sins and rebellions, he hath given
them cleanness of teeth: that is, dearth and scar-
city; and yet they did not turn unto him. Also he
withheld the rain from them, and punished them
with drought, and yet they did not turn unto him.
Moreover he smote their corn, their great gardens,
their orchards, vineyards, fig-trees, and olive-trees,
with blasting and mildew, and the palmer-worm
did devour them; and yet they did not return
unto him. Last of all, he smote them with
pestilence, and with the sword, and overthrew
them, as he overthrew Sodom and Gomorrah, and
they were as a firebrand plucked out of the burning: yet, for all this, they did not turn unto him.
"Ye have not turned unto me, saith the Lord."
But now to come to the point. Out of this I
gather, that if we multiply our transgressions,
God will multiply his plagues upon us; but on
the contrary, if we would unfeignedly turn unto
the Lord our God with all our hearts, all plagues
should be stayed, all dangers prevented: and no
evil should fall upon us. For because they would
not turn, therefore he smote them. If therefore
they had turned, he would not have smote them.
But now I pray you briefly conclude this point,
and declare in few words, what it is that doth
most materially concern our peace, and public
good.

Theol. These few then briefly I take to be
things which belong to our peace: Let Solomon
execute Joab and Shimei. Let John and Elijah
slay the priests and prophets of Baal. Let Aaron
and Eleazar minister before the Lord faithfully.
Let Jonas be cast out of the ship. Let Moses
stand fast in the gap, and not let down his hands.
Let Joshua succeed him. Let Cornelius fear

God, and all his household. Let Tabitha be full of good works, and alms-deeds. Let Deborah judge long in Israel, prosper, and be victorious. Let us all pray that the light of Israel may not be quenched. And this I take to be the sum of all that belongeth to our peace.

MARKS AND EVIDENCES OF SALVATION.

Phil. The sum of all our conferences hitherto, as I remember, may be reduced unto these few heads:—first, man's natural corruption hath been laid open; secondly, the horrible fruits thereof; thirdly, their evil effects and workings, both against our souls and bodies, goods, name, and the whole land; lastly, the remedies of all. Now therefore I would grow to some conclusion of that which you touched by the way, and made some mention of; namely, the signs of salvation and damnation; and declare unto us plainly, whether the state of a man's soul, before God, may not by certain signs and tokens, be certainly discerned even in this life?

Theol. Besides those which before have been mentioned, we may add these nine following:— reverence of God's name—keeping of his Sabbaths—truth—sobriety—industry—compassion —humility—chastity—contentment.

Phil. These indeed, I grant, are very good signs: but yet all of them are not certain. For some of them be in the reprobates.

Theol. What say you then to St. Peter's signs, which are set down in the first chapter of his

Second Epistle? which are these eight:—faith—
virtue — knowledge — temperance — patience—
godliness—brotherly-kindness—love.　St. Peter
saith, "If these be in us, and abound, they will
make us neither idle nor unfruitful in the knowledge of our Lord Jesus;" which is as much as
if he had said, They will make us sound and
sincere professors of the gospel.

Phil. All these, I grant, are exceeding good •
signs and evidences of a man's salvation; but yet
some of them may deceive; and an hole may be
picked in some of these evidences.　I would,
therefore, hear of some such demonstrative and
infallible evidences as no lawyer can find fault
with; for I hold that good divines can as
perfectly judge of the assurances and evidences
of men's salvation, as the best lawyer can judge
of the assurances and evidences whereby men
hold their lands and livings.

Theol. You have spoken truly in that; and
would to God all the Lord's people would bring
forth the evidences of their salvation, that we
might discern of them.

Phil. Set down, then, which be the most certain and infallible evidences of a man's salvation,
against the which no exception can be taken.

Theol. I judge these to be most sound and
infallible:—assured faith in the promises—sincerity of heart—the spirit of adoption—sound
regeneration and sanctification—inward peace—
groundedness in the truth—continuance to the
end.

Phil. Now you come near the quick, indeed;
for, in my judgment, none of these can be found
truly in any reprobate.　Therefore, I think no
divine can take exception against any of these.

Theol. No, I assure you; no more than a lawyer can find fault with the tenure of men's lands and fee-simples, when as both the title is good and strong by the law, and the evidences thereof are sealed. subscribed, delivered, conveyed, and sufficient witness upon the same, and all other signs and ceremonies—in the delivering and taking possession thereof—according to strict law observed. For if a man have these forenamed evidences of his salvation, sure it is, his title and interest to heaven is good, by the law of Moses and the prophets—I mean the word of God. God himself subscribeth to them; Jesus Christ delivereth them as his own deed; the Holy Ghost sealeth unto them; yea, the three great witnesses which bear record in the earth—that is, water, blood, and the Spirit—do all witness the same.

Phil. Now, you have very fully satisfied me touching this point; and one thing more I do gather out of all your speech, to wit, that you do think a man may be assured of his salvation, even in this life.

Theol. I, do think so, indeed. For he that knoweth not in this life that he shall be saved, shall never be saved after this life; for St. John saith, 1 Epis. iii. 2, " Now are we made the sons of God."

Phil. But because many doubt of this, and the papists do altogether deny it, therefore I pray you to confirm it unto us out of the scriptures.

Theol. The apostle saith, 2 Cor. v. 1, " We know that if our earthly house of this tabernacle be destroyed, we have a building given us of God; that is, an house not made with hands, but eternal in the heavens." Mark that he saith, both he and the rest of God's people, did certainly know, that heaven was provided for them. "For the Spirit of adoption beareth witness with our spirits, that we are the children of God." And again, the same apostle saith, 2 Tim. iv. 8, "From henceforth is laid up for me the crown of right-eousness, which the Lord the righteous judge shall give me at that day; and not to me only, but to all them that love his appearing." Here we see that he knew there was a crown prepared for him, and for all the elect. And the same Spirit which did assure it unto Paul, doth assure it also to all the children of God. For they all have the same Spirit, though not in the same measure. St. John saith also, 1 Epis. ii. 2–3, "Hereby we are sure we know him; if we keep his commandments." In which words, he telleth us thus much; that if we do unfeignedly endeavour to obey God, there is in us the true knowledge and fear of God; and consequently, we are sure we shall be saved. St. Peter saith, "Give all diligence to make your calling and election sure." Wherefore should the apostle exhort us to make our election sure, if none could be sure of it? In the second of the Ephesians, the apostle saith flatly, "that in Christ Jesus we do already sit together in the heavenly places." His meaning is not, that we are there already in possession; but we are as sure of it, as if we were there already. The reasons hereof are these: Christ our head is in possession; therefore he will draw all his members unto him, as he him-self saith. Secondly, we are as sure of the thing which we hope for, as of that which we have. But we are sure of that which we have, which is the work of grace; therefore we are sure of that we look for, which is the crown of glory. Many other places of the holy scriptures might be alleged to this purpose: but I suppose, these may suffice.

Phil. As you have shewed this by the scriptures, so also shew it yet more plainly, by evident reason out of the same.

Theol. How can a man in truth call God his Father (when he saith, "Our Father, which art in heaven,") and yet doubt, whether he be his Father or no? For if God indeed be our Father, and we his children, how can we perish? how can we be damned? Will a father condemn his own children? or shall the children of God be condemned? No, no; "There is no condemnation to them that are in Christ Jesus. And, who can lay any thing to the charge of God's elect? It is God that justifieth, who can condemn?" Rom. viii. 1, 33–34. It is therefore most certain and sure, that all such as do in truth call God their Father, and have God for their Father, shall be saved. Again, how can a man say, in truth and feeling, that he believeth the forgiveness of sin, and yet doubt whether he shall be saved? For if he be fully persuaded that his sins are forgiven, what letteth why he should not be saved? Moreover, as certainly as we know that we are called, justified, and sanctified; so certainly we know we shall be glorified. But we know the one certainly, and therefore the other.

Asun. I will never believe, that any man can certainly know in this world, whether he shall be saved, or damned; but all men must hope well, and be of a good belief.

Theol. Nay, we must go further than hope well. We may not venture our salvation upon uncertain hopes; as, if a man should hope it would be a fair day to-morrow: but he cannot certainly tell. No, no. We must in this case, being of such infinite importance as it is, grow to some certainty, and full resolution. We see worldly men will be loath to hold their lands and leases uncertainly, having nothing to shew for them. They will not stand to the courtesy of their landlords, nor rest upon their good wills. They will not stay upon uncertain hope. No; they are wiser than so. "For the children of this world are wiser in their generation, than the children of light." They will be sure to have something to shew. They will have it under seal. They will not stay upon the words and promises of the most honest men, and best landlords. They cannot be quiet till they have it in white and black, with sound counsel upon their title; and every way made as sure unto them, as any law of the land can make it. Are then the children of this world so wise in these inferior things, and shall not we be as wise in matters of ten thousand times more importance? Are they so wise for earth, and shall not we as wise for heaven? Are they so wise for their bodies, and shall not we be as wise for our souls? Shall we hold the state of our immortal inheritance by hope well; and have no writings, nor evidences, no seal, no witnesses, nor any thing to shew for it? Alas, this is a weak tenure, a broken title, a simple hold indeed.

Asun. Yet for all that a man cannot be certain.

Theol. Yes, St. John telleth us, we may be certain; for he saith, "Hereby we know we dwell in him, and he in us; because he hath given us of his Spirit," 1 Epis. iv. 13. He saith not, we hope; but we know certainly. For he that hath the Spirit of God, knoweth certainly he hath it; and he that hath faith, knoweth that he hath faith; and he that shall be saved, knoweth he shall be saved. For God doth not work so darkly in men's hearts by his Spirit, but that they may easily know whether it be of him or no, if they would make a due trial. Again, the same apostle saith, v. 10, "He that believeth in the Son of God, hath the witness in himself;" that is, he hath certain testimonies in his own conscience that he shall be saved; for we must fetch the warrant of our salvation from within ourselves, even from the work of God within us. For look, how much a man feeleth in himself the increase of knowledge, obedience, and godliness, so much the more sure he is that he shall be saved. A man's own conscience is of great force this way, and will not lie or deceive; for so saith the wise man, Prov. xxvii. 19, "As water sheweth face to face, so doth the heart man unto man; that is, the mind and conscience of every man telleth him justly, though not perfectly, what he is. For the conscience will not lie, but accuse or excuse a man—being instead of a thousand witnesses. The apostle also saith, 1 Cor. ii. 11, "No man knoweth the things of man, but the spirit of a man that is in him." And again, the scripture saith, Prov. xx. 27, "Man's soul is, as it were, the candle of the Lord; whereby he searcheth all the bowels of the belly." So then, it is a clear case that a man must have recourse to the work of God's grace within him, even in his own soul; for thereby he shall be certainly resolved one way or another; for even as Rebecca knew certainly, by the striving and stirring of the twins in her womb, that she was conceived and quick of child; so

God's children know certainly, by the motions
and stirrings of the Holy Ghost within them,
that they have conceived Christ, and shall undoubtedly be saved.

Phil. I pray you, let us come to the ground-
work of this certainty of salvation, and speak
somewhat of that.

Theol. The ground-work of our salvation is
laid in God's eternal election, and in respect thereof it standeth fast and unmoveable; as it is
written, 2 Tim. ii. 19, "The foundation of God
standeth fast;" and again, ver. 13, "He is faithful
that hath promised, though we cannot believe,
yet he abideth faithful." So then, as we know
it certainly in ourselves, by the consequents of
election; so it standeth most firm in respect of
God, and his eternal and immutable decree. And
a thousand infirmities, nay, all the sins in the
world, nor all the devils in hell, cannot overthrow
God's election; for our Lord Jesus saith, John
vi. 37, "All that the Father hath given me, shall
come unto me;" and again, ver. 39, "This is
the Father's will that hath sent me: that of all
which he hath given me, I should lose nothing;
but should raise it up again at the last day;"
and in another place, our Saviour Christ saith,
John x. 27, "My sheep hear my voice, and I
know them, and they follow me; and I give unto
them eternal life, and they shall never perish;
neither shall any pluck them out of my hand.
My Father which gave them me, is greater than
all; and none is able to take them out of my
Father's hand." We ought, therefore, to be as
sure of our salvation as of any other thing which
God hath promised, or which we are bound to
believe; for to doubt thereof, in respect of God's

truth, is blasphemous against the immutability of his truth.

Phil. But are there not some doubts, at some times, even in the very elect, and in those which are grown to the greatest persuasion?

Theol. Yes, verily; for he that never doubted, never believed; for whosoever believeth in truth, feeleth sometimes doubtings and waverings. Even as the sound body feeleth many grudgings of diseases, which if he hath not health, he could not feel; so the sound soul feeleth some doubtings, which if it were not sound, it could not so easily feel; for we feel not corruption by corruption, but we feel corruption by grace; and the more grace we have, the more quick are we in the feeling of corruption. Some men of tender skins, and quick feeling, will easily feel the slightest feather, in softer manner laid upon the ball of their hands; which others, of more slow feeling and hard flesh, cannot so easily discern. So then it is certain, that although the children of God feel some doubtings at sometimes, yet the same do no whit impeach the certainty of their salvation; but rather argue a perfect soundness and health of their souls; for when such little grudgings are felt in the soul, the children of God oppose against them the certainty of God's truth and promises, and so do easily overcome them. For the Lord's people need no more to fear them, than he that rideth through the streets upon a lusty gelding, with his sword by his side, needs to fear the barking and bawling of a few little curs and whappets.*

Phil. Show yet more plainly how, or in what

---

* Little dogs.

respects, the child of God may both have doubtings, and yet be fully assured.

Theol. Even as a man set in the top of the
highest steeple in the world, and so fast bound
unto it that he cannot fall though he would—
yet, when he looketh downward, he feareth,
because man's nature is not acquainted nor
accustomed to mount so high in the air, and to
behold the earth so far beneath—but when he
looketh upward and perceiveth himself fast bound
and out of all danger, then he casteth away all
fear: even so, when we look downward to ourselves, we have doubts and fears; but when we
look upward to Christ, and the truth of his
promises, we feel ourselves quite sure, and cease
to doubt any more.

Phil. Declare unto us what is the original of
these doubts and fears, and from whence they
spring in the children of God.

Theol. They spring from the imperfection
of our sanctification, and from that strife
which is in the very mind of the elect between
faith and infidelity; for these two do mightily
fight together in the regenerate, and strive to
over-master and over-shadow one another; by
reason whereof sometimes it cometh to pass,
through the prevailing of unbelief, that the most
excellent servants of God may fall into fits and
pangs of despair, as Job and David, in their
temptations, did. And even in these days, also,
some of God's children at sometimes are shrewdly
handled this way, and brought very low, even
unto death's door; but yet the Lord in great
mercy doth recover them, both from total and
final despair. Only they are humbled and tried
by these sharp fits for a time, and that for their

great good. For as we use to say, that an ague in a young man is a sign of health; so these burning fits of temptations in the elect, for the most part, are signs of God's grace and favour; for, if they were not of God, the devil would never be so busy with them.

Phil. Is it not mere presumption, and an overmuch trusting to ourselves, to be persuaded of our salvation?

Theol. Nothing less. For the ground of this persuasion is not laid in ourselves, or any thing within us, or without us; but only in the righteousness of Christ, and the merciful promises of God. For is it any presumption for us to believe that which God hath promised, Christ hath purchased, and the Holy Ghost hath sealed? No verily, it is not any presumption; but a thing which we all stand bound unto, as we will answer it at the dreadful day of judgment, As for ourselves we do freely confess that in God's sight we are but lumps of sin and masses of all misery; and cannot of ourselves move hand or foot to the furtherance of our salvation; "But being justified by faith, we are at peace with God," and fully persuaded of his love and favour toward us, in Christ.

Phil. Cannot the reprobates and ungodly be assured of their salvation?

Theol. No; for the prophet saith, "There is no peace to the wicked," Isa. lvii. 21. Then I reason thus: they which have not the inward peace cannot be assured; but the wicked have not the inward peace; therefore they cannot be assured. Stedfast faith in the promises doth assure; but the wicked have not stedfast faith in the promises; therefore they cannot be assured.

The Spirit of adoption doth assure; but the wicked have not the spirit of adoption; therefore they cannot be assured. To conclude, when a man feeleth in himself an evil conscience, blindness, profaneness, and disobedience, he shall, in despite of his heart,—sing this doleful song, I know not whether I shall be saved or damned.

Phil. Is not the doctrine of the assurance of salvation a most comfortable doctrine?

Theol. Yes, doubtless. For except a man be persuaded of the favour of God, and the forgiveness of sins, and consequently of his salvation, what comfort can he have in any thing? Besides this, the persuasion of God's love towards us, is the root of all our love and cheerful obedience towards him; for, therefore, we love him and obey him, because we know he hath loved us first, and written our names in the book of life. But, on the contrary, the doctrine of the papists, which would have men always doubt and fear in a servile sort, is most hellish and uncomfortable. For so long as a man holds that, what encouragement can he have to serve God? what love to his Majesty? what hope in the promises? what comfort in trouble? what patience in adversity?

Antil. Touching this point, I am flat of your mind. For I think verily a man ought to be persuaded of his salvation. And for mine own part, I make no question of it. I hope to be saved, as well as the best of them all. I am out of fear for that; for I have such a stedfast faith in God, that if there should be but two in the world saved, I hope I should be one of them.

Theol. You are very confident, indeed. You are persuaded before you know. I would your

ground were as good as your vain confidence.
But who so bold as blind Bayard? Your hope is
but a fancy, and as a sick man's dream. You
hope you cannot tell what. You have no ground
for what you say; for, what hope can you have
to be saved, when you walk in no path of salvation? What hope can a man have to come to
London speedily, that travelleth nothing that
way, but quite contrary? What hope can a man
have to reap a good crop of corn, that useth no
means—neither ploweth, soweth, nor harroweth?
What hope can a man have to be fat and well-
liking of his body, that seldom or never eateth
any meat? What hope can a man have to escape
drowning, which leapeth into the sea? Even so,
what hope can you have to be saved, when you
walk nothing that way, when you use no means,
when you do all things contrary unto the same?
For, alas! there is nothing in you of those things
which the scriptures do affirm must be in all
those that shall be saved. There be none of the
forenamed signs and tokens in you. You are
ignorant, profane, and careless. God is not worshipped under your roof. There is no true fear
of God in yourself nor in your household. You
seldom hear the word preached. You content
yourself with an ignorant minister. You have no
prayers in your family, no reading, no singing of
psalms, no instructions, exhortations, admonitions,
or any other Christian exercises. You make no
conscience of the observation of the Sabbaths;
you use not the name of God with any reverence;
you break out sometimes into horrible oaths and
cursings; you make an ordinary matter of swearing by your faith, and your troth. Your wife is
irreligious; your children dissolute and ungracious;

your servants profane and careless. You are an
example in your own house of all atheism and
conscienceless behaviour. You are a great game-
ster, a rioter, a spendthrift, a drinker, a common
ale-house hunter, an whore hunter; and, to conclude, given to all vice and naughtiness. Now
then, I pray you tell me, or rather let your conscience tell me, what hope you can have to be
saved, so long as you walk and continue in this
course? Doth not St. John say, 1 Epis. i. 6, "If
we say we have fellowship with him, and walk in
darkness, we are liars?" Doth not the same
apostle avouch, that such as say "They know
God, and keep not his commandments, are liars?"
ii. 4. Again, doth he not say, iii. 8, 10, "He
that committeth sin is of the devil;" and "Whosoever doeth not righteousness, is not of God?"
Doth not our Lord Jesus flatly tell the Jews,
which bragged that Abraham was their father,
that they were of their father the devil, because
they did his works? Doth not the apostle Paul
say, "His servants we are to whom we obey;
whether it be of sin unto death, or of obedience
unto righteousness?" Rom. vi. 16. Doth not
the scriptures say, "He that doeth righteousness,
is righteous?" 1 John iii. 7. Doth not our Lord
Jesus affirm, that "Not every one that saith, Lord,
Lord, shall enter into the kingdom of heaven;
but he that doeth the will of my Father which is
in heaven?" Matt. vii. 21. Therefore, I conclude,
that forasmuch as your whole course is carnal,
careless, and dissolute, you can have no warrantable hope to be saved.

Phil. I do verily think that this man's case,
which now you have laid open, is the case of
thousands.

Theol. Yea, doubtless of thousand thousands — the more is the pity.

Asun. Soft and fair, sir; you are very round indeed: soft fire maketh sweet malt. I hope you know we must be saved by mercy, and not by merit. If I should do all myself, wherefore serveth Christ? I hope that which I cannot do, he will do for me; and I hope to be saved by Jesus Christ as well as the best of you all.

Theol. Oh, now I see which way the game goeth. You would fain make Christ a cloak for your sins. You will sin that grace may abound. You will sin frankly, and set all upon Christ's score. Truly there be many thousands of your mind, which, hearing of God's abundant mercy in Christ, are thereby made more hold to sin; but they shall know one day, to their cost, what it is so to abuse the mercy of God. The apostle saith, "The mercy and loving-kindness of God should lead us to repentance," Rom. ii. 4; but we see it leadeth man to further hardness of heart. The prophet saith, "With him is mercy, that he may be feared;" but many thereby are made more secure and careless. But to come nearer the mark: you say you hope to be saved by Jesus Christ; and I answer, that if those things be found in you, which the scriptures do avouch to be in all that shall be saved by him, then you may have good confidence and assured hope; otherwise not. Now the scriptures do thus determine it, and set it down, that if a man he in Christ, and look to be saved by him, he must be endued with these qualities following:—first, he must be "a new creature," 2 Cor. v. 17; secondly, he must live, "not after

the lusts of men, but after the will of God,"
1 Peter iv. 2; thirdly, he must be "zealous of
good works," Tit. ii. 14; fourthly, he must "die
to sin, and live to righteousness," Rom. vi. 11;
fifthly, he must be "holy and unblameable," Col.
i. 12; sixthly, he must "so walk as Christ hath
walked," John ii. 6; seventhly, he must "crucify
the flesh with the affections and lusts," Gal. v.
24; eighthly, he must "walk not after the flesh,
but after the Spirit," Rom. viii. 1; last of all,
he must "serve God in righteousness and true
holiness all the days of his life," Luke i. 75.
Lo, then, what things are required of all that
shall be saved by Christ. Now, therefore, if
these things be in you in some measure of truth,
then your hope is current, sound, and good;
otherwise, it is nothing worth: for in vain do
men say they hope to be saved by Christ, when
as they walk dissolutely. The reason hereof is,
because the members must be suitable to the
head; but Christ our head is holy; therefore,
we his members, must be holy also; as it is
written, "Be ye holy, for I am holy." Otherwise, if we will join profane and unholy members to our holy head Christ, then we make
Christ a monster. As if a man should join unto
the head of a lion, the neck of a bear, the body
of a wolf, and the legs of a fox; were it not a
monstrous thing? would it not be a monstrous
creature? Even such a thing do they go about,
which would have swearers, drunkards, whoremongers, and such like, to be the members of
Christ, and to have life and salvation by him.
But since you do so much presume of Christ, I
pray you, let me ask you a question.

Antil. What is that?

Theol. How do you know that Christ died for you particularly, and by name?

Antil. Christ died for all men, and therefore for me.

Theol. But all men shall not be saved by Christ: how, therefore, do you know that you are one of them that have special interest in Christ, and shall be saved by his death?

Antil. This I know, that we are all sinners, and cannot be saved by any other than by Christ.

Theol. Answer directly to my question. How do you know in yourself, and for yourself, that you are one of the elect, and one of those for whom Christ died?

Antil. I know it by my good faith in God; because I put my whole trust in him, and in none other.

Theol. But how know you that you have faith? or how shall a man know his faith?

Antil. I know it by this, that I have always had as good a meaning, and as good a faith to Godward as any man of my calling, and that is not book learned. I have always feared God with all my heart, and served him with my prayers.

Theol. Tush! now you go about the bush, and hover in the air. Answer me to the point: how do you know, certainly and assuredly, that Christ died for you particularly, and by name?

Antil. You would make a man mad. You put me out of my faith; you drive me from Christ. But if you go about to drive me from Christ, I will never believe you; for I know we must be saved only by him.

Theol. I go not about to drive you from

Christ, but to drive you to Christ: for how can
I drive you from Christ, seeing you never came
near him? how can I drive you out of Christ,
seeing you were never in him? But this is it
that deceiveth you and many others, that you
think you believe in Christ, because you say
you believe in Christ; as though faith consisted
in words, or as though a man had faith because
he saith so. If every one that saith he hath
faith, therefore hath faith; and every one that
saith he believeth in Christ, doth therefore
believe; then who will not have faith? who
will not believe? But, in very deed, your faith,
and the faith of many others, is nothing else but
a mere imagination. But all this while you
have not answered my question touching your
particular knowledge of Christ.

Antil. I can answer you no otherwise than I
have answered you; and I think I have answered
you sufficiently.

Theol. No, no; you faulter in your speech:
your answer is not worth a button; you speak
you know not what; you are altogether befogged
and benighted in this question. But if there
were in your heart the true knowledge and lively
feeling of God, then I am sure you would have
yielded another and a better answer—then you
would have spoken something from the sense
and feeling of your own heart, and from the
work of God's grace within you; but, because
you can yield no sound reason that Christ died
for you particularly, and by name, therefore I
suspect you are none of them which have proper
interest in him, and in whom his death taketh
effect indeed.

Phil. I think this question would gravel a

great number; and few there be that can answer
it aright.

Theol. It is most certain. I do know it by
lamentable experience that not one of an hundred
can soundly and sufficiently answer this question;
none, indeed, but only those in whom the new
work is wrought, and do, by the inward work
of the Spirit, feel Christ to be theirs. I have
talked with some which are both witty, sensible, and learned, who, notwithstanding, when
they have been brought to this very point and
issue, have stuck sore at it, and staggered very
much; and howsoever they might by wit and
learning shuffle it over, and, in a plundered sort
speak reason; yet had they no feeling of that
which they said, and therefore no assurance; and
consequently as good never a whit, as never the
better. It is the sanctifying Spirit that giveth
feeling in this point; and therefore, without the
feeling of the operation of the same Spirit, it
can never be soundly answered. Thus then, I
do close up this whole matter; as the vine-
branch cannot live and bring forth fruit, except
it abide in the vine; no more can we, except we
abide in Christ, and be truly grafted into him by
a lively faith. None can have any benefit by
him, but they only which dwell in him. None
can live by Christ, but they which are changed
into Christ. None are partakers of his body,
but they which are in his body. None can be
saved by Christ crucified, but they which are
crucified with Christ. None can live with him
being dead, but those which die with him being
alive. Therefore, let us root downward in mortification, that we may shoot upward in sanctification. Let us die to sin, that we may live to

righteousness. Let us die while we are alive, that we may live when we are dead.

Asun. If none can be saved by Christ, but only those which are so qualified as you speak of, then Lord have mercy upon us; then the way to heaven is very strait indeed, and few at all shall be saved; for there be few such in the world.

Theol. You are no whit therein deceived; for, when all comes to all, it is most certain that few shall be saved; which thing I will shew unto you, both by scripture, reason, and examples.

Asun. First, then, let us hear it proved by the scriptures.

Theol. Our Lord Jesus saith, "Enter in at the strait gate: for, it is the wide gate and broad way that leadeth to destruction; and many there be which go in thereat; because the gate is strait, and the way narrow, that leadeth unto life, and few there be that find it," Matt. vii. 13. Again he saith, "Many are called, but few are chosen," xx. 16. In another place, we read of a certain man which came to our Saviour Christ, and asked him of purpose whether few should be saved. To whom our Lord Jesus answered thus, "Strive to enter in at the strait gate: for many, I say unto you, will seek to enter in, and shall not be able," Luke xiii. 24. In which answer, albeit, our Saviour doth not answer directly to his question, either negatively or affirmatively; yet doth he plainly insinuate by his speeches that few shall be saved. For, first, he bids us to strive earnestly; noting thereby, that it is a matter of great strife against the world, the flesh, and the devil. Secondly, he affirmeth, that the gate is very strait; noting, that, none can enter in, without vehement crowding, and almost breaking their shoulder-bones. Lastly, he saith, that many which seek to enter in, shall not be able; noting thereby, that even of them that seek, many shall step short; because they seek him not aright. Isaiah also saith, "Except the Lord of Hosts had left us a seed, we had been as Sodom, and had been like to Gomorrah." The apostle also allegeth, out of the prophet, "That the Lord will make a short account in the earth, and gather it into a short sum, with righteousness." These scriptures, I think, are sufficient to prove that few shall be saved.

Asun. Now let us hear your reasons.

Theol. If we come to reason, we may rather wonder that any should be saved, than so few shall be saved. For we have all the lets and hindrances that may be, both within us and without us. We have, as they say, the sun, moon, and seven stars against us. We have all the devils in hell against us, with all their horns, heads, marvellous strength, infinite wiles, cunning devices, deep sleights, and methodical temptations. Here runs a sore stream against us. Then have we this present evil world against us, with her innumerable baits, snares, nets, gins, and grins to catch us, fetter us, and entangle us. Here have we profits and pleasures, riches and honour, wealth and preferment, ambition and covetousness. Here comes in a camp royal of spiritual and invisible enemies. Lastly, we have our flesh, that is, our corrupted nature against us; we have ourselves against ourselves. For we ourselves are as great enemies to our salvation, as either the world or the devil. For, our understanding, reason, will, and affections, are altogether against us. Our

natural wisdom is an enemy unto us. Our concu-
piscences and lusts do minister strength to Satan's
temptations. They are all in league with Satan
against us. They take part with him in every
thing against us and our salvation. They fight
all under his standard, and receive their pay of
him. This then goeth hard on our side, that the
devil hath an inward party against us; and we
carry always within us our greatest enemy, which
is ever ready, night and day, to betray us into the
hands of Satan; yea, to unbolt the door, and let
him in to cut our throats. Here then we see an
huge army of dreadful enemies, and a very legion
of devils, lying in ambush against our souls. Are
not we therefore poor wretches in a most pitiful
case, which are thus betrayed and besieged on
on every side? All things then considered, may
we not justly marvel that any shall be saved?
For who seeth not, who knoweth not, that thousand thousands are carried headlong to destruction, either with the temptations of the world,
the flesh, or the devil? But yet, further, I will
shew, by another very manifest and apparent
reason, that the number of God's elect upon the
face of the earth are very few in comparison;
which may thus be considered; first, let there
be taken away from amongst us all papists,
atheists, and heretics; secondly, let there be
shoaled out all vicious and notorious evil livers,
as swearers, drunkards, whoremongers, worldings,
deceivers, cozeners, proud men, rioters, gamesters,
and all the profane multitude; thirdly, let there
be refused and sorted out, all hypocrites, carnal
protestants, vain professors, backsliders, decliners,
and cold Christians; let all these I say, be separated, and then tell me how many sound, sincere,

faithful and zealous worshippers of God will be found among us. I suppose we should not need the art of arithmetic to number them: for I think there would be very few in every village, town, and city: I doubt they would walk very thinly in the streets, so as a man might easily tell them as they go. Our Lord Jesus asketh a question in the gospel of St. Luke xviii. 8, saying, "Do you think, when the Son of man cometh, that he shall find faith on the earth?" to the which we may answer, surely very little.

Asun. Now, according to your promise, shew this thing also by examples!

Theol. In the first age of the world, all flesh had so corrupted their ways that God could no longer bear them, but even vowed their destruction by the overflowing of waters. When the flood came, how few were found faithful? Eight persons only were saved by the ark. How few righteous were found in Sodom, and the cities adjoining; but one poor Lot and his family? How few believers were found in Jericho, but one Rahab? How few of the old Israelites entered into the land of promise, but two, Caleb and Joshua? The rest could not enter in, because of unbelief. The true and invisible church was small, during the government of the Judges; as appeareth plentifully in that book. In Elias's time, the church was so small that it did not appear. In the reign of the kings of Israel and Judah, the sincere worshippers were very few; as appeareth by all the prophets. During the captivity, the church was as the moon under a cloud, she was driven into the wilderness where she hid herself. During the persecutions of the Greek empire, by Gog, Magog, and Egypt, they were fewest of all. In Christ's time, what a silly company did he begin withal! How were all things corrupted by the priests, scribes, and pharisees! In the beginning of the apostle's preaching there were few believers. After the first six hundred years, what an eclipse was in the church during the height of antichrist's reign! How few true worshippers of God were in the world, for the space of almost seven hundred years! Since the gospel was broached and spread abroad, how few do believe! and as the prophet saith, "Lord, who hath believed our report?" Thus then you see it is apparent, both by scripture, reason, and examples of all ages, that the number of the elect is very small; and, when all comes to all, few shall be saved.

Phil. I pray you tell us how few, and to what scantling they may be reduced: whether one of a hundred, or one of a thousand, shall be saved?

Theol. No man knoweth that, neither can I give you any direct and certain answer unto it; but I say that, in comparison of the reprobate, there shall be but a few saved; for all that profess the gospel are not the true church before God: there be many in the church which are not of the church.

Phil. How do you prove that?

Theol. Out of the ninth to the Romans, where the apostle saith, ver. 6, "All are not Israel, that are of Israel;" and again, Isaiah crieth concerning Israel, "Though the number of the children of Israel were as the sand of the sea, yet but a remnant shall be saved," v. 27.

Phil. How do you balance it in the visible church? or in what comparison do you take it? Let us hear some estimate of it. Some think one of a hundred; some but **one of** a thousand shall be saved.

Theol. Indeed, I have heard some learned and godly divines give such conjectures; but for that matter I can say nothing to it; but only let us observe the comparison of the Holy Ghost betwixt a remnant and the sand of the sea, and it will give some light into the matter.

Phil. Doth not the knowledge of this doctrine discourage men from seeking after God?

Theol. Nothing less. But rather it ought to awake us, and stir up in us a greater care of our salvation, that we may be of the number of Christ's little flock, which make an end of their salvation in fear and trembling.

Phil. Some make light of all these matters; others say, as for the life to come, that is the least matter of an hundred to be cared for. As for that matter, they will leave it unto God, even as pleaseth him, they will not meddle with it; for they say, God that made them must save them. They hope they will do as well as others, and make as good shift as their neighbours.

Theol. It is lamentable that men should be so careless, and make so light of that which, of all other things, is most weighty and important; for it shall not profit a man to win the whole world, and lose his own soul, as the author of all wisdom testifieth.

Asun. I pray you, sir, under correction, give me leave to speak my mind in this point: I am an ignorant man; pardon me if I speak amiss, for a fool's bolt is soon shot.

Theol. Say on.

Asun. I do verily think that God is stronger than the devil; therefore I cannot believe that

P

he will suffer the devil to have more than himself; he will not take it at his hands; he loveth mankind better than so.

Theol. You do carnally imagine that God will wrestle and strive with the devil about the matter. As for God's power it doth never cross his will· for God can do nothing against his will and decree, because he will not.

Asun. Yea, but the scripture saith, "God will have all men saved."

Theol. That is not meant of every particular man, but of all sorts some. Some Jews, some Gentiles, some rich, some poor, some high, some low, &c.

Asun. Christ died for all; therefore, all shall be saved.

Theol. Christ died for all, in the sufficiency of his death, but not in efficacy unto life; for only the elect shall be saved by his death; as it is written, "This is my blood in the new testament, which is given for you," meaning his disciples and chosen children. And, again, Christ, being consecrated, is made " the author of salvation to all that obey him."

Asun. God is merciful; and, therefore, I hope he will save the greatest part, for his mercy's sake.

Theol. The greatest part shall perish; but all that shall be saved shall be saved by his mercy; as it is written, "He will have mercy on whom he will have mercy, and whom he will he hardeneth." And, again, "It is not in him that willeth, or in him that runneth, but in God that sheweth mercy," Rom. ix. 16. Therefore, though God be infinite in mercy, and Christ infinite in merit, yet none shall have mercy but only the vessels of mercy.

Antil. Can you tell who shall be saved, and who shall be damned? Do you know God's secrets? When were you in heaven? When spake you with God? I am of the mind that all men shall be saved; for God's mercy is above all his works. Say you what you will, and what you can, God did not make us to condemn us.

Theol. You are very peremptory indeed: you are more bold than wise; for Christ saith few shall be saved; you say all shall be saved. Whether, then, shall we believe Christ or you?

Antil. If there should come two souls, one from heaven and another from hell, and bring us certain news how the case stood, then I would believe it indeed.

Theol. Put case: two souls of the dead should come—the one from heaven, the other from hell —I can tell you aforehand, certainly, what they would say, and what news they would bring.

Antil. What, I pray you?

Theol. They would say there be few in heaven and many in hell—heaven is empty and hell is full.

Antil. How know you that? how know you they would say so?

Theol. I am sure, if they speak the truth, they must needs say so.

Antil. Must they needs? Why, I pray you, must they needs?

Theol. Because the word of God saith so; because Moses and the prophets saith so: "If you will not believe Moses and the prophets, neither will you believe though one, though two, though an hundred should rise from the dead."

Antil. Yes, but I would.

Theol. I pray you, let me ask you a question:

whether do you think that God and his word, or the souls of dead men, are more to be credited?

Antil. If I were sure that God said so then I would believe it.

Theol. If his word say so, doth not he say so? Is not he and his word all one?

Antil. Yet, for all that, if I might hear God himself speak it, it would move me much.

Theol. You shew yourself to be a notable infidel. You will not believe God's word without signs and miracles, and wonders from the dead.

Antil. You speak as though you knew certainly that hell is full. You do but speak at random; you cannot tell: you were never there to see. But for mine own part, I believe there is no hell at all, but only the hell of a man's conscience.

Theol. Now you shew yourself in kind what you are. You say you believe no hell at all; and I think, if you were well examined, you believe no heaven at all, neither God nor devil.

Antil. Yes; I believe there is an heaven, because I see it with mine eyes.

Theol. You will believe no more belike than you see; "but blessed is he that believeth and seeth not," John xx. 29. You are one of the rankest atheists that ever I talked withal.

Antil. You ought not to judge; you know not men's hearts.

Theol. Out of the abundance of the heart the mouth speaketh. You have sufficiently bewrayed your heart by your words; for the tongue is the key of the mind. As for judging I judge you only by your fruits, which is lawful; for we may justly say it is a bad tree which bringeth forth bad fruit, and he that doth wickedly is a wicked man; but it is you, and such as you are, that will take upon you to judge men's hearts; for though a man's outward actions be religious and honest, yet you will condemn him; and, if a man give himself to the word and prayer, reformeth his family, and abstaineth from the gross sins of the world, you will by and by say he is an hypocrite. And thus you take upon you to judge men's hearts, as though you knew with what affection these things are done.

Antil. I confess I am a sinner; and so are all others for aught I know. There is no man but he may be amended. I pray God send us all of his grace, that we may please him, and get to heaven at last.

Theol. Now you would shuffle up altogether, as though you were as good as the best, and as though there were no difference of sinners; but you must learn to know that there is great difference of sinners; for there is the penitent, and the unpenitent sinner; the careful, and the careless sinner; the sinner whose sins are not imputed, and the sinner whose sins are imputed; the sinner that shall be saved, and the sinner that shall be damned. For it is one thing to sin of frailty, another thing to live in it, dwell in it, and trade in it, (as the Holy Ghost speaketh) to suck it in, as the fish sucketh water, and to draw it unto us with cart ropes and and cords of vanity, Isa. v. 18. To conclude, therefore, there is as great difference betwixt a sinner and a sinner, as betwixt light and darkness; for, though God's children be sinners, in respect of the remnants of sin within them, yet the scriptures call them just and righteous, because they are justified by Christ, and sanctified by his grace and Holy Spirit. And for this cause it is, that St. John saith, "He that is born of God sinneth not," iii. 6–9.

Antil. What, I pray you, did you never sin?

Theol. Yes, and what then? what are you the better?

Antil. You preachers cannot agree amongst yourselves; one saith one thing, and another saith another thing; so that you bring the ignorant people into a mammering;* and they know not on which hand to take.

Theol. The preachers, God be thanked, agree very well together in all the main grounds of religion, and principal points of salvation; but if they dissent in some other matters, you are to try the spirits whether they be of God or no; you must try all things, and keep that which is good.

Antil. How can plain and simple men try the spirits and doctrines of the preachers?

Theol. Yes; for the apostle saith, 1 Cor. ii. 15, "The spiritual man discerneth all things;" and St. John saith to the holy Christians, ii. 27, "You have received an ointment from that Holy One, and know all things," that is, all things necessary to salvation; those, therefore, which have the Spirit of God, can judge and discern of doctrines, whether they be of God or no.

Antil. I am not book-learned, and therefore I cannot judge of such matters; as for hearing of sermons, I have no leisure to go to them; I have somewhat else to do; let them that are bookish, and hear so many sermons, judge of such matters; for I will not meddle with them, they belong not unto me.

Theol. Yet for all that, you ought to read the

Perplexity.

scriptures, and hear the word of God preached, that you may be able to discern betwixt truth and falsehood in matters of religion.

Antil. Belike you think none can be saved without preaching; and that all men stand bound to frequent sermons; but I am not of your mind in that.

Theol. Our Lord Jesus saith, "My sheep hear my voice;" and again, he saith, "He that is of God, heareth God's words; ye therefore hear it not, because you are not of God;" you see therefore how Christ Jesus maketh it a special note of God's child, to hear his word preached.

Antil. But I think we may serve God well enough without a preacher; for preachers are but men, and what can they do? A preacher is a good man, so long as he is in the pulpit; but if he is out of the pulpit, he is but as another man.

Theol. You speak contemptuously of God's messengers, and of God's sacred ordinance; but the apostle doth fully answer your objection, saying, Rom. x. "Faith cometh by hearing, and hearing by the word of God; and how can they hear without a preacher." In which words, the apostle telleth us flatly, that you can neither have faith, nor serve God aright, without preaching.

Antil. When you have preached all that you can, you can make the word of God no better than it is; and some put in and put out what they list; the scriptures are but men's inventions, and they made the scriptures.

Theol. We preach not to make the word better, but to make you better; as for putting in and putting out, it is a mere untruth; and whereas you say the scriptures were made by men, it is blasphemy once to think it; and you are worthy to receive your answer at Tyburn.

Antil. Now I see you are hot: I perceive, for all your godliness, you will be angry.

Theol. I take it to be no sin to be angry against sin; for your sin is very great, and who can bear it?

Antil. All this while you speak much for preaching, but you say nothing for prayer. I think there is as much need of prayer as preaching; for I find in the scriptures, "Pray continually," but I find not preach continually.

Theol. No man denieth but that prayer is most needful, always to be joined unto preaching and all other holy exercises, for it is the handmaid to all; but yet we prefer preaching above it, because preaching is both the director and whetstone of prayer; yea, it stirreth us aright in all spiritual actions and services whatsoever, without the which we can keep no certain course, but are ever ready to err on this hand, or that. Now, whereas you say you find "Pray continually," but not preach continually, you might, if you were not wilfully blind, find also preach continually; for the apostle saith, 2 Tim. iv. 2, "Be instant: preach the word in season, and out of season:" that is always, as time and occasion shall serve.

Antil. You extol preaching, but you say nothing for reading. I believe you condemn reading.

Theol. Doth he that highly commendeth gold condemn silver? I do ingenuously confess that both public and private reading of the scriptures are very necessary and profitable, and would to God it were more used than it is; for it is of singular use, both to increase knowledge and judgment, and also to make us more fit to hear the word preached. For such men as are altogether ignorant of the history of the bible can hear the word with small profit or comfort.

Phil. It seemeth that this man neither regardeth the one nor the other; because, for ought that I can see, he careth not greatly if the scriptures were burnt.

Antil. Oh sirrah, you speak very malapartly; you may speak when you are bidden. Who made you a judge? You are one of his disciples, and that makes you to speak on his side.

Phil. No sir, I hope I am Christ's disciple, and no man's; but assuredly, I cannot hold my peace at your vile cavilling, and most blasphemous speeches.

Antil. I cry your mercy, sir; you seem to be one of these scripture-men; you are all of the Spirit: you are so full of it, that it runneth out at your nostrils.

Phil. You do plainly shew yourself to be a scoffing Ishmaelite.

Antil. And you do plainly shew yourself to be one of these folk of God which know their seats in heaven.

Phil. I pray God be merciful unto you, and give you a better heart. For I see you are in the gall of bitterness, and in the bond of iniquity.

Antil. You think there is none good but such as yourself, and such as can please your humour. You will, forsooth, be all pure; but, by God, there be a company of pure knaves of you.

Theol. Nay, now you do manifestly shew of what spirit you are; for you both swear and rail with one breath.

Antil. God forgive me! why did he anger me, then? There be a company of such controllers as he in the world, that nobody can be quiet for them.

Theol. I perceive a little thing will anger you, since you will be angry with him for speaking the truth.

Antil. What hath he to do with me? He is more busy than needs. Why doth he say I am in a bad case? I will not come to him to learn my duty. If I have faults he shall not answer for them; I shall answer for mine own faults, and every tub shall stand on his own bottom: let him meddle with that he hath to do withal.

Theol. You are too impatient; you take matters at the worst. We ought friendly, and in love, to admonish one another; for we must have a care one of another's salvation. I dare say for him that he speaketh both of love and compassion towards you.

Antil. I care not for such love; let him keep it to himself. What doth he think of me? doth he suppose that I have not a soul to save as well as he, or that I have no care of my salvation? I would he should know that I have as great care for my salvation as he, though I make no such outward shew; for all is not gold that glistereth. I have as good a meaning as he, though I cannot utter it.

Theol. These words might well be spared. I hope you will be pacified, and amend your life, and draw nearer to God hereafter.

Antil. Truly, sir, you may think of me what you please; but, I assure you, I have more care that way than all the world wonders at, I thank God for it. I say my prayers every night when

I am in my bed; and if good prayers will do us no good, God help us. I have always served God duly and truly, and had him in my mind. I do as I would be done to; I keep my church, and tend my prayers while I am there; and, I hope, I am not so bad as this fellow would make me. I am sure, if I be bad, I am not the worst in the world: there be as bad as I. If I go to hell, I shall have fellows, and make as good shift as others.

Theol. You think you have spoken wisely, but I like not your answer; for your words smell strongly both of ignorance, pride, and unbelief. For, first, you justify yourself in your faithless and ignorant worshipping of God; and. secondly, you justify yourself by comparison with others, because others are as bad as you, and you are not the worst in the world.

Antil. Now I know you speak of ill-will; for you never had any good opinion of me.

Theol. I would I could have as good an opinion of you as I desire, and that I might see that wrought in you which might draw my love and liking towards you; and as for ill-will, the Lord knoweth I bear you none. I desire your conversion and salvation with my whole heart; and I would think myself happy if I might save your soul with the loss of my right arm.

Antil. I hope I may repent; for the scripture saith, at what time soever a sinner doth repent, God will have mercy on him; therefore, if I may have space and grace, and time to repent before death, and to ask God forgiveness, and say my prayers, and cry God mercy, I hope I shall do well enough.

Theol. You speak as though repentance were

in your power, and at your commandment, and that you can put it into your own heart when you list; and that makes you, and many others, presume of it three hours before death. But you must know that repentance is the rare gift of God; and it is given but to a few. For God will know him well that he bestoweth repentance upon, since it is proper only to the elect. It is no word matter. It is not attained without many and fervent prayers, and much hearing, reading, and meditating in the word of God. It is not so easy a matter to come by, as the world judgeth. It is not found but of them that seek it diligently, and beg it earnestly. It is no ordinary three hours' matter. Cry God mercy a little, for fashion, will not do it. Cursory saying of a few prayers a little before death availeth not; for, though true repentance be never too late, yet late repentance is seldom true. Herein delays are dangerous; for the longer we defer it the worse is our case. The further a nail is driven in with a hammer, the harder it is to get out again. The longer a disease is let run, the harder it is to cure. The deeper a tree is rooted, the harder it is to pluck up again. The longer we defer the time of our repentance, the harder it will be to repent; and therefore it is dangerous driving it off to the last cast. For an ancient father saith, (Augustine) "we read but of one that repented at the last, that no man should presume: and yet of one, that none might despair." Well then, to conclude this point, I would have you to know, that the present time is always the time of repentance; for, time past cannot be recovered, and time to come is uncertain.

Antil. Sir, in mine opinion, you have uttered some very dangerous things, and such as were enough to drive a man to despair.

Theol. What be they, I pray you?

Antil. There be divers things; but one thing doth most of all stick in my stomach, and that is, the small number that shall be saved, as you say; but I can hardly be persuaded that God made so many thousands to cast them away when he hath done. Do you think that God hath made us to condemn us? will you make him to be the author of condemnation?

Theol. Nothing less; for God is not the cause of men's condemnation, but themselves; for every man's destruction cometh of himself; as it is written, Hosea xiii. 9, "O Israel, thy destruction is of thyself." As for God, he doth, in great mercy, use all possible means to save souls; as he saith by the prophet, Isaiah v. 4, "What could I have done more to my vineyard, that I have not done unto it?" but to come nearer to your question: I deny that God hath created the most part of men only and solely unto perdition, as the proper end which he did aim at in creating them; but he hath created all things for the praise of his glory, as it is written, Prov. xvi. 4, "He hath created all things for himself, and the wicked also for the evil day." Then it followeth, that the cause and end why the wicked were created, neither was nor is only the destruction of his creature, but his own praise and glory; that that only might appear and shine forth in all his works.

Yet certain it is, that God, for just causes, albeit unknown and hid to us, hath rejected a great part of men. The causes, I say, of reprobation are hid in the eternal counsel of God, and known to his godly wisdom only. They are secret and hid from us; reserved in his eternal wisdom to be revealed at the glorious appearing of our Lord Jesus. His judgments, saith the scriptures, are as a great deep, and his ways past finding out. It is as possible for us to comprehend the ocean sea in a little dish, as to comprehend the reason of God's counsel in this behalf.

Antil. What reason, justice, or equity is there that sentence of death should be passed upon men before they be born, and before they have done good or evil?

Theol. I told you before that we can never comprehend the reason of God's proceeding in this behalf, yet we must know that his will is the rule of righteousness, and must be unto us instead of a thousand reasons; for whatsoever God willeth, inasmuch as he willeth it, is to be holden just. We cannot conceive the reason of many natural things, and things subject to sense, as the motion of the celestial bodies, their inconceivable swiftness, their matter and substance, their magnitude, altitude, and latitude. We cannot thoroughly find out the cause of the thunder, lightning, winds, earthquakes, ebbing and flowing of the sea, and many other things under the sun. How then can we possibly ascend up into the privy chamber and council-house of God, to sift and search out the bottom of God's secrets, which no wit or reach of man can any way attain unto? Let us therefore learn in God's fear to reverence that which we cannot in this life comprehend.

This one thing I must say unto you, that whatsoever God decreeth, yet doth he execute no man till he have ten thousand times deserved it. For betwixt the decree and the execution thereof, cometh sin in us, and most just causes of condemnation.

Antil. If God have decreed men's destruction, what can they do withal? who can resist his will? why then is he angry with us? For all things must needs come to pass according to his decree and determination.

Theol. First, I answer you with the apostle, Rom. ix. 20, " O man, who art thou which pleadest against God! Shall the thing formed say to him that formed it, why hast thou made me thus ? Hath not the potter power of the clay, to make of the same lump one vessel to honour, and another to dishonour?" Moreover, I answer, that God's decree doth not enforce the will of man, but it worketh and moveth of itself. It hath in itself the beginning of evil motion, and sinneth willingly. Therefore, though the decree of God imposeth a necessity upon all secondary causes, so as they must needs be framed and disposed according to the same, yet no co-action or constraint, for they are all carried with their voluntary motion. Even as we see the plumb of a clock, being the first mover, doth cause all the other wheels to move, but not to move this way or that way, for in that they move some one way and some another, it is of themselves—I mean of their own frame. So God's decree doth move all secondary causes, but not take away their own proper motion; for God is the author of every action, but not of any evil in any action. As the soul of man is the original cause of all motion in man, as the philosophers dispute, but yet not of lame and impotent motion, for that is from another cause, to wit, some defect in the body; so I say, God's decree is the root and first cause of motion, but not of defective motion, that is from ourselves. Likewise that a bell soundeth, the cause is in him that ringeth it, but that it jarreth, the cause is in itself. Again, that a instrument soundeth, is in him that playeth upon it, but that it jarreth is in itself, that is in its own want of tuning. So then, to shut up this point, all instruments and middle causes are so moved of God, being the first mover, that he always doth well, holily, and justly in his moving. But the instruments moved are carried in contrary motions, according to their own nature and frame. If they be good they are carried unto that which is good, but if they be evil, they are carried unto evil. So that, according to the double beginning of motion and will, there is a double and divers work and effect.

Antil. But from whence cometh it that man of himself, that is of his own free motion, doth will that which is evil?

Theol. From the fall of Adam, whereby his will was corrupted.

Antil. Who was the cause of Adam's fall?

Theol. The devil, and the deprivation of his own will.

Antil. How could his will incline unto evil, it being made good, and he being made good?

Theol. He and his will were made good, yet mutably good ; for to be immutably good is proper only to God; and Adam did so stand that he might fall, as the event declared.

Antil. Was not the decree of God the cause of Adam's fall?

Theol. No, but the voluntary inclination of his will unto evil. For Adam's will was neither forced, nor by any violence of God's purpose, compelled to consent; but he, of free will and ready mind, left God and joined with the devil. Thus then I do determine that Adam sinned necessarily, if you respect the decree or event, but if you respect the first mover and inherent cause, which was his own will, then he sinned voluntarily and contingently; for the decree of God did not take away his will or the contingency thereof, but only order and dispose it; therefore, as a learned writer (Beza) says, "*Volens peccavit et motu.* He sinned willingly, and of his own motion." And therefore no evil is to be attributed unto God, or his decree.

Antil. How then do you conceive and consider of the purpose of God in all these things?

Theol. Thus, that God decreed with himself, *uno actu*, at once, that there should be a world. —that Adam should be created perfect—that he should fall of himself—that all should fall with him—that he would save some of the lost race— that he would do it of mercy through his Son— that he would condemn others for sin.

Antil. But how do you prove the decree of reprobation? to wit, that God hath determined the destruction of thousands before the world was.

Theol. The scriptures calleth the reprobates, Rom. ix. 22, "The vessels of wrath prepared to destruction." The scriptures saith, 1 Thes. v. 9, "God hath not appointed us unto wrath;" therefore it followeth; that some are appointed unto wrath. The scriptures saith, 1 Pet. ii. 8, of the reprobates, "That they were even ordained to stumble at the word." The scriptures saith,

"They were of old ordained to this condemnation,
Jude 4.

Antil. But how do you answer this? "God
willeth not the death of a sinner," Ezek. xviii;
therefore he hath predestinated none to destruction.

Theol. God willeth not the death of a sinner
simply and absolutely, as it is the destruction of
his creature, but as it is a means to declare his
justice and to set forth his glory.

Antil. God did foresee and foreknow that the
wicked would perish through their own sin, but
yet he did not predestinate them unto it.

Theol. God's prescience and foreknowledge
cannot be separated from his decree; for whatsoever God hath foreseen and foreknown in his
eternal counsel, he hath determined the same shall
come to pass; for as it appertaineth to his wisdom to foreknow and foresee all things, so doth
it appertain to his power to moderate and rule
all things according to his will.

Antil. What do you call prescience in God?

Theol. Prescience in God is that whereby all
things abide present before his eyes, so that to his
eternal knowledge nothing is past, nothing to
come, but all things are always present. And so
are they present, that they are not as conceived
imaginations, forms, and motions, but all things
are always so present before God that he doth
behold them in their verity and perfection.

Antil. How can God justly determine of men's
destruction before they have sinned?

Theol. This objection hath been answered in
part before; for I told you that God condemneth
none but for sin, either originally only, or else
both original and actual; for howsoever he doth

in himself, before all time, determine the reprobation of many, yet he proceedeth to no execution,
till there be found in us both just deserts and
apparent cause. Therefore they deal unsoundly
and foolishly which confound the decree of reprobation with damnation itself, since sin is the
cause of the one, and only the will of God of the
other.

Phil. Well, sir, since we are so far proceeded
in this question, by the occasion of this man's
objections and cavils, I pray you now, as you have
spoken much of reprobation and the causes thereof,
so let us hear somewhat of election and the causes
thereof; and show us out of the scriptures that
God hath before all worlds chosen some to eternal life.

Theol. Touching the decree of election there
are almost none that make any doubt thereof,
therefore small proof shall serve for this point.
Only I will confirm it by one or two testimonies
out of the holy scriptures. First, the apostle
saith, Ephes. i. 3, 4, "Blessed be God, even the
Father of our Lord Jesus Christ, who hath blessed us with all spiritual blessings in heavenly
things in Christ, as he hath chosen us in him before the foundation of the world, that we should
be holy and without blame before him in love."
You see the words are very plain and pregnant
for this purpose. Another confirmation is taken
out of the 8th chap. to the Romans, in the 29th
verse, "Those whom he knew before did he also
predestinate to be like to the image of his own
Son, that he might be the first-born of many
brethren."

Phil. Which be the causes of election?

Theol. The causes of election are to be found

only in God himself. For his eternal election dependeth neither upon man, neither yet upon anything that is in man, but is purposed in himself, and established in Christ, in whom we are elected. This is fully proved in these words, Eph. i. 5, 6, "Who hath predestinated us to be adopted through Jesus Christ in himself, according to the good pleasure of his will, to the praise of his glory, wherewith he hath made us freely accepted in his Beloved." Where we see the apostle telleth us, that his free grace and the good pleasure of his will, are the first motives or moving causes of our election.

Phil. But the papists fetch the first motive of election out of man's merits and foreseen works; for, say they, God did forsee who would repent, believe, and do well, and therefore he made choice of them.

Theol. But they are greatly deceived. For I say, again and again, that there was nothing in us which did ever move God to set his love upon us and choose us unto life, but he ever found the original cause in himself; as it is written, Rom. ix. 18, "He will have mercy upon whom he will have mercy, and whom he will he hardeneth;" and again, ver. 16, " It is neither in him that willeth, nor in him that runneth, but in God that sheweth mercy." The Lord himself, in Deut. vii. 7, also testifieth that he did choose his people, not for any respect in them, but only because he loved them, and bore a special favour unto them. So, then, it is a certain truth that God's eternal predestination excludeth all merits of man, and all power of his will, thereby to attain eternal life; and that his free mercy and undeserved favour is both the beginning, the middle, and the end of our salvation: that is to say, all is of him, and nothing of ourselves.

Phil. Whether then doth faith depend upon election, or election upon faith? that is, whether did God choose us because we do believe? or whether do we believe, because we are chosen?

Theol. Out of all doubt, both faith and all fruits of faith do depend upon election. For, therefore we believe, because we are elected, and not therefore elected, because we believe; as it is written, " So many as were ordained to everlasting life believed," Acts xiii. 48.

Antil. If men he predestinate before they be born, to what purpose serve all precepts, admonitions, laws, &c.? It forceth not how we live; for neither our godly or ungodly life can alter the purpose of God.

Theol. This is a very wicked and carnal objection, and sheweth a vile and dissolute mind in them that use it. But I would wish such men to consider the end of our election, which is that we should lead a godly life; as it is plainly set down in the first to the Ephesians, where the apostle saith, ver. 3, 4, " God hath chosen us before the foundation of the world." But to what end? that we should live as we list? No, no, saith he, " But that we should be holy and unblameable before him in love." Again, he saith, Rom. viii. 29, " We are predestinate to be made like the image of his Son;" that is, to be holy and righteous; for most certain it is that we can judge nothing of predestination but by the consequents, that is, by our calling, justification, and sanctification; for when once we feel the work of grace within us, that is, that we are washed by the new birth, and renewed by the

Holy Ghost, finding in ourselves an unfeigned hatred of sin, and love of righteousness, then are we sure, and out of all doubt, that we are predestinated to life; and it is even as much as if God had personally appeared unto us, and whispered us in the ear, and told us that our names are taken and written in the book of life: " For, whom he hath predestinated, them hath he called; and whom he hath called, them he hath justified; and whom he hath justified, them he hath glorified," verse 30. Now, therefore, till we feel these marks of election wrought in us, we can be at no certainty in this point; neither are we to take any notice of it, or middle in it; but we must strive, according to that power and faculty we have, to live honestly and civilly, waiting upon God till he have mercy on us, and give us the true touch. As for them that are careless and dissolute, setting all at six and seven, there is small hope that they are elected, or ever shall be called.

Antil. I think the preaching and publishing of this doctrine of predestination hath done much hurt; and it had been good it had never been known to the people, but utterly concealed; for some it driveth to despair, and others it maketh more secure and careless.

Theol. You are in a great error, for this doctrine is a part of God's revealed truth, which he would have known to his people; and, in good sooth*, it is of very great and comfortable use to the children of God against all the assaults of the devil, and temptations of desperation whatsoever; for, when a man hath once in truth felt, by the effects, that God hath chosen him to life.

* Truth

then though the devil lie sore at him, and the
conscience of sin and his own frailties most vehe-
mently assault him, yet he knoweth certainly
that the eternal purpose and counsel of God is
immutable; and that because his salvation is not
grounded upon himself, nor his own strength, but
upon the unchangeable decree of God, which is a
foundation unmoveable, and always standing sure
and firm; therefore, do the devil and sin what
they can, yet he shall be upheld in righteousness
and truth, and, as it were, born up in the
arms of God, even to the end; for whom God
loveth, to the end God loveth them. Moreover,
when once the Lord's people perceive, by their
sanctification and new birth, both that the Lord
hath rejected and reprobated so many thousand
thousands, and made choice of them to be heirs
of his most glorious kingdom, being in themselves
of the same mould and making that others are,
and that he hath done all this of his free grace
and undeserved mercy towards them, oh how
doth it ravish their hearts with the love of him!
Again, how frankly and cheerfully do they serve
him! how willingly and faithfully do they obey
him! yea, how are they wholly enwrapt and in-
flamed with the desire of him! for it is the persuasion and feeling of God's love toward us that
draweth up our love to him again, as St. John
saith, iv. 19, " We love him, because he hath loved
us first." Moreover, it is said of Mary Magdalene
" That she loved much, because much was forgiven;" for, after she felt her many and great sins
freely pardoned, her affections were kindled with
the love and obedience of Christ. So likewise the
church in the Canticles, after she had been in
the banqueting house of all spiritual grace, and

felt the banner of Christ's love displayed upon
her, forthwith she was enwrapt therewith, and
cried out, as it were in a swoon, " That she was
sick of love." So again, when Christ put in his
hand by the hole of the door, that is, touched
the very inward parts of her heart, by his
Spirit, then her heart yearned, and her bowels
were affectioned towards him. This is it which St.
Paul prayeth for upon his knees, that it may be
granted to the Ephesians, "That they may be
able to comprehend with all the saints, what is
the breadth and length, heighth and depth of
God's love towards us, and to know the love of
Christ, which passeth knowledge, and to be filled
with all the fulness of the God." Thus you then
see the great and comfortable use of this doctrine
of election, both in that it ministereth strength
and comfort against all temptations; as also
because it constraineth us to love God, and of
very love to fear him and obey him.

Phil. Well, sir, I think now you have spent
time enough in answering the objections and
cavils of Antilegon; in all which I do observe
one thing, that there is no end of cavilling and
objecting against the truth; and that a man may
object more in an hour than a learned man can
well answer in a day.

Theol. You say truth; and the reason hereof
is because men have sin in them out of measure,
and the Spirit of God but in measure; therefore
they can by the one object, and conceive more
against the truth, than by the other they shall
be able to answer and say for it.

Phil. It appeareth, indeed, that errors be infinite, and objections innumerable, and that there
is no end of men's cavilling against God's sacred

truth. It is good for us, therefore, to be thoroughly settled in the truth, that we be not entangled or snarled with any cavils, or sophistications whatsoever; but I do verily think, notwithstanding all his objections and exceptions, that he doth in his conscience desire, with Balaam, to die the death of the righteous, and to be as one of them whom he seemeth to despise.

Theol. I am so persuaded too; for this is the triumph that virtue hath over vice, that, where she is most hated, there she is often desired and wished for. And this is the great punishment that God bringeth upon the wicked, "*Virtutem ut videant, intabescantque relictà,*" as saith the poet, "That they shall see virtue and pine away, having no power to follow it."

HINDRANCES IN THE WAY OF MAN'S SALVATION.

Phil. Now let us return to the point we were in hand with before we fell into these objections and cavils, which was concerning the small number of them which shall be saved; and as you have shewed us many reasons thereof, so proceed to speak yet more unto that point.

Theol. As I have shewed you of sundry lets, both within us and without us, which do keep us back from God, and hold us fast in our sins; so now, unto all that hath been said before, I will add nine great hindrances unto eternal life, which may not unfitly be termed nine bars out of heaven, and nine gates into hell.

Phil. Which be they?

Theol. They be these:—infidelity—presumption of God's mercy—example of the multitude
—long custom of sin—long escaping of punishment — hope of long life — conceitedness — ill-
company—evil example of ministers.

Phil. These, indeed, be strong bars out of
heaven, and wide gates into hell. I pray you,
therefore, prove them out of the scriptures, and
lay them forth somewhat more largely.

Theol. The first, which is infidelity, is proved
out of the fourth chapter to the Hebrews, where
it is written, " Unto us was the gospel preached,
as unto them; but the word which they heard
profited them not, because it was not mixed with
faith in those that heard it;" and again, " They
could not enter in, because of unbelief." Here
we see that unbelief did bar out the old people
from entering into the land of promise, which
was a figure of God's eternal kingdom; and sure
it is that the same unbelief doth bar out thousands
of us; for many will believe nothing but their
own fancies; they will not believe the word of
God, especially when it is contrary to their lusts
and likings, profits and pleasures. Though things
be manifestly proved to their faces, and both the
chapter and the verse shewed them, yet they will
not believe; or though they say they believe, yet
will they never go about the practice of anything,
but reply against God in all their actions; and,
for the most part, when God saith one thing
they will say another; when God saith yea, they
will say nay; and so give God the lie. Some
again will say, if all be true that the preachers
say, then God help us. Thus you see how infidelity doth bar men out of heaven, and cast them
into hell.

Phil. Let us hear of the second gate, which is presumption of God's mercy.

Theol. This is set down in the twenty-ninth chapter of Deuteronomy, where the Lord saith thus, "When a man heareth the words of this curse, and yet flattereth himself in his heart, saying, I shall have peace, although I walk according to the stubbornness of mine own heart (thus adding drunkenness to thirst, that is, one sin to another,) the Lord will not be merciful unto him, but the wrath of the Lord and his jealousy shall smoke against that man; and every curse that is written in this book shall light upon him, and the Lord shall put out his name from under heaven." Here we see how the mighty God doth thunder down upon such as go on in their sins, presuming of his mercy, and saying in their hearts, if I may have but a "Lord have mercy upon me," three hours before death I care not. But it is just with God, when those three hours come, to shut them up in blindness and hardness of heart, as a just plague for their presumption; therefore the prophet David, seeing the grievousness of this sin, prayeth to be delivered from it, " Keep me, O Lord, (saith he) from presumptuous sins; let them not reign over me," *P*salm xix. Let all men, therefore, take heed of presumptuous sins: for though God be full of mercy, yet will he shew no mercy to them that presume of his mercy; but they shall once know, to their cost, that justice goeth from him as well as mercy.

Phil. Let us come to the third gate, which is the example of the multitude.

Theol. This is proved in the twenty-third chapter of Exodus, ver. 2, where the Lord saith flatly, "Thou shalt not follow a multitude to do

evil." In another place, the Lord saith, Levit.
xviii. 3, "After the doings of the land of Egypt,
wherein ye dwelt, shall ye not do; and after the
manner of the land of Canaan, whither I will
bring you, shall ye not do, neither walk in their
ordinances." Against this law did the children
of Israel offend when they said, in the stubbornness of their heart, to the prophet Jeremiah, xliv.
16, 17, "The word that thou hast spoken unto us
in the name of the Lord we shall not hear. But
we will do whatsoever goeth out of our own
mouth; and we will do as we have done, both we
and our fathers, our kings, and our princes, in the
cities of Judah, and in the streets of Jerusalem."
Note here how they do altogether refuse the word
of the Lord, and how to follow the example of the
multitude. We see, in these our days, by lamentable experience, how thousands are violently carried down this stream, and for defence of it some
will say, "Do as the most men do, and the fewest
will speak of you;" which is a very wicked speech,
for if we will follow the course of the most we
shall have the reward of the most, which is eternal perdition. Let us, therefore, take heed of
bending with the sway; for the sway of the world
doth weigh down all things that can be spoken
out of the word of God, and openeth a very wide
passage into hell.

Phil. Proceed to the fourth gate into hell, which
is the long custom of sin.

Theol. This is noted by the prophet Jeremiah
to be a very dangerous thing; for he saith, xiii.
23, "Can the black Moor change his skin, or the
leopard his spots? then may ye also do good,
which are accustomed to do evil:" noting thereby that it is as hard a matter to leave an old

custom of sin as to wash a black Moor white, or
to change the spots of a leopard, which, because
they are natural, are most impossible: so, when
men through custom have made swearing, lying,
adultery, and drunkenness, as it were natural
unto them, oh how hard it is to leave them! for
custom maketh another nature, and taketh away
all sense and feeling of sin.

Phil. Let us hear of the fifth gate, which is
the long escaping of punishment.

Theol. This is avouched by the wise man in
these words, Eccles, viii. 11, "Because sentence
against an evil work is not executed speedily,
therefore the hearts of the children of men are set
in them to do evil;" where he sheweth that one
cause why men are so hardened in their sins is
because God winketh at them, and letteth them
alone, not punishing them immediately after they
have sinned; for if God should forthwith strike
down one, and rain fire and brimstone upon another, and cause the earth to swallow up the third,
then men would fear indeed. But it hath been
shewed before that God taketh not that course;
but though he meet with some in this life, yet he
lets thousands escape; and that makes them more
bold, thinking they shall never come to their
answer; even as an old thief, which hath a
long time escaped both prison and gallows, thinks
he shall always so escape, and therefore goeth
boldly on in his thefts. But let men take heed;
for, as the proverb saith, "Though the pitcher
goeth long to the well, yet at last it cometh broken
home;" so, though men escape long, yet they
shall not escape always; for there will come a
day of reckoning, a day that will pay it home for
all. Thus you see how impunity leadeth num-

bers to destruction; that is, when men are let
alone, and neither smitten by the hand of God
nor punished by the law of the magistrate.

Phil. Let us come to the sixth gate, which is
the hope of long life.

Theol. This is affirmed by our Lord Jesus concerning that rich worldling who, when he felt
the world come in upon him with full stream, said
he would pull down his barns and build greater,
and say to his soul, "Soul, thou hast much goods
laid up for many years. Live at ease, eat, drink,
and take thy pastime," Luke xii. 19. But our
Saviour calleth him fool, for flattering himself in
security, and promising unto himself long life.
Moreover, he plainly told him that the same night
he should make a miserable end in hell. Note,
I pray you, how Jesus Christ, the fountain of all
wisdom, calleth this man a fool, and yieldeth a
reason thereof, to wit because he gathered riches
to himself, and was not rich in God: he had great
care of this life, and none at all for that which is
to come. So then, it followeth that all such are
right fools indeed, and may be chronicled for fools,
how wise soever they may be taken and reputed
in the world, which have much care for their
bodies, and none for their souls: great care for
this life, and little for that which is to come.
Well, let all such profane worldlings as dream
and dote of long life, and therefore defer the
day of their repentance and conversion unto
God, take heed by this man's example that they
reckon not without their host, and be suddenly snatched away in the midst of all their
pleasures and gaities: as Job saith, xxi. 23, 24,
"Some die in their full strength, being in all
ease and prosperity; their breasts run full of milk,

and their bones run full of marrow;" we see, therefore, how dangerous a thing it is for men to flatter and sooth up themselves with hope of long life.

Phil. Proceed to the seventh gate, which is conceitedness.

Theol. This is, indeed, a very broad gate into hell; for the scripture saith, "Seest thou a man wise in his own conceit? there is more hope of a fool than of such a one." And again, "The fool is wiser in his own eyes, than seven men that can give a sensible reason," *Prov.* xxvi. 12, 16. The Holy Ghost, we see, affirmeth that such as are puffed up with an overweening* of their own gifts are farthest of all others from the kingdom of heaven; for they despise the wisdom of God to their own destruction. They hold scorn to be taught; they will say they know as much as all the preachers can tell them; for, what can all the preachers say more than this? we are all sinners—we must be saved by Christ—we must do as we would be done to. There is no more but do well, and have well, &c. Alas! poor souls, they look aloft; they are desperately hoven up with conceitedness, not knowing that they are poor, naked, blind, and miserable, *Rev.* iii. 17. These men trust altogether to their own wit, learning, policy, riches, and great reputation in the world; and because all men crouch to them, and clap their hands at them, therefore they swell like turkey cocks, set up their feathers, and draw their wings upon the ground, with a kind of snuff and disdain of all men, as if they were the only wights† of the

---

High conceit.   † Persons.

world. Moreover, when men do praise them for their gifts, sooth them, and applauded unto them, then is it a wonder to see how they streak* themselves, as though they would forthwith take their flight and mount up into the clouds. But let all insolent and conceited men hearken unto the woe that is pronounced against them, by the eternal King of glory, saying, "Woe unto them that are wise in their own eyes, and prudent in their own sight," Isa. v. 21. Again, let them hearken to the counsel of God, which saith, "Trust unto the Lord with all thy heart, but lean not unto thine own wisdom. Be not wise in thine own eyes; but fear God and depart from evil," Prov. iii. 5. These silly conceited fools think that because they have the cast of this life, and can cunningly compass the things of this world, and go through stitch with them, therefore they can compass heaven also by their fine wits and deep devices; but, alas! poor wretches, they are greatly and grossly deceived; "For the wisdom of the world is foolishness with God; and he catcheth the wise in their own craftiness," 1 Cor. iii. 19. And again the Lord saith, "I will destroy the wisdom of the wise, and will cast away the understanding of the prudent," 1 Cor. i. 19. Let not these men, therefore, stand too much in their own light: let them not trust to their own policies; for they are all but as an ice of one night's freezing, which will deceive them that trust unto it. Let them, therefore, become fools themselves, that God may make them wise. Let them deny themselves, that God may acknowledge them; let them be humbled in them-

---

* Stretch themselves up.

selves, that God may exalt them. For assuredly, there is no use after this life, of the exquisite wisdom of the flesh; it all endeth when we end. For how dieth the wise man? even as dieth the fool, saith the Holy Ghost, Eccles. ii. 16; and where all worldly wisdom endeth, there all heavenly wisdom beginneth. Thus, therefore, we see what a wide gate into hell conceitedness is, and how many enter in thereat.

Phil. Now, let us understand of the eighth gate into hell, which is ill company.

Theol. The Spirit of God, forseeing the great danger of this, and knowing how ready we are to be carried away with ill company, doth give us most earnest warning to take heed of it as a most dangerous thing. " Enter not (saith he) in the way of the wicked; and walk not in the way of evil men. Avoid it, go not by it, turn from it, and pass by," *Prov.* iv. 14, 15. The reason hereof is yielded in another place, where it is said, " A companion of fools shall be destroyed," xiii. 20. Let men, therefore, take heed of ill company; for many thereby have been brought to the gallows, and have confessed upon the ladder that ill company hath brought them unto it, and therefore have admonished all by their example to take heed, and beware of, lewd company. Moreover, the scriptures saith, "He that followeth vain companions shall be filled with poverty," *Prov.* xxviii. 19; and again, in the same chapter, "He that keepeth company with banqueters, shameth his father." Let us, therefore, with David say, "I am a companion of all them that fear God and keep his commandments," *Psalm* cxix. 63. And, on the contrary, let us say with him, "I have not haunted with vain persons,

R

neither kept company with the dissemblers. I hate the assembly of the evil, and have not companied with the wicked," Psalm xxvi. 4. Let us, therefore, by David's example, shun the company of the wicked; for as a man is so is his company. It is the surest note to discern a man by; for, as all unlike things are unsociable, so all like things are sociable. Herein let us beware we deceive not ourselves with vain words, and an opinion of our own strength; as if we were as strong as Christ, and could not be drawn away with any company. No, no; we are more apt to be drawn than to draw: to be drawn to evil by others, than to draw others to good; therefore, God saith by his prophet, Jeremiah, xv. 19, "Let them return unto thee, but return not thou unto them." Undoubtedly, he is an odd man that is not made worse with ill company, For can a man touch pitch and not be defiled therewith? Can a man carry coals in his bosom and not be burnt? Daily and lamentable experience sheweth that many of them which think themselves strong, are this way most grievously smutted.* Let a man think, therefore, he never abandoneth evil, till he abandon ill company; for no good is concluded in this parliament; for ill company is the suburbs of hell. Furthermore, it is to be observed that some, upon admonitions and some inward compunctions of their own conscience, do leave their sins until they have new provocations, and until they come amongst their old copesmates† and sin companions; and then are they carried back again to their old bias, and return to their folly as a dog returneth to his vomit. For we see

---

* Corrupted, disgraced.   † Wild companions.

some, which otherwise are of good natures and
dispositions, most pitifully and violently carried
away with ill company; for even as green wood
of itself is unapt to burn, yet being laid on the
fire with a great deal of sear* wood, it burneth
as fast as the rest; so many toward youths,
which of themselves are not so prone unto evil as
others, yet with this violent stream and blustering
tempest of ill company, are carried clean away.

Phil. Let us come to the last gate, which is
the evil example of ministers.

Theol. It grieveth me, and I am almost
ashamed to speak of this point; for is it not a
woful and lamentable thing that any such should
be found amongst the sons of Levi? Is it not a
corsey,† that the ministers of Christ should be of
a scandalous conversation? for if the eye be
dark, how great is the darkness? If they be examples of all evil to the flock, which should be
patterns, lights, and examples of all goodness,
must it not needs strengthen the hands of the
wicked, so as they cannot return from their
wickedness? But this is an old disease and evil
sickness which hath always been in the church.
The prophet Jeremiah doth most grievously complain of it in his time, and saith, xxiii. 14, that
"from the prophets of Jerusalem is wickedness
gone forth into all the land; for both the prophet
and the priest do wickedly. I have seen, (saith
he) in the prophets of Jerusalem, filthiness; they
commit adultery, and walk in lies; they strengthen
also the hands of the wicked, that none can return from his wickedness; they are all unto me
as Sodom, and the inhabitants thereof as Gomor-

---

* Dry wood.
† A fretting burning plaster to a sore—a painful grievance.

rah." And in the ninth verse of the same chapter, he sheweth that it was no pleasure or joy
unto him so publicly to reprove them; but that
he did it with exceeding grief, as being forced
thereunto, both in regard of God's glory, and the
good of his church. His words are these, "Mine
heart breaketh within me, because of the prophets;
and all my bones shake." Moreover, in the same
chapter is set down how the Lord would feed
them with wormwood, and make them drink the
water of gall, and sundry other ways plague them
for their flatteries, seducements, corrupt doctrine,
and evil example of life.

Phil. Most certain it is that the evil example
of ministers, and especially of preachers, is very
dangerous and offensive: for thereby thousands
are hardened in their sins. For men will say,
such a minister and such a preacher doth thus
and thus, and therefore, why may not we do so
too? They are learned, and know the word of
God; therefore, if it were evil, I hope they
would not do it; for they should be lights to
us, and give us good examples; therefore, since
they do such things, we cannot tell what to think,
or what to say to the matter: they bring such
simple folks as we are into a mammering.*

Theol. Oh that I could, with the prophet
Jeremiah, quake and shake to think of these
matters! Oh that I could mourn as a dove, in
penning of it! Oh that I had in the wilderness
a cottage, and could with Job be a brother to the
dragons, and a companion to the ostriches,
whilst I have any thoughts of those things! Oh
that I could weep and mourn without sin, before

---

* Perplexity.

I yield you an answer. For weep indeed I may, but answer I cannot. Alas, with much grief I speak it, all is too true that you say; and herein the people have a vantage against us. if I may call it vantage. But let this be mine answer, " If the blind lead the blind, both shall fall into the ditch," Matt. xv. 14. Blind guides and blind people, shall perish together. If because we are wicked they will be more wicked, then both they and we shall burn in hell-fire together. Then, let them reckon their gains and see what they have got. They have small cause so to triumph over us; for thereby their market is never a whit amended: let them take this for answer. And let us that are the ministers of Christ, and preachers of the gospel, look narrowly to ourselves, and make straight steps to our feet: for, if we tread never so little awry, we may see how many eyes are upon us. Let us, therefore, with David pray continually, " Order my goings, O Lord, that my footsteps slip not. For when my foot slipped, they rejoiced against me." And as for the people, let them follow the example of those which walk unblameably, as God be thanked, some such there be, and let them fly the examples of such as are offensive. So shall God have more glory, and they more peace in their own hearts. Thus have we heard what a wide gate is opened into hell by the evil example of ministers, and especially of preachers.

THE SIN AND DANGER OF IGNORANCE:

WITH THE VAST IMPORTANCE OF THE GOSPEL MINISTRY AS A REMEDY.

Phil. Well, since there be so many bars out of heaven and so many gates into hell, it is a very hard matter to break through all these bars, and so to enter into life; and as hard a matter to miss all these gates and escape hell. He quits him well that can do it.

Theol. True indeed; and as hard a thing as this is, so hard a thing is it for flesh and blood to enter into the kingdom of heaven; and yet most men make light of it, and think it is the easiest matter of an hundred.

Asun. As hard as it is, yet I hope by the grace of God I shall be one of them that shall enter in; for, so long as I do as I would be done to, and say nobody no harm, nor do nobody no harm, God will have mercy on my soul. And I doubt not but my good deeds shall weigh against my evil deeds, and that I shall make even with God at my latter end; for, I thank God for it, I have always lived in his fear, and served him with a true intent; therefore I know that so long as I keep his commandments, and live as my neighbours do, and as a Christian man ought to do, he will not damn my soul.

Theol. Can you then keep God's commandments?

Asun. As near as God will give me grace.

Theol. Nay, but I ask you whether you keep them or no?

Asun. I do say, to keep them as near as I can, I do my true intent. Though I keep them not all, yet I am sure I keep some of them.

Theol. Because you say you keep some of them, I pray you let me be so bold with you as to examine you in the particulars. You know the first commandment is this, " Thou shalt have none other gods in my sight." How say you, do you keep this?

Asun. I am out of all fear of it; for I never worshipped any God but one. I am fully persuaded there is but one God.

Theol. What say you to the second commandment? " Thou shalt make to thyself no graven image," &c.

Asun. I never worshipped any images in my life: I defy them. I know they cannot help me, for they be but stocks and stones.

Theol. What say you to the third commandment? which is this, " Thou shalt not take the name of the Lord thy God in vain," &c.

Asun. Nay certainly, I was never counted a swearer in my life, but I have feared God always of a child, and have had a good faith in him ever since I could remember. I would be sorry else.

Theol. What say you then to the fourth commandment? " Remember that thou keep holy the Sabbath-day," &c.

Asun. Nay, for that matter, I keep my church as well as any man in the parish where I dwell, and mind my prayers as well when I am there. I thank God for it, though I say it myself, I have been always well given, and have loved God's word with all my heart; and it doth me good to hear the epistles and gospels read every Sunday by our vicar.

Theol. Tell me, what say you to the fifth commandment? which is, "Honour thy father and thy mother," &c. do you keep this?

Asun. I have always loved and obeyed my father and mother from my heart; I hope there is nobody can accuse me for that, and I am sure if I keep any commandment it is this; for when I was a boy every body said that I was well given, and a toward child; therefore, if I should not keep this commandment, it would be a great grief to me, and go as near my heart as any thing that came to me this seven years.

Theol. What say you to the sixth commandment? "Thou shalt not kill."

Asun. It were strange if I should not keep that.

Theol. What say you to the seventh? "Thou shalt not commit adultery."

Asun. I thank God for it, I was never given to women; God hath always kept me from that, and I hope will so still.

Theol. What say you to the eighth? "Thou shalt not steal."

Asun. I am neither whoremaster nor thief.

Theol. What say you to the ninth? "Thou shalt not bear false witness," &c.

Asun. I defy all false witness-bearing from my heart.

Theol. What say you to the last? "Thou shalt not covet," &c.

Asun. I thank God for it, I never coveted any man's goods but mine own.

Theol. Now, I perceive you are a wonderful man; you can keep all the commandments. You are like that blind ruler which said unto Christ, Matt. xix. 20, "*A*ll these things have I kept from my youth." I perceive now, indeed, that it is no marvel though you make so light of preaching, for you have no need of it: you are whole, you need not the physician; you feel no misery, and therefore you care not for mercy; for where misery is not felt, there mercy is not regarded; but I see you need no Saviour.

Asun. You say not well in that: I need a Saviour, and it is my Lord Jesus that must save me, for he made me.

Theol. What! need you a Saviour since you are no sinner?

Asun. Yes, believe me, I am a sinner; we are all sinners; there is no man but he sinneth.

Theol. How can you be a sinner since you keep all the commandments?

Asun. Yes, I am a sinner for all that.

Theol. Can you both be a sinner and be without sin too? for he that keepeth the commandments is without sin! which thing you say you do. But I see how the case standeth, that a great number of such ignorant and sottish men as you are will in general say you are sinners, because your conscience telleth you so; but when it cometh to particulars, you know not how you sin, nor wherein. I pray you, therefore, let me lead you through the commandments again, and deal with you in particulars, that I may bring you to the sight of your sin. How say you, therefore, do you upon your knees, every morning and evening, give God thanks for his particular mercies, and manifold favours towards you? And do you call much upon him privately, and much also with your family? Answer me, plainly and simply.

Asun. I cannot say so.

Theol. Then you have broken the first com-

mandment, which chargeth us to give God his
due worship, whereof prayer and thanksgiving
are a part; so then, here, at the very entrance,
you are found guilty. Further, I demand of you
whether you never had any by-thoughts in your
prayers, and your heart hath not been upon
other matters, even then while you were in
prayer.

Asun. I cannot deny that: for it is a very hard
matter to pray without by-thoughts.

Theol. Then, by your own confession, you have
broken the second commandment, which doth command the right manner of God's worship; that is,
that as we must worship God, so we must do it
in faith, love, zeal, and pure affections. So that
here you are guilty also, because when you pray
your mind is of other matters, and you do it not
in sincerity and truth. Further, I demand of you
whether you did never swear by your faith, or
truth, or by our lady, St. Mary, and such other
oaths?

Asun. Yes, by St. Mary have I—I must needs
confess it.

Theol. We need no further witness. Your
very answer proveth it, for your answer is an oath;
therefore, here also you are guilty, because you
swear by idols. Further, I demand of you
whether you did never travel to fairs on the Sabbath-day, or make bargains on that day, or take
journeys, or talk of worldly matters, neglecting
holy duties?

Asun. Yes, God forgive me, I have.

Theol. Then you are guilty of the breach of
the fourth commandment, which chargeth us, on
pain of death, to spend the Sabbath-day in holy
and religious duties, both publicly and privately.

Further, I demand whether you instruct your wife, children, and servants in the true knowledge of God, and pray with them or no?

Asun. I am sure you would have me speak the truth; I must needs confess I do not, neither am I able to do it.

Theol. Then you are guilty of the breach of the fifth commandment, which commandeth all duties of superiors to inferiors, and of inferiors towards their superiors, whereof prayer and instructions are a part. Moreover, I demand whether you were never angry or no?

Asun. Yes, an hundred times in my days. And I think there is nobody but will be angry at one time or other, especially when they have cause.

Theol. Then you have broken the sixth commandment, which chargeth us to avoid wrath, anger, malice, desire of revenge, and all such like forerunners unto murder. Further, I ask you whether you did never look upon a woman with a lust in your heart?

Asun. Yes, for I think there is no man free from thoughts that way. I had thought thoughts had been free.

Theol. No, thoughts are not free before God; for God knoweth our thoughts, and will punish us, arraign us, and condemn us for thoughts. Men know not thoughts, and therefore can make no laws against thoughts; but because God is privy to all our most secret thoughts, therefore he hath made laws against them, and will condemn them. Therefore, I conclude that if you have nourished adulterous thoughts in your heart you are guilty of the breach of the seventh commandment, which forbiddeth all secret thoughts

and provocations whatsoever to adultery. But
further, I demand whether you did never pilfer,
purloin, and steal some small things from your
neighbour: as pasture, poultry, conies, apples,
and such like?

Asun. I cannot clear myself in these things,
for I had thought they had been no sin.

Theol. Then have you broken the eighth commandment, and stand guilty of eternal death;
for God in his commandment chargeth us to
have as great care of our neighbour's goods as of
our own; and not to injure him in any manner of
way, in thought, word, or deed; therefore, all
deceit, pilfering, oppressing, and all unjust dealing
with our neighbour's goods, is here condemned.
Moreover, let me ask you whether you did never
lie, or dissemble?

Asun. Yes, assuredly.

Theol. Then you have broken the ninth commandment, wherein God chargeth us, both in
witness-bearing and all other matters, to speak
the plain truth from our heart, without lying or
dissembling. Last of all, I demand whether you
did never in your heart desire something that was
not your own: as your neighbour's house, or
ground, kine, or sheep, &c. therein bewraying
the discontentment of your heart?

Asun. I am as guilty in this as in any thing,
for, God forgive me, I have often desired and
lusted after this and that, which was none of mine
own, and so have bewrayed my discontentment.

Theol. Then I perceive, by your own confession, that you are guilty of the breach of all the
commandments.

Asun. I must needs confess it; for I see now
more into that matter than ever I did. I never

heard so much before in my life, nor was ever asked any such questions as you ask me. I had thought many of those things which you asked me had been no sins at all.

Theol. I could have convicted you in a thousand other particulars, wherein you do daily and hourly break the law of God. But my purpose was only to give you a taste of some particular transgressions, and therewithal some little light by the way into the meaning of the law, that thereby you might be brought to some better sight of yourself, and might a little perceive in what case you stand before God; and by that little conceive a great deal more.

Asun. Well, now I do plainly see that I have been deceived, and am not in so good estate before God as I thought I had been. Moreover, I see that thousands are out of the way which think they are in a good case before God; whereas, indeed, they are in blindness and in their sins. But, Lord have mercy upon us, I do now plainly see that I am far from keeping the commandments; and I think no man doth keep them.

Theol. You may take your oath of that, I warrant you; for neither Saint Paul, David, or the Virgin Mary, could ever keep any one of the commandments. I am glad you begin to see into the law of God, and to have some taste that way; for, as a man's knowledge and insight is into the law, so is the knowledge and insight into himself. He that hath a deep insight into the law of God, hath also a deep insight into himself. He that hath no sight into the law, can have no insight into himself; for the law is that glass wherein we do behold the face of our souls before God.

The apostle saith, Rom. iii. 20, "By the law cometh the knowledge of sin;" therefore, those which are altogether ignorant of the law, and never behold themselves in this glass, do commit an hundred sins a day, which they know not of; and therefore are not grieved for them; for how can a man be grieved for that which he knoweth not? but now further, I pray you, give me leave to ask you some more questions of the principles of religion, to the end that you, knowing and feeling your ignorance, may be humbled therewith, bewail it in time, and seek after the true knowledge of God. But yet, by the way, I will ask Antilegon a question or two; because I desire to understand what knowledge he hath in the grounds of religion. Tell me, therefore, Antilegon, what was the reason why Christ was conceived by the Holy Ghost?

Antil. I could answer you, but I will not; what authority have you to examine me? shew your commission; when I see your warrant I will answer you; in the meantime you have nothing to do to examine me; meddle with that you have to do withal.

Theol. I perceive you are not only ignorant, but wilful and obstinate, and refuse all instructions; therefore I will leave you to God, and to your galled conscience; but, I pray you, Asunetus, answer that question: what think you, what is the reason that Christ was conceived by the Holy Ghost?

Asun. Believe me, sir, that is an hard question; you may ask a wise man that question, for I cannot answer it.

Theol. What say you then to this, who was Christ's mother?

Asun. Mary, sir; that was our blessed ladv.

Theol. What was Pontius Pilate?

Asun. I am somewhat ignorant, I am not book-learned; but if you will have my simple opinion, I think it was the devil; for none but the devil would put our sweet Saviour to death.

Theol. What is the holy catholic church, which you say you do believe?

Asun. The communion of saints, the forgiveness of sins.

Theol. What do you pray for when you say "thy kingdom come?"

Asun. I do pray that God would send us all of his grace, that we may serve him, and do as we ought to do, and keep us in a good mind to Godward, and to have him much in our mind; for some, God bless us, have nothing but the devil in their mind: they do nothing in God's name.

Theol. What is a Sacrament?

Asun. The Lord's Supper.

Theol. How many sacraments be there?

Asun. Two.

Theol. Which be they?

Asun. Bread and wine,

Theol. What is the principle end of your coming to receive the sacrament?

Asun. To receive my Maker.

Theol. What is the principal use of a sacrament?

Asun. The body and blood of Christ.

Theol. What profit and comfort have you by a sacrament?

Asun. In token that Christ died for us.

Theol. I can but pity you for your ignorance; for it is exceeding gross and palpable. Your answers are to no purpose, and bewray a wonderful blindness and senselessness in matters of religion. I am sorry that now I have not time and leisure to let you see your folly and extreme ignorance, as also to lay open unto you the sense and meaning of the articles of the faith, the Lord's prayer, and the sacraments, and all the other grounds of Christian religion.

Asun. What course would you wish me to take, that I may come out of ignorance, and attain unto the true knowledge of God?

Theol. Surely I would wish you to be diligent in hearing of sermons, and reading the scriptures, with prayer and humility. Also, that you would peruse catechisms, and other good books; and especially Virel's Grounds of Religion, and works of the two worthy servants of God, Master Gyffard and Master Perkins, and other men's that have done great service to the church, and for whom thousands are bound to give God thanks. If you take this course, you shall by God's grace, within a short time, grow to some good measure of knowledge, in all the main grounds of Christian religion.

Phil. I had not thought any man had been so ignorant as I now perceive this man is.

Theol. Yes, verily; there be thousands in his case; and I do know by experience that many will use the very same answers, or at least very little differing.

Phil. I warrant you if you had questioned with him of kine, or sheep, purchasing of lands, taking of leases, or any other matter under the sun, you should have found him very ripe and ready in his answers.

Theol. I am so persuaded too; for let a man talk with worldly men of worldly matters, and their answer is never to seek. They will talk

very freshly with you of such matters, if it be all
the day long; for they have a deep insight into
earthly things, and do wholly delight to talk of
them, being never weary; for it is their joy
their, meat, and their drink. But come once to
talk with them of God's matters, as of faith, repentance, regeneration, &c., you shall find them
the veriest dullards and dunces in the world;
for, when speech is had of these things, they are
so befogged* that they cannot tell where they
are, nor what they say.

Phil. In my judgment, such men's case is very
pitiful and dangerous. And so is this man's case
also, if God do not very speedily pull him out of it.

Theol. Questionless; for God saith, Hosea
iv. 6, " My people perish for want of knowledge."
Our Lord Jesus saith that ignorance is the cause
of all errors: " Ye do err, saith he, not knowing
the scripture, nor the power of God," Matt. xxii.
29. The apostle saith that ignorance doth alien-
ate us from the life of God; for, saith he, "The
Gentiles were darkened in the cogitation, being
strangers from the life of God, through the ignorance that is in them," Eph. iv. 18. So then, it
is clear that ignorance is not the mother of devo-
tion, as the papists do avouch; but it is the mother
of error, death, and destruction, as the scriptures
affirmeth. Our Lord, forseeing the great danger
of ignorance, how thereby thousands are carried
headlong into hell, doth admonish all men to
search the scriptures, John v. 39, which do testify of him; that so they might get out of the
most dangerous gulf of ignorance, wherein multitudes are implunged. Therefore, the noble men

* Lost, set fast.

of Berea are commended by the Holy Ghost, Acts xvii. 11, because they received the word with all readiness; and searched the scriptures daily, whether those things were so. Oh therefore, that men would earnestly seek after the know- ledge of God in time, and, as the prophet saith, "Seek the Lord while he may be found; call upon him whilst he is near," Isa. lv. 6.

Phil. I do see that all ignorance in matters of faith is dangerous; but I think wilful ignorance is of all others most dangerous.

Theol. Wilful ignorance, no doubt, is a plain prognostication, and demonstrative argument of eternal death; for it is a most horrible and fear- ful thing for men to refuse instructions, despise counsels, harden their hearts, stop their ears, and close up their eyes against God. This is the very upshot of our decay.

Phil. I pray you, what call you hardness of heart?

Theol. An hard heart is that which is neither moved with God's mercies, nor scared with his judgments; neither feareth the law, nor regardeth the gospel; neither is holpen by threatenings, nor softened by chastenings; which is unthankful for God's benefits, and disobedient to his counsels; made cruel by his rods, and dissolute by his favours; unshameful to filthiness, and fearless to perils; uncourteous to men and retchless* to God; forgetful of things past, negligent in things pres- ent, and improvident in things to come.

Phil. Lay forth yet more plainly the state of ignorant and hard-hearted men; and shew how lamentable it is.

---

* Careless, hardened.

Theol. If a man be outwardly blind we do pity him, and say, there goeth a poor blind man; but if he be both blind and deaf, do we not more pity him? and say, oh, in how miserable a case is that man! but if he be both blind, deaf, and dumb, do we not most of all pity him? and say, oh, that man is in a most woful taking, and in a most pitiful plight! How much more then are they to be pitied, which, as concerning their souls, are both blind, deaf, and dumb? for the diseases of the soul are far more dangerous, and more to be pitied than those of the body. Would it not pity a man's heart to see a poor sheep in a lion's mouth, whilst he teareth him, renteth him, and pulleth him in pieces? Even such is the case of ignorant men in the claws of the devil; for the devil hath them under him, rideth them at his pleasure, and teareth their souls in pieces! Oh, that we had eyes to see these things, hearts to feel them, and affections to be thoroughly moved with them, even unto mourning and tears.

Phil. Few do think that ignorant men are in so woful case as you speak of; for they think that ignorance will excuse them; and some will say they are glad they have so little knowledge; for if they should have much knowledge of their master's will, and do it not, they shall be beaten with many stripes; but now, being ignorant, they think all is safe.

Theol. God willed his people to offer sacrifice for their sins of ignorance, Levit. iv; therefore, ignorance is a sin, and excuseth no man: and as for the state of their souls before God, it is most miserable; if we could see into their souls as we see their bodies; for, assuredly, there be multitudes which ruffle it out in velvets and silks, and most brave and glittering outsides, but inwardly are full of filthiness and sin; they have fine and delicate bodies, but most ugly, black, and filthy souls. If a man could see into their souls as he doth into their bodies, he would stop his nose at the stink of them; for they smell rank of sin in the nostrils of God, his angels, and all good men.

Phil. Then I perceive by your speech that the case of all ignorant and profane men is fearful in the sight of God, and that all good men are to pity them, and pray for them.

Theol. If two blind and deaf men should walk in a beaten path that leadeth to a great deep pond wherein they are like to be drowned, if they go forward, and two men afar off should whoop unto them, and will then not go forward least they be drowned; yet they neither seeing any man, nor hearing any man, go forward and are drowned: were not this a lamentable spectacle to behold? Even so it is with all the ignorant, blind, and deaf souls of the world: for they cast no perils, but walk on boldly to destruction; and though the preachers of the gospel whoop never so loud unto them, or give them never so many warnings and caveats to take heed; yet they, being inwardly blind, see nothing; and spiritually deaf, hear nothing; and therefore go on forward in their sins and ignorance, till they suddenly fall into the pit of hell. Put case also, two great armies should pitch in a field, and fight a main battle upon a plain, and that some man should stand upon the top of a mountain hard by, and behold all, and should see with his own eyes how thousands and ten thousands went to wreck, and fell down on every side as thick as hail, the whole plain swim-

ming in blood; and should also hear the groanings
of soldiers wounded, and the doleful sighs and
groanings of many captains and colonels giving
up the ghost; were not this a most woful spectacle? Even so, when we do clearly see Satan
wound and murder thousand thousands souls, is
it not a far more tragical and lamentable sight?
and ought it not even to kill our hearts to behold
it? but, alas! men have no eyes to see into these
things; and yet certain it is, that Satan doth
continually, and in most fearful manner, massacre
innumerable souls. Thus have I shewed you the
woful estate of profane and ignorant men.

Phil. If it be so, you that be ministers and
preachers of the gospel, and have taken upon you
the cure and charge of souls, have need to look
about you, and to do what in you lieth to save
souls; and, as good shepherds, in great pity and
compassion, to labour to pull them out of the paws
of this roaring lion, which goeth about continually
seeking whom he may devour.

Theol. It standeth upon us, indeed, very seriously and carefully to look to it, as we will answer
it at the dreadful day of judgment; for it is no
small matter that we have taken in hand, which
is, to care for the flock which Christ hath bought
with his blood. Would to God therefore that we
would leave striving about other matters, and
strive together all about this—who can pull most
out of the kingdom of Satan, sin, and ignorance—
who can win most souls—and who can perform
best service to the church. This were a good
strife indeed,—and would to God that we might
once at last with joined forces go about it, and
with one heart and hand, join together to build
up God's house. If through our own follies the

work hath been hindered, or any breach made, let us in wisdom and love labour to make it up again. If there hath been any declining and coldness, let us now at last revive: let us stir up ourselves, that we may stir up others. Let us be zealous and fervent in spirit, that we may through God's grace put life into others, and rouse up this dead, declining, and cold age wherein we live: so shall God be glorified, his church edified, his saints comforted, his people saved, his throne erected, and the kingdom of the devil overthrown.

Phil. What think you were the best course to effect this which you speak of?

Theol. This is a thing that must be exceedingly laboured in of us which are the ministers and preachers of the gospel. And here is required diligence and, as we say, double diligence; for the people are every where ignorant. Some are stones, altogether incapable of instruction: others are froward and wilful. Some will receive the doctrine, but not the practice: some again are altogether set upon peevishness and cavilling. So that a man were better take upon him the charge of keeping wolves and bears than the charge of souls; for it is the hardest thing in the world, to reform men's disorders, and to bring them into order; to pull men's souls out of the kingdom of Satan, and to bring them to God. It is as we say, an endless piece of work, an infinite toil, a labour of all labours: I quake to think of it. For, men are so obstinate and irrefragable that they will be brought into no order: they will come under no yoke. They will not ruled by God, nor bridled by his word. They will follow their own swing. They will run after their own lusts and pleasures. They will kick and spurn if they be reproved.

They will rage and storm if you go about to curb them, and restrain them of their wills, likings, and liberties. They will have their wills, and follow their old fashions, say what you will, and do what you can. Is it not, think you, a busy piece of work, to smooth and square such timber logs, so full of knots and knobs? Is it not a tedious and irksome thing to think upon? and would it not kill a man's heart to go about it? for, how hard a thing is it to bring such into frame as are so far out of frame!

Phil. Well sir, you can but do your endeavour, and commit the success to God. You can but plant and water: let God give the increase. You are ministers of the letter, but not of the Spirit. You baptize with water, but not with the Holy Ghost. If you therefore preach diligently, exhort. admonish, and reprove, publicly and privately; studying by all good example of life, and seeking with all good zeal, care, and conscience, to do the uttermost that in you lieth, to reduce them from their evil ways; I take it, you are discharged, though they remain stubborn and incorrigible; for you know, what the Lord saith by his prophet, "If you do admonish them and give them warning, then you shall be discharged, and their blood shall be required at their own hands," Ezek. xxxiii.

Theol. You have spoken the truth; and, therefore, since some must needs take upon them this so great a charge, it will be our best course to labour much with them in catechising and private instructions, and that in most familiar and plain manner, for much good hath been done, and is done this way. The ignorant sort must be much laboured upon this way: and so, no doubt, much good may be done; "For, in all labour there is profit," Prov. xiv. 23. Herein, we that are the ministers of Christ must be content to be abased, and to teach the poor ignorant people in most plain manner, asking them many easy questions, and often questioning with them in most plain and loving manner, till we have brought them to some taste and smack of the principles of the Christian religion. We must not be ashamed to use repetitions and tautologies, and tell them one thing twenty times over and over again; here a line, and there a line; here a little, and there a little; precept upon precept, as the prophet speaketh, Isa. xxviii. 10. I know right well nothing goeth more against the stomach of a scholar, and him that is learned indeed, than to do thus. It is as irksome and tedious as to teach A B C: some can, at no hand, endure it. But truly, truly, I find now, after long experience, that if we will do any good to these simple and ignorant souls, we must enter into this course, and we may not be ashamed of it; for, it will be our crown and our glory to win souls, howsoever we be abased. Let us, therefore, be well content to stoop down, that Christ may be exalted. Let us be abased, that God may be honoured. Let us do all things in great love to Christ, who hath said, "If thou lovest me, feed, feed, feed my flock," John xxi. 15–17. Let us, therefore, testify our love to him by feeding his flock. Let us do all things in great love and deep compassion towards the poor souls that go astray. As it is said that our Lord Jesus was moved to pity, and his bowels did yearn, to see the people as sheep without a shepherd; let it likewise move us thoroughly, and make our hearts to bleed, to see so many poor sheep of

Christ wandering and straying in the mountains, and wilderness of this world, caught in every bramble, and hanged in every bush, ready to be devoured of the wolf. Thus have I shewed you, what course, in my judgment, is best to be taken, for the delivering of poor ignorant souls out of the captivity of Satan and sin.

Phil. Now, as you have declared what course is best to be followed of your part, which are the ministers and preachers of the gospel; so I pray you shew what is best to be done of us, which are the people of God.

Theol. The best counsel that I can give you, if it were for my life, is to be much exercised in the word of God, both in the hearing, reading, and meditation thereof; and also to purchase unto yourself the sincere ministry of the gospel, and to make conscience to live under it, esteeming yourself happy if you have it, though you want other things; and unhappy if you have it not, though you have all other things. For it is a peerless pearl, an incomparable jewel; for the purchasing whereof, we are advised by our Lord Jesus to sell all that we have, rather than to go without it, Mat. xiii. 44. Again, our Saviour Christ giveth the same counsel to the church of Laodicea, in these words, "I counsel thee, to buy of me gold tried by the fire, that thou mayest be rich: and white raiment, that thou mayest be clothed, and that thy filthy nakedness do not appear; and anoint thine eyes with eye-salve, that thou mayest see," Rev. iii. 18; where you see the word of God is compared to most precious gold, whereby we are made spiritually rich; and to glittering attire, wherewithal our naked souls are clothed; and to an eye-salve, wherewith our spiritual blindness is

cured. We are advertised also by Jesus Christ,
whose counsel is ever the best, that we should
buy these things, whatsoever they cost us. The
same counsel also giveth wise Solomon, saying,
" Buy the truth, but sell it not," Prov. xxiii. 23.
So then you see, the counsel which herein I give
you is not mine own, but the counsel of Jesus
himself, and Solomon the wise; and who can, or
who dare, except against their counsel?

Asun. Is your meaning that men must of necessity frequent preaching of the word? will not
bare reading serve the turn?

Theol. I told you before that reading is good,
profitable, and necessary, but yet it is not sufficient.
We must not content ourselves with that only;
but we must go further, and get unto ourselves
the sound preaching of the gospel, as the chiefest
and most principal means which God hath ordained and sanctified for the saving of men; as
it is plainly set down, 1 Cor. i. 21, "When as
the world, by wisdom, knew not God, in the wisdom of God, it pleased God, by the foolishness of
preaching, to save them that believe." The meaning of it is that—when as men, neither by natural
wisdom, nor the contemplation of the creatures,
could sufficiently attain to the true knowledge of
God—the Lord, according to his heavenly and infinite wisdom, thought of another course; which
is to save men by preaching, which the world
counteth foolishness. And by the way, note that
the preaching of the word is not a thing of human
invention; but it is God's own device, and came
first out of his wisdom as the best and nearest way
to save men's souls. Wise Solomon, also, in the
book of the Proverbs, xxix. 18, telleth us that the
preaching of God's word, which is called vision,

using the word of the prophets, which called their sermons visions, is not a thing that may be spared, or that we may be at choice whether we have it or no; but he maketh it to be of absolute necessity unto eternal life; for he saith, "Where vision faileth, the people are left naked." So indeed, it is in the original; but the old translation giveth us the sense, thus, "Where the word of God is not preached there the people perish." Then you see that Solomon striketh it dead, in telling us that all they which are without preaching of the word are in exceeding danger of losing their souls. Oh that men could be persuaded of this! Saint Paul also saith that faith cometh by hearing the word preached; for he saith, Rom. x. 14, "How can they hear, without a preacher?" If faith come by hearing the word preached, then I reason thus—no preaching, no faith; no faith, no Christ; no Christ, no eternal life, for eternal life is only in him. Let us then put them together, thus: take away the word, take away faith; take away faith, take away Christ; take away Christ, and take away eternal life. So then it followeth, take away the word and take away eternal life. Or we may read them backward, thus: if we will have heaven, we must have Christ; if we will have Christ, we must have faith; if we will have faith, we must have the word preached. Then it followeth thus: if we will have heaven, we must have the word preached. Then I conclude, that preaching generally, and for the most part, is of absolute necessity unto eternal life; as meat is of absolute necessity for the preservation of our bodies; as grass and fodder are of absolute necessity for the upholding of the life of beasts; and water of absolute necessity for the life of fishes. Then, this being so, men are

with great care and conscience to hear the gospel
preached, to frequent sermons, to resort much to
God's house and habitation, where his honour
dwelleth; with David to say, Psalm xxvii. 4,
"One thing have I desired of the Lord, that I will
require: even that I may dwell in the house of
the Lord, all the days of my life; to behold the
beauty of the Lord, and to visit his holy temple."
With godly Mary to say, Luke x. 42, "One thing
is necessary; and so choose the better part."
With the poor cripple of Bethesda, John v. 7,
to wait for the moving of the waters by the angel,
that his impotency may be cured: I mean that
we should tie ourselves to the first moving of the
spiritual waters of life, by the preachers of the
gospel, that our spiritual impotency may be
holpen and relieved. For the ministry of the
gospel is that golden pipe whereby and where,
through the goodness of God, all the sweetness
of Christ, and all heavenly graces whatsoever are
derived unto us.   Which thing was shadowed
in the law by the pomegranates in the skirts of
Aaron's garments, and the golden bells between
them round about: that is "a golden bell and
a pomegranate; a golden bell and a pomegranate," Exod. xxviii. 34. The golden bells did
signify the preaching of the gospel, and the pomegranates the sweet savour of Christ's death; noting thereby, that the sweet savour of Christ's
death, and all the benefits of his passion, should
be spread abroad by the preaching of the gospel.
Thus you see, that if ever men purpose to be saved,
they must make more account of the preaching of
the gospel than they have done; and not think,
as most men do, that they may be without it,
and yet do well enough.   And some had as leave

be without it as have it; for it doth but disquiet them, and trouble their consciences; but woe be unto such.

Phil. Yet we see, where the word is soundly preached there be many bad people; and the reasons thereof, in mine opinion, are two; the one, that God taketh his Holy Spirit from many in hearing the word, so that their hearing is made unfruitful; the other, that the devil hath an hundred devices to hinder the effectual working of the word, so as it shall do no good at all, nor take any effect in multitudes of men. But you, master Theologus, can better lay open this matter than I. I pray you therefore speak something of it.

Theol. The sleights of Satan, in this behalf, are more and more sly than I. or any man else, can possibly discover. For who is able to descry, or in sufficient manner, to lay open the deep subtilties, and most secret and sinful suggestions of the devil in the hearts of men: he is so cunning a craftmaster this way that none can perfectly trace him. His workings, in the hearts of men, are with such close and hid deceits, and most methodical and crafty conveyances, that none can sufficiently find them out; but yet, notwithstanding, I will bewray so much as I know, or can conceive of his dealings with men that hear the word, that he may steal it out of their hearts, and make it fruitless and unprofitable. First of all, he bestirreth him and laboureth hard to keep men fast asleep in their sins, that they may have no care at all of their salvation; and therefore dissuadeth them from hearing, or reading the word at all, lest they should be awaked. If this will not prevail, but that they must needs hear, then his craft is to make their hearing unprofitable,

by sleepiness, dulness, by thoughts, conceitedness, and a thousand such like. If this will not
serve the turn, but that the word doth get within
them, and work upon them, so as thereby they
grow to some knowledge and understanding of the
truth, then he practiseth another way, which is,
to make them rest themselves upon their bare
knowledge, and so become altogether conscienceless. If this will not suffice, but that men fall to
doing, and leave some sins, especially the gross
sins of the world, and do some good, then he
persuadeth them to trust to those doings without
Christ, and to think themselves well enough,
because they do some good, and leave some evil.
If this be not enough, but that men attain unto
the true justifying faith which apprehendeth
Christ, and resteth upon his merits, then he de-
viseth how to blemish the beauty of their faith,
and weaken their comfort, through many frailties
and wants, yea, gross downfalls, and rank evils:
so as they shall be but spotted and leprous Christians. If this weapon will not work, but that
Christians do join all good virtues with their faith,
and abundantly shine forth in all fruits of righteousness, then he casteth about another way: which
is, to daunt and damp them with discouragements:
as poverty, necessity, sickness, reproaches, contempts, persecutions, &c. If none of all these will
do the deed, but that men constantly believe in
Christ, and patiently and joyfully endure all afflictions, then his last refuge is to blow them up
with gunpowder: that is to puff them up with a
pride of their gifts, graces, and strength, and so
to give them an utter overthrow whilst they do
not walk humbly, and give God the praise of his
gifts. Thus have you a little taste of Satan's

cunning, in making the word unfruitful amongst us.

Asun. I pray you, good sir, seeing I am ignorant and unlearned, give me some particular directions out of the word of God, for the good guiding and ordering of my particular actions, in such sorts as that I may glorify God in the earth, and after this life be glorified of him for ever.

Theol. It were an infinite thing to enter into all particulars; but briefly do this: first, seek God earnestly in his word; pray much; in all things give thanks; eschew evil, and do good; fear God, and keep his commandments; reform yourself, and your household; love virtue, and virtuous men; keep company with the godly, and avoid the society of the wicked. Live soberly, justly, and holily, in the present evil world. Speak always graciously, and beware of filthy communications. Recompense to no man evil for evil; but recompense evil with good. Be courteous and pitiful towards all men. Take heed of swearing, cursing, and banning.* Beware of anger, wrath, and bitterness. Praise your friend openly; reprove him secretly. Speak no evil of them that are absent, nor of the dead. Speak evil of no man; speak always the best, or at least, not the worst. Reverence God's name, and keep his Sabbaths. Avoid all the signs of condemnation, and labour after all the signs of salvation. Above all things, take heed of sin, for that is the very cutthroat of the soul, and bane of all goodness. Tremble therefore, and sin not. For if you sin, mark what followeth—God seeth—his angels bear witness—the conscience pricketh—death

---

Cursing, blasting.

threateneth—the devil accuseth—hell devoureth. You see then that sin is no scarecrow, or
jesting matter. Every sin that a man committeth
is as a thorn thrust deep into the soul, which will
not be got out again but with many a sigh, and
many a sorrowful—oh, oh! "Every sin is written
with a pen of iron: and the point of a diamond
upon the conscience," Jer. xvii. 1; and shall in
the last day, when the books shall be opened, accuse us, and give in evidence against us. If a man
commit sin with pleasure, the pleasure passeth
away, but the conscience and sting of the sin
abideth, and tormenteth deadly; but if a man do
well, though with labour and painfulness, the pain
passeth away, yet the conscience of well-doing remaineth with much comfort; but the best end of
sin is always repentance, if not in this life, then
with woe, and alas! when it is too late: therefore
take heed in time; take heed, I say, of sin. Sin
hardeneth the heart, Heb. iii. 13; sin gnaweth
the conscience, 1 Sam. xxv. 31; sin fighteth
against the soul, 1 Peter ii. 11; sin bringeth
forth death, James i. 15; sin maketh ashamed,
Rom. vi. 21; sin procureth all plagues of body
and soul, Deut. xxviii. Behold, therefore, the
evil effects of sin: for this cause, Zophar, the
Naamathite, speaketh very wisely to Job, saying,
xi. 15, "When thou shalt lift thy face out of thy
sin, thou shalt be strong, and shall not fear; thou
shalt forget all sorrow; thou shalt remember it
as the waters that are past;" where Zophar
plainly sheweth that the avoiding of sin is our
strength, and the committing of it our weakening;
according to that of Solomon, Prov. x. 29, "The
way of the Lord is the strength of the upright
man." Therefore, walk in the way of God, and

take heed of the ways of sin; for God punisheth every sin his way; some one way, and some another; and no sin can escape unpunished; for because God is just, therefore he must needs punish sin in all men, though in divers manners: as the wicked, in their own persons; the godly, in Christ. Beware of it, therefore, and flatter not yourself in your sins. Remember how every disobedience and every transgression hath had a just recompence of reward. God hath, in all ages, matched the causes with the effect; that is, sin with the punishment of sin. The Israelites, for breaking the first commandment, in making other gods, were often smitten by the hand of God. Nadab and Abihu, the sons of Aaron, for the breach of the second commandment, in offering strange fire upon God's altar, were consumed with fire. He that blasphemed and transgressed the third commandment, was stoned to death. He that brake the fourth commandment, in gathering sticks upon the Sabbath, was likewise stoned. Absalom, transgressing the fifth commandment, was hanged in his own hair. Cain, transgressing the sixth, in slaying his brother Abel, was branded with the mark of God's wrath. Shechem, the son of Hamor, transgressing the seventh, in defiling Dinah the daughter of Jacob, was slain by Simeon and Levi, the sons of Jacob. Achan, sinning against the eighth commandment, in stealing the wedge of gold, and the Babylonish garment, was stoned to death. Ananias and Sapphira, sinning against the ninth commandment, in lying and dissembling, were suddenly smitten with death. Ahab, transgressing the tenth commandment, in coveting and discontentment, was devoured of dogs. Or if you will have original sin therein only forbidden, then infants are therefore punished with death, Rom. v. 14. Thus we see there is no dallying with God; but if we sin, we are as sure to be jerked* for it, as the coat is on our back. Therefore let us not deceive ourselves nor make light of sin; for sin is no scarecrow, and we shall one day find it so. And howsoever we make light of some sins, yet, in every deed, all sin is odious in the sight of God, yea all sin is heinous and capital, in this respect, that it is against a person of infinite being; it is against God himself; it is against the highest majesty. For the greatness of the person offended doth enhance and increase the greatness of the sin: as for example, if a man rail at a justice of peace, he shall be stocked; if he rail at one of his majesty's privy council, he shall be imprisoned; but if he rail at his own majesty, he shall be hanged. So then, you see how a sin is increased by the dignity of the person offended. Now then, since all mortal princes are but dust in the sight of God, and he is a person of infinite and incomparable majesty, how heinous and how flagitious a thing is it, in any wise, or after any sort to sin against his most royal and sacred person! Well then, to grow to some conclusion, this I do advise you; as to shun all vice, so to embrace all virtue; as to put of the old man, so to put on the new man. Remember, often and always, what shall become of you after this life, and where you shall be forty years hence—in hell or in heaven. Look well to that in time; and therefore so live that you may live always. Consider often in your secret cogitations what you have been; what you

* Lashed, or sharply checked   † Set in the stocks.

are; what you shall be; what God hath done for you; what he doth; what he will do; God's judgments past; God's judgments present; God's judgments to come. Awake at last; and take care for your salvation. Sleep no longer in sin, lest ye perish eternally; for, verily, there is a reward for the righteous; doubtless, there is a God that judgeth the earth. And this is the best counsel that I can give you.

Asun. Your counsel is very good. I pray God give me grace to follow it; and so to live that I may please God, and go to heaven in the end.

Theol. You must take heed you speak not these words of course, and for fashion's sake, having no settled purpose in your heart to follow these directions. For there be numbers that can skill to give good words, but they will do nothing. They think they highly please God with their good words, and that God will take them for payment; as though God regarded words. They would fain go to heaven, but they will take no pains, they will leave no sins, they will not forego their lusts and pleasures: they would have the reward of God's children, but they will not do the works of God's children; they would have the sweet, but none of the sour; they would have the crown, but they will fight never a stroke; they would fain come to Canaan, but they are loth to travel that long and dangerous way, which leadeth unto it. Therefore, these men, being the sons of idleness, will stop short in the end, of that they looked for; for the Spirit saith, Prov. xiii. 4, "The sluggard lusteth, but his soul hath nought." We must therefore leave bare words, and come to deeds; for our Lord Jesus saith, Matt. vii. 21,

"Not every one that saith Lord, Lord, shall enter into the kingdom of heaven, but he that doeth the will of my Father which is in heaven;" where we see Christ, in plain terms, doth exclude out of his kingdom all those whose religion consisteth only in good words and smooth speeches, but make no conscience to practise the commandments of God. David, having made some good preparation for the building of the temple, and perceiving his son Solomon to have stuff and provision enough to perfect and finish it, doth most wisely encourage him to the work, in these words: "Up, and be doing, and the Lord shall be with thee," 1 Chron. xxii. 16. Oh that men would follow this counsel of David! that they would up, and be doing; and not sit still, and do nothing: that they would leave words and countenances, and set upon the practice of God's law; and study, with all care and conscience, to be obedient to his will. Then, assuredly, God would be with them, and bless them; and much good would come of it; for the scriptures saith, Prov. xiv. 23, "In all labour there is profit, or increase, but the talk of the lips only bringeth want."

Phil. Most men's minds are so wholly drowned in the love of this world, that they have no heart to obey God, nor any delight in his commandments.

Theol. The greatest part of men are like unto the Gadarenes, which esteemed their swine more than Christ. As we see in these our days, how many make more account of their kine and sheep than of the most glorious gospel of Christ! They highly esteem dung, and contemn pearls. They are careful for trifles, and regard not the things of greatest moment; and, therefore, may very

fitly be compared to a man who, having his wife
and children very sick, doth utterly neglect them,
and is altogether careful for the curing of his
hogs.

———

CHRIST'S COMING TO JUDGMENT.

Phil. We have somewhat digressed from the
matter we had in hand: I pray you, therefore, if
you have any more matter of good counsel to
give unto Asunetus, that you would presently
deliver it.

Theol. I have little more to say, save only I
would advise him often to remember, and much
to muse, of these nine things:—The evil he hath
committed—the good he hath omitted—the
time he hath mis-spent—the shortness of this
life—the vanity of this world—the excellency
of the world to come—death, than which nothing
is more terrible—the day of judgment, than
which nothing is more fearful—hell-fire, than
which nothing is more intolerable.

Phil. This is short and sweet indeed: you have
touched some of these points before in these our
conferences; but I am very desirous to hear somewhat more of the two last, which yet have not
been touched.

Theol. Since you are desirous, I will briefly
deliver unto you that which I have received
from the Lord.   First, concerning the day of
judgment, I find in the volume of God's book
that it shall be very terrible and dreadful, for
" The Son of Man shall come in the clouds of
heaven, with power and great glory," Matt. xxiv.

30. St. Peter saith, 2 Epis. iii. 10, "The day
of the Lord shall come as a thief in the night,
in the which the heavens shall pass away with a
noise, the elements shall melt with heat, and the
earth, with the works that are therein, shall be
burnt up." The apostle telleth us that at the
coming of Christ all the whole world shall be
of a light fire; and that all castles, towers, goodly
buildings, gold, silver, velvet, silks, and all the
glittering hue, glory, and beauty of this world
shall be consumed to powder and ashes; for he
saith plainly, "The heavens and the earth which
are now, are reserved unto fire, against the day
of judgment, and of the destruction of ungodly
men," ver. 7· Moreover, he doth strongly prove,
that as the world was once destroyed by water,
so the second time, in the end thereof, it shall be
destroyed by fire. The apostle Paul doth witness
the same thing; for he saith, 2 Thess. i. 7,
"Christ shall come from heaven, with all his
mighty angels, in flaming fire." And in another
place, 1 Thess. iv. 16, he noteth the terror of his
coming to judgment, saying, "He shall come
with a shout, with the voice of the archangel,
and the trumpet of God." We see, by experience, that the coming of mortal princes to
any place, is with great pomp and glory, They
have great trains and troops behind them and
before them. They are accompanied with
many nobles; gallant lords and goodly ladies
do attend upon them. The sword-bearer, trum-
peters, and harbingers go before; many flaunting
and stately personages follow after. Now then,
if the coming of mortal princes be so pompous
and glorious, how much more glorious shall the
coming of the Son of Man be, in whose sight all

mortal princes are but dust? The scriptures do affirm that his second coming unto judgment, shall be with such resplendent and unspeakable glory, that even the most excellent creatures shall blush at it; for "The sun shall be darkened; the moon shall not give her light; and the stars shall fall from heaven," Matt. xxiv. 29; meaning thereby, that the most glorious and bright-shining creatures shall be clouded and obscured by the unconceivable brightness of Christ's coming. Moreover, is noted unto us the error of Christ's coming in this, that immediately before it the very sea shall quake and tremble, and in his kind cry out; for it is said, Luke xxi. 25, 26, "That the sea shall roar, and make a noise in most doleful and lugubrious manner, and men's hearts shall fail them for fear, and for looking after those things which shall come on the world; for the powers of heaven shall be shaken." Oh what shall become of swearers, drunkards, whoremongers, and such like, in that day! they shall seek to creep into an auger-hole, to hide their heads; they shall then cry woe and alas, that ever they were born! they shall wish that they never had been born, or that their mother had born them toads. And, as it is said in the Apocalypse, "They shall say to the mountains and rocks fall on us, and hide us from the presence of him that sitteth on the throne, and from the wrath of the Lamb; for the great day of his wrath is come, and who can stand?" Rev. vi. 16, 17. We see, therefore, that the coming of Christ shall not be base and contemptible, as in his first visitation; but it shall be most terrible, princely, and glorious. And as the scriptures do affirm that his coming shall be with great terror and dread, so also they do shew that it shall be very sudden and unlooked for; for "The day of the Lord shall come as a thief in the night," 1 Pet. iii. 10; "As the travail that cometh upon a woman," 1 Thess. v. 2, 3; "As a snare shall it come on all them that dwell on the face of the earth," Luke xxi. 35: that is, it shall suddenly catch and entangle all men, wheresoever they be in the world. As the earthquake, which was some twenty years ago, did suddenly take the world tardy, they not thinking of any such matter; so shall the coming of the Son of Man to judgment take the world tardy and unprepared; for few there be that think of any such matter. Since, therefore, the second appearance of Christ shall be with such suddenness, let us fear and tremble; for all sudden things are to be feared.

Phil. Well, sir, as you have shewed us the terror and suddenness of Christ's coming, so shew us the purpose and end of his coming.

Theol. The principal end of his coming shall be to keep a general audit, to call all men to an account, to have a reckoning of every man's particular actions, and to reward them according to their deeds; as it is written, Matt. xvi. 27, "The Son of Man shall come in the glory of his Father, with his angels: and then shall he give to every man according to his deeds." Again, the apostle saith, 2 Cor. v. 10, "We must all appear before the judgment-seat of Christ, that every man may receive the things which are done in his body, according to that which he hath done, whether it be good or evil." Here we do plainly see that the end of Christ's coming shall be to judge every man according to his works; that is, as his works shall declare him, *and testify of him and of his faith.* In another place, the apostle saith, 2 Thess. i. 7–9, "That the end of his coming shall be to render vengeance unto them which know not God, and which obey not the gospel of our Lord Jesus Christ; which shall be punished with everlasting perdition from the presence of the Lord, and from the glory of his power." Woe, then, unto two sorts of men!—the ignorant and the disobedient; for, the apostle saith flatly, they both shall be damned. Methinketh both the ignorant and disobedient, and all other profane men, should tremble to think of this—that Christ shall come to render vengeance unto them. If we did certainly know that the Spaniard should invade our nation, overrun it, and make a conquest of it—that he should shed our blood, destroy us, and make a massacre amongst us— yea, that we should see our wives, our children, our kindred, and dear friends slain before our faces, so as their blood should stream in the streets, what a wonderful fear and terror would it strike into us! We would quake to think of it. Shall we not, then, be much more afraid of the damnation of our souls? shall we not quake to think that Christ shall come to take vengeance? If the lion roar, all the beasts of the field tremble; and shall not we be afraid of the roaring Lion of the tribe of Judah? But, alas, we are so hard-hearted, and so rocked asleep in the cradle of security, that nothing can move us, nothing can awake us.

Phil. Now, as you have shewed us the terror and end of Christ's coming, so also declare the manner of it.

Theol. The manner of it is this, that the whole world shall be cited to appear personally

at the general assizes, before the great Judge.
No man shall be admitted to appear by his
attorney, but all must appear personally. None
shall be suffered to put in sureties, but all must
come in their own persons, without bail or main
prize; as it is written, 2 Cor. v. 10, " We must
all appear," high and low, rich and poor, king
and beggar, one and other; as it is plainly set
down in the 20th chapter of the Revelation,
where the Spirit saith, " I saw the dead, both
great and small, stand before God; and the sea
gave up the dead which were in her, and death
and hell delivered up the dead which were in
them." So, then, it is clear that all, without exception, shall make their appearance at the great
and dreadful assizes. Oh what a great day will
that be when as the whole world shall appear
together at once! • If a king marry his son, and
bid other kings, emperors, dukes, and nobles, to
the marriage, with all their pomp and train, we
use to say—oh what a marriage! what a meeting!
what a do! what a great day will there be! but
when the universal world shall be assembled
together, not only all monarchs, kings, and princes, but all others that ever have been from the
beginning of the world, all that are and shall be,
what a day will that be! No marvel, therefore,
that the scriptures call it the day of God, and
the great day of the Lord! Now then, when all
flesh is come together, to make their personal appearance, then shall the Son of God ascend unto
his tribunal seat, with great majesty and glory;
for a "fiery stream shall issue, and come forth
before him; thousand thousand angels shall accompany him, and minister unto him; and ten
thousand thousand shall stand before him; the

judgment shall be set, and the books opened,"
Dan. vii. 10.   All the saints also, and true worshippers of God, shall attend him, and accompany
him unto his judgment seat; and not only so
but they shall sit upon the bench and throne with
him, as it is written, 1 Cor. vi. 2, 3, "The saints
shall judge the world; they shall judge the angels;"
that is the devils, the angels of darkness.   Our
Lord Jesus himself doth avouch the same thing,
when he said to his disciples, and in them to all
true Christians, "Verily, I say unto you, that when
the Son of Man shall sit in the throne of his majesty, ye which followed me in the regeneration,
shall sit upon twelve thrones, and judge the twelve
tribes of Israel," Matt. xix. 28; that is, the
saints of God shall bear witness that the judgment
of Christ, and sentence of condemnation which
he passeth against all unbelievers, is according to
justice and equity.   Thus then, we see how
Christ shall be accompanied to his throne; and
with what glory and majesty he shall ascend unto
it.   Experience teacheth, that when mortal
judges hold their sessions and general assizes,
they are brought unto the bench and judgment
seat with pomp and terror; for the sheriff of the
shire, and holbard-men, with many justices of
peace, and trains of others, do accompany them
unto the bench.   Then, with how much more
glory and majesty shall the Son of God be
brought unto his royal throne!   Thus, then,
Christ being set upon his judgment seat, all the
ungodly shall be convented before him, and he
shall stand over them with a naked sword in his
hand.   The devil shall stand by them on the one
side, to accuse them; and their own conscience,
on the other side; and the gaping gulf of hell,

underneath them, ready to devour them.   Then
shall the books be opened; not any books of
paper and parchment, but the books of men's
consciences.   For every man's sins are written
and recorded in his conscience, as it were in a
register book.   Then will God bring every work
to judgment, with every secret thought, and set
them in order before all the reprobates.   Then
"will God lighten the things that are hid in darkness, and make the counsels of the heart manifest," 1 Cor. iv. 5.   Then shall all the ungodly
be arraigned, convicted, and hold up their hands
at the bar of Christ's tribunal seat, and shall cry,
guilty.   Then shall that most dreadful sentence of
death and condemnation be pronounced against
them by the most righteous Judge, Matt. xxv.
41, "Go, ye cursed, into everlasting fire, which
is prepared for the devil and his angels."   Oh
doleful sentence! oh heavy hearing!   Whose
heart doth not tremble at these things? whose
hair doth not stand upon his head? for then
shall thousands, which in this world have flou-
rished as the cedars of Libanus, be cast down for
evermore; and shall drink, as a just recompense
for their iniquity, of the bitter cup of God's
eternal wrath and indignation, in the kingdom of
darkness, and in the fearful presence of Satan,
and all the cursed enemies of God's grace.

Phil. Well, now, as you have declared unto
us the terror, the suddenness, the end, and the
manner of Christ's coming to judgment; so lastly,
shew unto us the right use of all these things.

Theol. St. Peter telleth and teacheth us the
right use of all; for, saith he, 2 Peter iii. 11,
"Seeing all these things must be dissolved, what
manner of persons ought we to be, in all holy

conversation and godliness?" as if he should
say, since the heavens shall pass away with a
noise, the elements shall melt with heat, and the
earth, with the works that are therein, shall be
burnt up; since also the coming of Christ shall
be with great terror, to a fearful end, and in
fearful manner, oh how ought we to excel in
goodness! So then, St. Peter telleth us, that the
true use of all is this, that hereby we be brought
nearer unto God, even to be more obedient to
his will, and to walk in all his commandments,
making conscience of all our ways, and studying
to please God in all things, and to be fruitful in
all good works, living soberly, justly, and holily
in this present evil world, and shewing forth the
virtues of him which hath called us out of darkness to this marvellous light; so that we may be
prepared against the day of his appearing, that
it may not take us tardy; for our life ought to
be a continual meditation of death; we should
always live as if we should die, or that our bed
should be our grave; we must live continually
as if Christ should come to judgment presently;
as it is reported of a godly man in the primitive church, that whether he ate or drank, or
whatsoever he did, he thought always he heard
the trumpet of the Lord, with these words,
"Arise, ye dead, and come unto judgment."
Put case—it were certainly known that Christ
would come to judgment the next midsummer-
day; oh what an alteration would it make in the
world! how men would change their minds and
affections! who would care for this world? who
would set his heart unto riches? who would regard brave apparel? who durst deceive or oppress?
who durst be drunk? who durst swear, lie,

and commit adultery? Nay, would not all men give up themselves to the obedience of God? would not all serve him diligently? would not all men and women flock to hear sermons? would they not give themselves to prayer and reading? would they not repent them of their sins? would they not cry for mercy and forgiveness? See then, what the knowledge of a certain day approaching would effect; and ought we not to do all these things with as great a care and zeal seeing the day is uncertain? for who knoweth whether Christ will come this month or the next, this year or next? He himself saith, Matt. xxiv. 44, " Be ready; watch; for in the hour that ye think not of, will the Son of man come." We think he will not come this year, nor next year, nor this hundred years. It may be, therefore, that he will come *suddenly upon us; we know not how soon.* For in an hour that we little think of, will he come. Therefore, our Saviour saith, in the 13th chapter of Mark, ver. 33, "Take heed, watch and pray; for you know not when the time is;" and in the gospel of St. Luke, xxi. 34, he saith, "Take heed that your hearts be not overcome with surfeiting and drunkenness, and the cares of this life, and so that day come upon you unawares; for as a snare shall it come upon all them that dwell upon the face of the earth." We hear, therefore, how many watch-words and caveats our Saviour giveth us, when he saith, Be in readiness, awake, take heed, watch and pray, and look about you, lest that day come suddenly upon you, and take you napping. It standeth us all therefore upon, to be at an hour's warning, upon pain of death, and as we will answer it at our uttermost peril.

Phil. Proceed to speak of the torments of hell.

Theol. Concerning the torments of hell, I do note three things, which I will briefly speak of, and they be these: the extremity, perpetuity, and remedilessness thereof. First, touching the extremity thereof, it standeth specially in these three things: first, that it is a separation from all joy and comfort of the presence of God; secondly, that it is an eternal fellowship with the devil and his angels; thirdly, it is a feeling of the horrible wrath of God, which shall seize upon body and soul, and shall feed on them, as fire doth upon pitch and brimstone, for ever. The scriptures do note the extremity of it, in calling it "a lake, that burneth with fire and brimstone for ever;" in saying "there shall be weeping and gnashing of teeth;" in affirming that "their worm dieth not," meaning the worm that gnaweth their conscience, or their torment of conscience; "and the fire never goeth out," in terming it "Tophet, which is deep and large, and the burning thereof is fire and much wood," and that "the breath of the Lord, as a river of brimstone, doth kindle it." All these things be terrible to our senses, and yet can they not fully express the thing as it is indeed. For no heart can conceive, or tongue express, the greatness and extremity of the torments of hell. As the joys of heaven never entered into the heart of man, no more did the torments of hell. All the torments and troubles that fall upon men in this life are but as sparkles of the furnace of God's total wrath. All fires are but, as it were, pictures of fire in comparison of hell-fire; for, as one writeth, "hell-fire is so extremely hot that it will burn up a man seven mile before he come at it;" yet the reprobates, being always in it, shall never be consumed of it.   As the salamander is always in the fire, and never consumeth ; so the wicked shall be always in the fire of hell, and never consume; for hell is a death always living, and an end always beginning.   It is a grievous thing to a man that is very sick to lie upon a feather-bed—how much more upon a hot gridiron! but how, most of all, to burn always in hell-fire, and never be consumed ? Another extremity of it consisteth in this, that the torments of hell are universal, that is, in every member at once; head, eyes, tongue, teeth, throat, stomach, back, belly, heart, sides, &c. All punishments of this life are particular: for some are pained in their head, some in their back, some in their stomachs, &c.; yet some particular pains are such as a man would not suffer to gain all the world; but for a man to be tormented in all parts at once, what sight more lamentable! who could but take pity of a dog in the street in that case! · Thus, then, we see that the extremity of hell-torments is greater than can be conceived or uttered; for who can utter that which is incomprehensible? we can go no further in comprehending that which is incomprehensible than to know it to be incomprehensible.

Phil. As you have shewn us the extremity of hell-torments, so now proceed to the perpetuity.

Theol. The scriptures do set forth the perpetuity of hell torments in saying they are for ever: the wicked shall be cast into the lake that burneth with fire and brimstone for ever. The fire never goeth out.   When as many hundred thousand years are expired as there be stones by the sea-side, yet still there be so many more to come; for that which hath no end can never come to an end. If all the arithmeticians in the world were set to work to do nothing but number all the days of their life, even the greatest numbers that they could possibly set down, and should in the end add all their numbers together; yet could they never come anything near to that length of time wherein the wicked shall be tormented. If the whole circumference of the heavens were written about with figures of arithmetic, from the east to the west, and from the west to the east again; yet could it not contain that infinite time and innumerable years, wherein all unbelievers shall suffer eternal torture; for, in things infinite, time hath no place; for time is the measure of those things which are subject to measure. Therefore, because hell torments are infinite, they cannot be measured by any time, neither can that which is infinite be diminished; for if you subtract from that which is infinite, ten thousand thousand millions of millions, yet it is hereby nothing diminished or made less. Put this case—a man should once in an hundred thousand years, take a spoonful of water out of the great ocean sea, how long would it be ere he had so emptied it? Yet shall a man sooner empty the sea, by taking out a spoonful once in a hundred thousand years, than the damned soul shall have any ease; therefore, a certain writer saith, "If a damned soul might be tormented in hell but a thousand years, and then have ease, there were some comfort in it, for then there would be hope it would come to an end;" but, saith he, this word "*ever*" killeth the heart. Oh consider this ye that forget God! Oh ye carnal worldlings, think on this in time! For if you will not now

U

be moved in hearing, you shall be then crushed in pieces in feeling. What availeth it to live in all possible pleasures, and carnal delights here, for some sixty years, and then to suffer this eternal torment? What shall it profit a man to win the whole world, and lose his own soul? They be more than mad which will hazard their souls for a little profit and a few stinking pleasures. But this is the nature of men: they will have the present sweet, come of it what will, though they pay never so dear it, though they go to the highest price, though they lose their souls for it. Oh the unspeakable blindness and madness of the men of this world! The devil hath put out their eyes, and therefore leadeth them whither he list; for who cannot lead a blind man whither he list? Nahash, the *Ammonite*, would make no covenant with the Israelites, but upon condition that he might put out all their right eyes, 1 Sam. xi. 2; so the devil doth covenant with all the wicked to put out both their eyes, that he may lead them directly into hell.

Phil. Now sir, a word or two more of the remedilessness of hell-fire.

Theol. The scriptures do affirm that as the torments of hell are extreme, so they are without all hope of remedy; as it is written, Ps. xlix. 8, " A man can by no means redeem his brother; he cannot give his ransom unto God; so precious is the redemption of the soul and the continuance for ever." To this purpose Abraham said to the rich man, being in hell torments, Luke xvi, 26, " Betwixt you and us there is a great gulf set, so that they which would go from hence to you cannot, neither can they come from thence to us." Our Lord Jesus also saith, " What shall a man

give for the recompense of his soul?" where
our Saviour doth plainly affirm that there is no
ransom or recompense, though never so great, to
be given for a damned soul. For the soul being
in hell can never be released: it is past remedy.
No means whatsoever can do any good. No gold,
no silver, no friends, no riches, no power, no policy,
no flattery, no bribery, no reach, no fetch or device
whatsoever can prevail one jot. For a man being
once in hell hath no remedy. He is in close
prison, he is shut up under the hatches for ever;
there is no getting out again: he must suffer
perpetual imprisonment. He cannot bring a writ
of false imprisonment, because he is laid in by
the most righteous and just Judge, who cannot
possibly do any wrong but he must lie by it.
For being there once he is there for ever. If all
the angels in heaven should entreat for a damned
soul; if Abraham, Isaac, and Jacob should make
great suit; if all the prophets, apostles, and mar-
tyrs should be continual solicitors of Christ for
release; if the father should make request for his
son, or the mother for her daughter; yet can none
of these be heard, they must all have the repulse.
For the sentence of Christ cannot be reserved;
his decree is unrepealable. The due consideration
of these things may make all hearts to quake,
and all knees to tremble. In the troubles and
afflictions of this life, though a man come in never
so great dangers, yet he may wind out again, by
one means or another, by money or friendship,
or rewards, or such like means: but in hell-fire
this is it that gripes, and maketh the heart despair,
that there is no remedy at all to be used. If we
should ask of a damned soul, or an afflicted conscience, what they would give for the ease and

redemption of their souls, they would answer, the whole world: howsoever, secure worldlings and wicked atheists (which see nothing, nor feel nothing) make nothing of it. Here, by the way, let us consider the greatness of the loss of a man's soul, which we shall the better perceive and see into if we can aright value and prize the soul. If therefore it be demanded what is the price of the soul? or what is it worth? our Lord Jesus answereth, that it is more worth than all the world; for, saith he, Matt. xvi. 26, " What shall it profit a man to win all the world and lose his soul?" Therefore the soul of the poorest beggar is worth more than all the world. Then I reason thus, if the soul be more worth than all the world, than the loss of it is greater than the loss of the whole world; for indeed it is a loss of all losses, an unrecoverable loss. If a man should have his house burnt over his head, and all that he hath consumed in one night, it were a great loss—if a merchant-venturer should lose twenty thousand pounds in one venture, in one ship, or as they say, in one bottom, it were a very great loss —if a king should lose his crown and kingdom, it were an exceeding great loss—but the loss of the soul is a thousand times more than all these; it is a matter of infinite importance. If a tenant be cast out of the favour of his landlord, it is a matter of grief—if a nobleman's secretary be cast out of favour with his lord, so that he taketh a pitch* against him, it is a matter of great sorrow—if a nobleman himself be discountenanced, and cast out of all favour with his prince, that was in great favour, it is a corsey,† a heart smart,

---

* An offence.   † A burning plaster of painful grievance.

and a matter of exceeding grievance—but to be eternally separated from God, to be shut out of his favour, and to be cast away from his presence, and the presence of his angels, is a matter of infinite more dolor and torment. Mark then, and behold, what a thing it is for a man to lose his soul! Oh therefore that men would be wise in God's fear, that they would look out in time, and make provision for their souls. Now then, to close up this whole point, the sum of all that hath been said is this: that the torments of hell are endless, easeless, and remediless.

CONVICTION AND CONVERSION—GOSPEL CONSOLATIONS; AND CONCLUSION.

Asun. The laying open of these doctrines of hell-fire, and the judgment to come, maketh me quake and tremble; I am thereby much perplexed —I feel great terror in my conscience—I am afraid I shall be damned.

Antil. Damned, man! what, speak you of damning? I am ashamed to hear you say so; for it is well known that you are an honest man, a quiet liver, a good neighbour, and as good a townsman as any is in the parish where you dwell, and you have always been so reputed and taken. If you should be damned, I know not who should be saved.

Asun. I regard not your flatteries; I believe God; I believe his word; I believe those things which Mr. Theologus hath alleged out of the holy scriptures, pointing me both to the chapter and the verse, and whether it be more meet that I should believe the scriptures or your soothings, judge you. No, no! now I do clearly see, by the glass of God's law, that my state is wretched and miserable; for I have lived in sin and ignorance all the days of my life, being utterly void of all religion and true knowledge of God. I am not the man indeed that you and others take me for; for, though outwardly I have lived honestly to the worldward, yet inwardly I have not lived religiously to Godward.

Antil. Tush, tush! now I see you are in a melancholy humour; if you will go home with me I can give you a speedy remedy, for I have many pleasant and merry books, which if you should hear them read, would soon remedy you of this melancholy passion: I have the Court of Venus, the Palace of Pleasure, Benas of Southampton, Ellen of Rummin, the merry Jest of the Friar and the Boy, the pleasant Story of Clem of the Clough, Adam Bell, and William of Cloudesley, the odd tale of William, Richard, and Humfry, the pretty conceit of John Splinter's last Will and Testament; which are all excellent and singular books against heart-qualms, and to remove such dumpishness as I see you are now fallen into.

Asun. Your vain and frivolous books of tales, jests, and lies, would more increase my grief, and strike the print of sorrow deeper into my heart.

Antil. Nay, if you be of that mind, I have done with you.

Phil. I pray you, if a man may be so bold with you, how came you by all these good books? I should have said so much trash and rubbish.

Antil. What mattereth it to you? what have
you to do to inquire? But I pray you, sir, what
mean you to call them trash and rubbish?

Phil. Because they be no better. They be
goodly gear, trim stuff: they are good to kindle
a fire, or to scour a hot oven withal; and shall
I tell you my opinion of them? I do thus think
that they were devised by the devil, seen and
allowed by the pope, printed in hell, bound up by
hobgoblin, and first published and dispersed in
Rome, Italy, and Spain; and all to this end, that
thereby men might be kept from the reading of
the scriptures; for even as a lapwing with her
busy cry draweth men away from her nest, so
the popish generation, by these fabulous devices,
draw men from the scriptures.

Antil. Ah, sir, I see now, a fool's bolt is soon
shot—you are more precise than wise—the vicar
of St. Fool's shall be your ghostly father. What!
tell you me of your opinion? I would you should
well know I neither regard you nor your
opinion: there be wiser men than you which
do both read, allow, and take pleasure in these
books.

Theol. Let him alone, good Philagathus, for
you see what he is; there is no end of his cross-
ing and cavilling; but he that is ignorant, let him
be ignorant; and he that is filthy, let him be more
filthy. Let us now turn our speech to Asunetus,
for I see he is heavy-hearted, and troubled in his
mind. How do you, Asunetus? how do you feel
yourself? methinketh you are very sad.

Asun. I am the better for you, sir, thank God:
I never knew what sin meant till this day. It
hath pleased God now to give me some sight and
feeling thereof: I am greatly distressed in my

conscience to think what I have been. The remembrance of my former sins doth strike an
horror into me. When I consider how ignorantly
and profanely, and how far off from God I have
lived all my life, it stings and gripes me to the
heart. I do now see that which I never saw, and
feel that which I never felt: I do plainly see,
that if I had died in that state wherein I have
lived all my life, I should certainly have been
condemned, and should have perished for ever in
my sin and ignorance.

Theol. I am very glad that God hath opened
your eyes, and given you the sight and feeling of
your misery, which indeed, is the very first step
to eternal life. It is a great favour and special
mercy of God towards you, that he hath so
touched your heart; you can never be thankful
enough for it. It is more than if you had a mil-
lion of gold given you. It is the only rare privilege of God's elect, to have the eyes of their souls
opened, that they may see into heavenly and
spiritual things: as for the world, it is just with
God to leave them in their blindness.

Asun. I do feel the burden of my sins, I am
greatly grieved for them, I am weary of them, I
am sorry that ever I sinned against God, or that
I should be such a wretch as to incur his displeasure, and provoke his Majesty against me;
but I pray you, good Mr. Theologus, since you
are a spiritual physician, and I am sick of sin,
that you would minister unto me out of God's
word, some spiritual physic and comfort.

Theol. Truly, I must needs think that the promises of mercy and forgiveness of sin made in the
gospel, do belong unto you, and that Jesus Christ
is yours: you are truly interested in him, and have

a proper right unto him; for he came not to call the righteous, but sinners to repentance. You do now feel yourself to be a sinner, you are grieved for your sins, you are weary of them; therefore Jesus Christ is for you, all the benefits of his passion belong to you. Again, he saith, Matt. xix. 12, "The whole need not the physician, but they that are sick." But you do acknowledge yourself to be sick of sin, therefore Christ Jesus will be your physician—he will swaddle you, and lap you—he will bind up all your sores—he will heal all your wounds—he will anoint them with the oil of his mercy—he will smile upon you and shew you a joyful countenance—he will say unto you, your sins are forgiven. In him you shall have rest and peace to your soul; through him you shall have ease and comfort; for he taketh pity of all such as mourn for their sins, as you do. He biddeth you, and all that are in your case, to come unto him, and he will help you. "Come unto me," saith he, Matt. xi. 28, "all ye that are weary and heavy laden, and I will ease you." You are one of them that are bid to come, for you are weary of your sins, you feel the burden of them. Christ is altogether for such as you are. He regardeth not the world, that is, the profane and unregenerate men; he bids not them come, he prayeth not for them; "I pray not for the world," saith he, John xvii. 9; they have no part nor interest in him; they have nothing to do with him, nor with his merits and righteousness. He is only for the penitent sinner, and such as mourn for their sins; he is a pillow of down to all aching heads, and aching consciences. Be of good comfort, therefore, fear nothing; for assuredly Christ and all his righteousness is yours; he will clothe you

with it; he will never impute your sins unto
you, or lay any of them to your charge, though
they be never so many or so great—he will forget
them and forgive them; as he saith by his prophet, Isa. i. 18, "Though your sins were as
crimson, they shall be made as white as snow;
though they were red like scarlet, they shall be as
wool." And again, he saith by the same prophet,
xliv. 22, " I have put away thy transgressions
as thick clouds, and thy sins as a mist." By
another prophet he saith, Mic. vii. 19, "He will
lay aside our iniquities, and cast all our sins into
the bottom of the sea." Again, he saith by the
prophet Isaiah, xliii. 25, "I, even I, am he that
putteth away thine iniquities for mine own sake,
and will not remember thy sins;" and yet more
sweetly he speaketh unto us by the prophet Jeremiah, iii. 12, saying, "Turn again unto me, and
I will not let my wrath fall upon you, for I am
merciful, and will not always keep mine anger;"
and again, by the prophet Hosea, xi. 9, he saith,
"I will not execute the fierceness of my wrath; I
will not return to destroy Ephraim; for I am God,
and not man." Be of good cheer, therefore;
comfort yourself with these promises; you have
cause to rejoice, seeing God hath wrought in you
a dislike and a grief for your sins, which is a
certain token that your sins shall never hurt you;
for sins past cannot hurt us, if sins present do not
like us. You are grown to a hatred and dislike of your sins; you mourn under the burden of
them; therefore you are blessed; for "blessed are
they that mourn." Why therefore should you be
so heavy and sad? Remember what St. John
saith, 1 John ii. 1, "If any man sin, we have an
advocate, Jesus Christ the righteous, and he is the

reconciliation for our sins." St. Paul saith, Rom. iii. 25, "That Jesus Christ is set forth to be a reconciliation through faith in his blood." Again, the Holy Ghost saith, Heb. vii. 25, " He is perfectly able to save all those that come unto God by him, seeing he ever liveth to make intercession for us." The apostle saith, 1 Cor. i. 30, "He is made of God for us, wisdom, righteousness, sanctification, and redemption:" mark that he saith all is for us, all is for his church, and for every member of his church, and therefore for you. Christ is made of God righteousness, sanctification, and redemption for you. Christ is your Mediator and your High Priest, and hath offered up the everlasting sacrifice, even for you, that he might pay your ransom, and redeem you from all iniquity: " By his own blood hath he entered once into the holy place, and obtained eternal redemption for you," Heb. ix. 12. Christ is not entered into the holy places which are made with hands, which are similitudes of the true sanctuary; but is entered into the very heaven, to appear now in the sight of God for you. The apostle saith, 2 Cor. v. 21, " He hath made him to be sin for you, that knew no sin, that you might be made the righteousness of God in him;" Gal. iii. 13, " Christ was made a curse for you, that he might redeem you from the curse of the law." Oh, therefore, how happy are you that have such a Mediator and High Priest. Rest therefore wholly upon him, and upon that perfect, eternal, and propitiatory sacrifice which he hath once offered. Apply Christ, apply his merits, apply the promises to yourself, and to your own conscience, so shall they do you good and bring great comfort to your soul. For put case—you had a most excellent and sovereign salve, which would cure any wound it were laid unto, yet if you should lock it up in your chest, and never apply it to your wound, what good could it do you? even so the righteousness and merits of Christ are a spiritual salve, which will cure any wound of the soul; but if we do not apply them to ourselves by faith they can do us no good. You must therefore apply Christ, and all the promises of the gospel to yourself by faith, and stand fully persuaded that whatsoever he hath done upon the cross, he hath done for you particularly: for what is justifying faith but a full persuasion of God's particular love to us in Christ? A general and confused knowledge of Christ and of his gospel availeth not to eternal life. Labour therefore to have the true use of all these great and precious promises; stick fast to Christ, for through him only we have remission of sins and eternal life. "To him all the prophets give witness," saith St. Peter, "that through his name, all that believe shall receive remission of their sins," Acts x. 43; where the apostle telleth us, that if a grand jury of prophets were pannelled to testify of the way and means to eternal life, they would all with one consent bring in a verdict, that remission of sins and eternal life are only in Christ. Let us hear the foreman speak, and one or two of the rest, "for in the mouth of two or three witnesses shall every word stand." The prophet Isaiah saith, " He was wounded for our transgressions; he was broken for our iniquities; the chastisement of our peace was upon him, and with his stripes we are healed." This great prophet, we see, doth plainly affirm that Christ suffered for our sins, and by his suffering we are saved. The prophet Jere-

miah testifieth the same thing, saying, xxiii. 5,
"Behold, the days come," saith the Lord, " that
I will raise unto David a righteous branch; and a
king shall reign and prosper, and shall execute
judgment and justice in the earth. In his days
Judah shall be saved, and Israel shall dwell safely:
and this is the name whereby they shall call him,
the Lord our righteousness." This prophet
trumpeth with the other, for he saith, that Christ
is the righteous branch, and that he is our righteousness, which is all one as if he had said our
sins are pardoned only through him, and through
him we are made righteous. Moreover, he affirmeth that Judah and Israel, that is, the church,
shall be saved by him. The prophet Zechariah,
that I may speak it with reverence, telleth the
same tale, word for word. He announceth the
same thing with the other two prophets, for he
saith, xiii. 1, "In that day a fountain shall be
opened to the house of David, and to the inhabitants of Jerusalem, for sin and for uncleanness:"
the meaning of the prophet is, that in the days
of Christ's kingdom, the fountain of God's mercy
in Christ should be opened, and let out to wash
away the sins and uncleanness of the church. So
then, we see that these three great witnesses do
all agree in this—that through Christ only we
are washed from our sins, and through him only
we are made righteous. Seeing then that eternal
life is only in the Son, therefore, " He that hath
the Son hath life." Be of good courage therefore,
O Asunetus, for no doubt you have the Son, and
therefore eternal life: fear not your sins, for they
cannot hurt you; for as all the righteousness of
Abraham, Isaac, and Jacob, and all the most righteous men that ever lived upon the face of the earth

if it were yours, could do you no good without
Christ; so all the sins in the world can do you no
hurt, being in Christ; "For there is no condemnation to them which are in Christ Jesus," Rom.
viii. 4. Pluck up a good heart, therefore; be no
more heavy and sad; for if you be found in Christ,
clothed with his perfect righteousness, being made
yours through faith—what can the devil say to
you? what can the law do? They may well hiss at
you, but they cannot sting you; they may grin at
you, but they cannot hurt you; for "Who shall
lay anything to the charge of God's elect? It is
God that justifieth; who shall condemn? It is
Christ which is dead, or rather which is risen
again, who is also at the right hand of God, and
maketh request for us," Rom. viii. 33. "Rejoice
in the Lord, therefore, and again I say, rejoice,"
Phil. iv. 4. For greater is he that is in you than
he that is in the world: our Lord Jesus is stronger
than all. None can pluck you out of his hands:
he is a strong Mediator; he hath conquered all our
spiritual enemies; he hath overcome hell, death,
and damnation; "He hath led captivity captive;
he hath spoiled principalities and powers, and hath
made an open show of them, and triumphed over
them in his cross," Col. ii. 15; he hath most
triumphantly said, "O death, I will be thy death;
O grave, I will be thy destruction," Hos. xiii. 14;
"O death, where is thy sting? O hell, where is thy
victory?" 1 Cor. xv. 52. Seeing then you have
such a Mediator and High Priest, as hath conquered the hellish army and subdued all infernal
power, what need you to doubt? what need you
to fear any more? Moreover, you are to understand, and to be persuaded, that God's mercy is
exceeding great towards penitent sinners, and all

such as mourn for their transgressions, according
as he saith, "At what time soever a sinner doth
repent him of his sins from the bottom of his
heart, he will put them all out of his remembrance." The prophet David doth most lively
and fully describe unto us the merciful nature of
God in the 103rd Psalm, where he saith, "The
Lord is full of compassion and mercy, slow to
anger, and of great kindness; he will not always
chide, neither keep his anger for ever; he hath
not dealt with us after our sins, nor rewarded us
according to our iniquities. For as high as the
heaven is above the earth, so great is his mercy
towards those that fear him. As far as the east
is from the west, so far hath he removed our sins
from us. As a father hath compassion on his
children, so hath the Lord compassion on them
that fear him. For he knoweth whereof we be
made; he remembereth that we are but dust."
The history of the lost son doth most notably set
forth the wonderful mercy of-God towards penitent
sinners. There is shewed how the Lord doth
embrace, tender, and make much of such poor
sinners as have broken and contrite hearts for
their sins; for it is said, Luke xv. that when the
father saw his repenting son a great way off, he
had compassion on him, and ran and fell on his
neck, and kissed him, and clothed him with the
best robe, put it on him, put a ring on his hand,
and shoes on his feet, and caused the fat calf to
be killed for him. Even so, the everlasting Father
doth rejoice at the conversion of any of his lost
sons. Yea, there is joy in the presence of the
angels of God for one sinner that converteth.
Moreover, the Lord doth most lively express his
merciful nature and disposition, in this, that he

is very loth we should perish and willingly cast away ourselves. Therefore, often in the holy scriptures, he doth mourn for us, bewail our wretchedness, and taketh up many pitiful complaints, and lamentations for us, saying, "Oh that my people had hearkened unto me, and Israel had walked in my ways," Ps. lxxxi. 13; and again, "Oh that thou hadst hearkened unto my commandments; then had thy prosperity been as the flood, and thy righteousness as the waves of the sea," Isa. xliii. 18; again, he mourningly complaineth by his prophet Hosea, saying, vi. 4, "O Ephraim, what shall I do unto thee? O Judah, how shall I entreat thee?" And in another place, "What could I do more unto my vineyard that I have not done? Mark here, how compassionately the Almighty God doth yearn over us, and even as it were bleed upon our wounds. The apostle also doth note the rich mercy, and marvellous love of God to mankind in this, that he doth beseech us, and pray us by the ministers of the gospel, that we would be reconciled unto him: the words are these, 2 Cor. v. "Now then, we are ambassadors for Christ, as though God did beseech you through us, we pray you in Christ's stead, that you be reconciled unto God." Is it not a strange thing that the omnipotent God should fall to entreating of us poor wretches? It is all one as if a king should entreat a beggar, whom he may will and command; but the abundant mercy of God towards mankind doth most of all consist in this, that he hath given his only Son for us, when we were his enemies; as it is written, John iii. 16, "God so loved the world, that he hath given his only begotten Son, that whosoever believeth in him should not perish, but have eternal life." Again, Rom. v. 8, "God setteth out his love towards us, seeing that while we were yet sinners, Christ died for us; much more then, being now justified by his blood, we shall be saved from wrath through him; for if when we were enemies we were reconciled to God by the death of his Son, much more being reconciled, we shall be saved by his life." In all this then we may clearly behold the infinite mercy of God towards us poor sinners; for is it not a great matter that the Son of God should take our nature upon him, should be so abased as he was, and should humble himself to death, even to the death of the cross? Phil. ii. 8; for as the shadow of the dial went back ten degrees that Hezekiah might receive length of days, and much happiness; so Christ, the sun of righteousness hath gone back many degrees, that we might have eternal life. His humiliation, therefore, is our exaltation; his sufferings our joy; his death our life; for we have no other remedy or refuge but only his merits and righteousness—he is our city of refuge, whither we must fly, and where we must take sanctuary—he is the balm of Gilead, whereby our souls are cured—he is that pool of Bethesda, where every man may be cured of what disease soever he hath—he is the river of Jordan, where Naaman may wash away all his leprosy —he is that pelican, who, by picking a hole in his own breast, doth restore his young to life again by his blood. Yet one thing we must note by the way, which hath been partly touched before, that all the mercy of God, and merits of Christ, are to be restrained only to the elect—only to the true members of the church—as plainly appeareth in the 103rd Psalm, where the mercies of God,

which there are largely described, are restrained
only to them that fear him, keep his covenant, and
think upon his commandments to do them. And
touching Christ, it is said that he is a Prince and
a Saviour unto Israel; and that he shall redeem
Israel from all his iniquities. Again, it is written,
that Christ being consecrate, was made "the author of eternal salvation to them that obey him."
None do or can obey him, but only the elect;
therefore, he is the author of salvation only to the
elect; and, consequently, the profane world, whatsoever they say, whatsoever they brag and boast,
have no true title or interest in him. This thing
was figured in the law, in this, that the mercy
seat, which was a type of God's mercy in Christ,
and the ark, which was a figure of the church,
were, by the express commandment of God, fitted
each to other, both in length and breadth; for
as the ark was two cubits and a half long, and a
cubit and a half broad, just so was the mercy
seat, Exod. xxv. 10, 17; noting thereby that
the mercy of God in Christ should only be fitted
to his church, and belong only to the church, so
as not one without the church should be saved;
for he that hath not the church for his mother
cannot have God for his father. Lastly, we are
to observe, that as God is infinite in mercy, and
of great compassion towards penitent sinners, so
also is he most constant in the course of his mercies towards his children; and, therefore, one of
the Psalms, cxxxvi. carrieth this foot, "His
mercy endureth for ever; his mercy endureth for ever; his mercy endureth for ever;" noting thereby both the constancy and eternity of
God's mercy. To the same purpose, it is thus
written, Lamen. iii. 22, "It is of the Lord's mer-

cies that we are not consumed; it is because his compassions fail not " Let us know, therefore, that God, as touching his mercy to his children, is of a most constant and unchangeable nature; as he saith, "I am the Lord, I change not;" for if God were of a changeable nature, as we are, and subject to passions, then were we in a most miserable case. Then must he needs smite us down, and take vengeance of us every day, and every hour in the day; because we provoke him every day, and every hour in the day. But the God of heaven is not as a man, that he should be subject to passions and affections; he is of a most constant and immutable nature; for though we provoke him every day with new sins, yet he is so far off from taking revenge, that the next day he rewardeth us with new mercies, and breaketh through all our unkindness, to shew kindness unto us, and through all our naughtiness to do us good. All our infirmities cannot make him break off with us, or cease to love us—he is content to take us with all faults; and to love us dearly, though we have great faults—he regardeth not our infirmities, though we be oftentimes wayward and elvish,* yet, for all that, he loveth us nevertheless. Even as a loving mother, though her young suckling cry all night, and be exceeding treafe† and wayward, so as she cannot rest an hour in the night; yea, though she endure much loathsomeness and trouble with it, yet in the morning, when she ariseth, she loveth it nevertheless, and dandles it, playeth with it, smileth and laugheth upon it; so the God of all mercies, whose love towards us far passeth the love of mothers, though we grieve

* Froward, wicked.   † Peevish, pettish.

him with our infirmities continually, yet loveth us nevertheless, and is content to put up all, to forget and forgive all; for he is a most constant lover. Where he once sets and settles his love, he loveth most constantly; nothing can alter him; nothing can remove him. Even as a father, when his little child catcheth a fall, breaketh his shins, and hurteth his face, is so far from being offended or displeased with him therefore, that he doth pity him, and bemoan him, seeking remedies for his hurt; so our merciful Father is so far from being angry and displeased with us for some slips and falls, that he doth the more pity us, and lament our case. Even as a loving and wise husband, though his wife have many infirmities, yet knowing that she loveth him dearly, and that her heart is with him, he is well content to wink at all her faults, to hide them, to bear with them, yea, and to make nothing of them, loving her nevertheless for them; so our dear husband and spouse, Jesus Christ, because he knoweth we love him, and that he hath our hearts, is content to bear with all our infirmities, and to make light of them. For this cause it is that he saith to his spouse in the Canticles, iv. 1, 7, though she was black and full of infirmities, "Behold, thou art fair, my love; behold, thou art fair; thou art all fair, my love; there is no spot in thee." Mark that he calleth his church fair, all fair, and without spot; not because she was so in herself, but because she was made so in him; and, assuredly, the eternal God, beholding her in his Son, doth so esteem and account of her; for as he that beholdeth any thing through a red glass doth take it to be red, as is the colour of the glass; so God the Father, beholding us in his Son, doth take us to be of the same nature and quality that he is: that is, perfectly right- eous; for this cause it is that he loveth us, and setteth his heart upon us, and will not be removed from us; for his love to his children is always one and the same, although we have not always the like sight and feeling of it; as the moon is always the same in substance and quality, though sometime it seemeth unto us to be wasted into a very small scantling. Let us know then, to our great comfort, that the love of God towards us, in his dear Son, is constant and always alike, and that he will not discountenance us, or shake us off for some infirmities, no, nor yet for many infirmities; for the merciful God doth accept of his children because their general care is good, and the universal tenor of their life tendeth unto righteousness, howsoever they may greatly fail in many particular actions. Two or three fits of an ague do not prove a diseased body; nor two or three good days a sound body; even so, some few infirmities do not argue a wicked man; nor two or three good actions a good man; but we must have an eye to the cer- tain and settled course of a man's life. Even as men are truly said to walk in a way when they go in it, although sometimes they trip and stumble; so God's children do walk in the way of righteousness, although sometimes they stumble, and step out of it; or sometimes be violently haled out of it by thieves; for Satan and the violence of our lusts, do often hail us out of the way, but we must get into it again as soon as we are escaped. Now then, to conclude, and draw to an end, since God is so infinitely merciful and constant in his mercy—since such great and precious promises are made to us in Christ—since the Lord doth not regard our infirmities when our hearts are with him—therefore, O Asunetus, be of good cheer; let nothing trouble you; fear not the assaults of the devil; regard not his temptations; for assuredly your sins are forgiven. Christ is yours, heaven is yours, and all the promises of life and salvation belong unto you; so as you need not to doubt. You cannot miscarry, your name is written in the book of life.

Asun. I am greatly comforted and cheered up with your words: your preaching of the gospel, and laying open of God's abundant mercy in Christ, and of the promises, do exceedingly revive me, and even as it were put new life into me: they are as sack and sugar unto my soul, and more sweet than the honey and the honey-comb; they are as physic to my sick soul, and as ointment to my spiritual wounds. I do now begin to see what misery is in man, and what mercy is in God. And I know, by woful experience, that where misery is not felt there mercy is not regarded; but now it hath pleased God to give me some feeling of mine own wretchedness and misery, and yet with good comfort in his mercy. For, I thank God for it, I begin now to grow to some persuasion, that the promises do belong unto me, my sins are forgiven, and that I am one of them that shall be saved.

Theol. I do greatly rejoice that God hath according to his rich mercy wrought this good work in you. I do, from the bottom of my heart, give him the praise and glory of it. Happy are you that ever you were born, in whom God hath wrought so gracious a work. It is of his high favour and special mercy towards you, for it is only the privilege and prerogative royal of God's own children, truly to repent and believe. I beseech God, therefore, to increase your faith, and to fill you full of joy and peace in believing, that you may abound in hope, through the power of the Holy Ghost.

Antil. The sun draweth low, Asunetus, it is time for you and me to be going.

Phil. Indeed the night will approach by and by; and therefore we must of necessity break off.

Theol. Since it is so, we will here surcease, and go no further.

Asun. Sir, I will now take my leave of you. I can never be thankful enough for all the good instructions and comforts which I have heard from you this day; I hope I shall remember some of them whilst I live: I do therefore praise God for you, and for your counsel, and for this day which I hope shall be the first day of my repentance, and true conversion unto God.

Theol. The Lord for his infinite mercies' sake grant it. And I most humbly beseech the Almighty God to establish you with his free Spirit, that you may proceed and go forward in a Christian course unto the end.

Phil. I pray you, good Mr. Theologus, pardon my boldness; for you see I have been very bold to propound many questions unto you, wherein you have fully satisfied me, to the great joy and comfort of my soul. I do therefore praise God for you, and I hope I shall never forget some things which you have uttered. But I will now commend you to God, and to the word of his grace, which is able to build further.

Theol. Farewell, good Philagathus. The Lord

bless you, and keep you in all your ways; and the God of Heaven preserve us all, and continue us in his fear unto the end. All glory be given to God!

A MORNING PRAYER:

TO BE USED IN PRIVATE FAMILIES.

O LORD our God, and heavenly Father! we, thy
unworthy children, do here come unto thy most
holy and heavenly presence, to give thee praise
and glory for all thy great mercies and manifold
blessings towards us; especially for that thou
hast preserved us this night past from all the
dangers and fears thereof—hast given us quiet
rest to our bodies, and brought us now safely to
the beginning of this day—and dost now afresh
renew all thy mercies upon us, as the eagle
reneweth her bill, giving us all things abundantly
to enjoy—as food, raiment, health, peace, liberty,
and freedom from many miseries, diseases, casualties, and calamities which we are subject unto in
this life every minute of an hour: and not only
so, but also for vouchsafing unto us many good
things, not only for necessity, but even for
delight also. But, above all, dear Father, we
praise thy name for the blessings of a better life;
especially for thy most holy word and sacraments, and all the good we enjoy thereby—for
the continuance of the gospel amongst us—for
the death of thy Son, and all that happiness
which we have thereby; also, because thou hast
chosen us to life before we were, and that of thy
mere goodness and undeserved favour towards us;
and hast called us in thine appointed time, justified us by thy grace, sanctified us by thy Spirit,
and adopted us to be thine own children, and

heirs apparent to the great crown. O Lord, open our eyes every day more and more to see and consider of thy great and marvellous love to us in all these things; that, by the due consideration thereof, our hearts may be drawn yet nearer unto thee—even more to love thee, fear thee, and obey thee; that, as thou art enlarged towards us in mercy, so we may be enlarged towards thee in thanksgiving; and as thou dost abound towards us in goodness, so we may abound towards thee in obedience and love. And since, dear Father, thou art never weary of doing us good, notwithstanding all our unworthiness and naughtiness, therefore let the consideration of thy great mercy and fatherly kindness towards us, even, as it were, force our hearts, and compel us to come into thy most glorious presence with new songs of thanksgiving in our mouths. We pray thee, O most merciful God, to forgive us all our unthankfulness, unkindness, profaneness, and great abusing of all thy mercies, and specially our abuse and contempt of thy gospel, together with all other the sins of our life, which, we confess, are innumerable, and more than can be reckoned up, both in omission of good things and commission of evil. We most humbly entreat thee to set them all over to the reckoning which thy Son Christ hath made up for them upon his cross, and never to lay any of them to our charge, but freely forget all, and forgive all; nail down all our sins and iniquities to the cross of Christ, bury them in his death, bathe them in his blood, hide them in his wounds, let them never rise up in judgment against us. Set us free of the miseries that are upon us for sin, and keep back the judgments to come, both of soul, body, goods, and good name. Be recon-

ciled unto us in thy dear Son, concerning all
matters past, not once remembering or repeating
unto us our old and abominable iniquities; but
accept us as righteous in him, imputing his
righteousness to us, and our sins to him. Let
his righteousness satisfy thy justice for all our un-
righteousness, his obedience for our disobedience,
his perfection for our imperfection. Moreover,
we humbly beseech thy good Majesty to give us
the true sight and feeling of our manifold sins,
that we may not be blinded in them through delight, or hardened in them through custom as the
reprobates are; but that we may be even weary
of them, and much grieved for them, labouring
and striving by all possible means to get out of
them. Good Father, touch our hearts with true
repentance for all sin. Let us not take any delight or pleasure in any sin, but howsoever we
fall through frailty, as we fall often, yet let us
never fall finally, let us never lie down in sin,
nor continue in sin; but let us get upon our feet
again, and turn to thee with all our hearts; and
seek thee whilst thou mayest be found, and
whilst thou dost extend grace and mercy unto
us. O Lord, increase in us that true and lively
faith whereby we may lay sure hold on thy Son
Christ, and rest upon his merits altogether. Give
us faith assuredly to believe all the great and
precious promises made in the gospel, and
strengthen us from above, to walk and abound
in all the true and sound fruits of faith. Let us
walk, not after the flesh, but after the Spirit.
Let us feel the power of thy Son's death killing
sin in our mortal bodies, and the power of his
resurrection raising us up to newness of life.
Let us grow daily in the sanctification of the

Spirit, and the mortification of the flesh.   Let us live holily, justly, and soberly, in this present evil world, shewing forth the virtues of thee in all our particular actions; that we may adorn our most holy profession, and shine as lights in the midst of a crooked and froward generation amongst whom we live, being gainful to all by our lives and conversations, and offensive to none.   To this end, we pray thee fill us with thy Spirit and all spiritual grace: as love, wisdom, patience, contentment, meekness, humility, temperance, charity, kindness, and affability; and stir us up to use prayer and watchfulness, reading and meditation in thy law, and all other good means whereby we may grow and abound in all heavenly virtues.   Bless us in the use of the means from day to day; make us such as thou wouldest have us to be, and such as we desire to be, working in us both will and deed, purpose and power; for thou, O Lord, art all in all, thou wilt have mercy upon whom thou wilt have mercy, and whom thou wilt thou hardenest. Have mercy upon us, therefore, dear Father, and never leave us to ourselves, nor to our own wills, lusts, and desires, but assist us with thy good Spirit, that we may continue to the end in a righteous course; that so at length,we may be received into glory, and be partakers of that immortal crown which thou hast laid up for all that love thee, and truly call upon thee.

Further, we entreat thee, O heavenly Father, to give us all things necessary for this life: as food, raiment, health, peace, liberty, and such freedom from those manifold miseries which we lie open unto every day, as thou seest meet.   Bless unto us all the means which thou hast put into our

hands for the sustenance of this frail life. Bless
our stock and store, corn and cattle, trades and
occupations, and all the works of our hands; for
thy blessing only maketh rich, and it bringeth
no sorrows with it. Give us, therefore, such a
competency and sufficiency of these outward
blessings, as thou in thy heavenly wisdom seest
most needful for us. Moreover, we humbly beseech
thee, most loving Father, in great mercy to look
down from heaven upon thy whole church, and
every member of it. Be favourable unto Zion,
and build up the walls of Jerusalem. Behold,
with the eye of pity, the great ruins and desol-
ations of thy church. Heal up the wounds, and
make up the breaches thereof in all nations.
Regard it as thine own flock, tender it as thine
family, dress it as thine own vineyard, love it as
thine own spouse. Think thoughts of peace to
it, and always look upon it in deep compassion.
Bless it with thy grace, guide it with thy Spirit,
and defend it always with thy mighty power: scatter
the devices, confound the counsels, and overthrow
the forces of all that fight against it. Specially, we
entreat thee, dear Father, to set thyself against
that antichrist of Rome, that man of perdition,
which setteth himself against thee, and against all
thy people. In thine appointed time we pray thee
give him a deadly downfall. Beat down all his
power and authority daily more and more: give
free passage to thy gospel in all kingdoms, that
Babylon may fall and never rise up again. The
more the favourites and adherents of Rome labour
to uphold their idolatrous kingdom, the more let it
fall down, even as Dagon before the presence of
thine ark. Pour down the vials of the fulness of
thy wrath upon the kingdom of the beast, and let

their riches, wealth, credit, and authority dry up
every day more and more, as the river Euphrates.
Let it pity thee, O Father, to see thine own spouse
sit as a deformed and forlorn woman here below,
weeping and mourning with her hair about her
neck; having lost all her beauty and comeliness:
cheer her up dear Father, glad her with the joy
of thy countenance, and so deck her and trim her
up, that thou mayest delight in her, as a bride-
groom in his bride. Specially we entreat thee to
have mercy upon thy church in this land; intend
good unto us and not evil; give us not over into
the hands of the cruel Spaniard, as our sins have
deserved. Scatter, we pray thee, O Lord, the
devices, and break the plots of all such as have
plotted the overthrow and utter subversion of this
church and commonwealth. Bless this church
more and more, with the continuance of true religion amongst us. For thy great name's sake,
and infinite mercies' sake, deal graciously and
favourably with us, and our posterity. Turn from
us that vengeance which is due to us for our sins.
For thou seest how iniquity prevaileth, and the
wicked go away with the goal. Atheism over-
spreadeth everywhere, and popery seemeth to get
ahead again. Now, therefore, dear Father, we
most humbly beseech thee to take order speedily
for the remedying and repressing of these manifold disorders and grievous enormities that are
amongst us. Be entreated of thy poor children to
be good to this English nation. Hear the cries
of thine elect: hear the mourning of them that
mourn in Sion. Let the cries of thy children cry
down all the cries of the sins of the land, and be
reconciled unto us in the multitude of thy compassions, so that thou mayest still continue a most

merciful protector of this thine English vineyard.
We pray thee, good Father, shew special mercy
to our most noble and gracious King James, thine
anointed servant: bless him, and keep him in all
his ways. Bless his government unto us. Let
thine angels encamp about him, and let thy holy
hand be always over him; keep him from treasons,
and deliver him from the treacheries of his enemies: give him to see what belongeth to his
peace, and give him a heart earnestly bent to set
upon the practice of the same: give him all graces
necessary for his peace, and necessary for his
salvation: continue his government peaceable and
prosperous amongst us: and as thou hast made
him the breath of our nostrils, and a gracious instrument for the saving of many thousand souls,
so let his own soul be saved in the day of thy Son
Christ. Bless his majesty's most honourable
privy counsellors, and give such good success
unto all their counsels and policies in matters of
state, that we may lead a quiet and peaceable life
in all godliness and honesty. Bless all the nobility; work in them a care to glorify thy name in
their places; make them faithful to thee, and
faithful to the land. Direct with thy good Spirit
all such as bear the sword of justice, that they
may draw it out to punish the wicked, and to defend the godly, and that they may, with all good
care and conscience, discharge the duties of their
places. Increase the number of faithful and zealous ministers in thy church. Send thy gospel
to those places where it is not, and bless it where
it is. Remember them in thy mercy, O Lord,
that are under any cross or affliction whatsoever:
be comfortable unto them, heal up their wounds,
bind up their sores, put all their tears into thy

bottle, and make their bed in all their sorrows; and put such a good end to all their troubles that they may redound to thy glory and the furtherance of their own salvation. In the meantime, give them patience and constancy to bear whatsoever it shall please thy merciful hand to lay upon them. Last of all, in a word, we pray thee, bless magistracy, ministry, and commonalty. Bless all thy people; do good to all that are true and upright in their hearts. And so, dear Father, we do commit and commend ourselves, our souls, and bodies into thy hands, for this day, and the rest of our life, praying thee to take care and charge of us; keep us from all evil; watch over us for our good; let thine angels encamp about us; let thy holy hand be over us, and keep us in all our ways, that we may live to thy praise and glory here on earth, keeping faith and a good conscience in all our actions; that after this life we may be crowned of thee, for ever in thy kingdom. Grant these things, good Father, to us here present, and to all thine absent; praying thee in special favour to remember our friends and kinsfolks in the flesh, all our good neighbours and well-wishers, and all those for whom we are bound to pray by nature, by deserts, or any duty whatsoever, for Jesus Christ's sake, our only Mediator; to whom with thee, and the Holy Ghost, be given all praise and glory, both now, and for evermore. *Amen.*

AN EVENING PRAYER,

O Eternal God, and our most loving and dear
Father! we, thy unworthy children, do here fall
down at the foot of thy great Majesty, acknow-
ledging from our hearts, that we are altogether
unworthy to come near thee, or to look towards
thee: because thou art a God of infinite glory,
and we are most vile and abominable sinners,
such as were conceived and born in sin and
corruption, such as have inherited our father's
corruptions, and also have actually transgressed
all thy holy statutes and laws, both in thoughts,
words, and deeds, before we knew thee; and
since, secretly and openly, with ourselves and
with others. Our particular sins are more than can
be numbered; for who knoweth how often he
offendeth? But this we must needs confess against
ourselves, that our hearts are full of pride, covetousness, and the love of this world; full of wrath,
anger, and impatience; full of lying, dissembling,
and deceiving; full of vanity, hardness, and profaneness; full of infidelity, distrust, and self-love;
full of lust, uncleanness, and all abominable desires; yea, our hearts are the very sinks of sin,
and dunghills of all filthiness. And besides all
this, we do omit the good things we should do;
for there are in us great wants of faith, of love of
zeal, of patience, of contentment, and of every
good grace; so as thou hast just cause to proceed
to sentence of judgment against us, as most

damnable transgressors of all thy holy commandments: yea, such as are sunk in our rebellions
and have many times and often committed high
treason against thy Majesty; and therefore, thou
mayest justly cast us all down into hell-fire, there
to be tormented with Satan and his angels for
ever. And we have nothing to except against
thy Majesty for so doing: since therein thou
shouldest deal with us but according to equity
and our just deserts. Wherefore, dear Father,
we do appeal from thy justice to thy mercy; most
humbly entreating thee to have mercy upon us,
and freely to forgive us all our sins past whatsoever,
both new and old, secret and open, known and
unknown, and that for Jesus Christ's sake, our
only Mediator. And we pray thee, touch our
hearts with true grief and unfeigned repentance
for them, that they may be a matter of continual
sorrow and heart-smart unto us, so as nothing
may grieve us more than this, that we have
offended thee, being our special friend and Father.
Give us, therefore, dear Father, every day more
and more sight and feeling of our sins, with true
humiliation under the same. Give us also that
true and lively faith whereby we may lay sure
hold on thy Son Christ, and all his merits,
applying the same to our own souls; so as we
may stand fully persuaded that whatsoever he
hath done upon the cross, he hath done for us
particularly, as well as for others. Give us faith,
good Father, constantly to believe all the sweet
promises of the gospel, touching remission of
sin and eternal life, made in thy Son Christ. O
Lord, increase our faith, that we may altogether
rest upon thy promises, which are all yea and
amen. Yea, that we may settle ourselves, and

all that we have wholly upon them: both our souls, bodies, goods, name, wives, children, and our whole estate, knowing that all things depend upon thy promises, power, and providence; and that thy word doth support and bear up the whole order of nature. Moreover, we entreat thee, O Lord, to strengthen us from above to walk in every good way, and to bring forth the fruits of true faith in all our particular actions, studying to please thee in all things and to be fruitful in good works, that we may shew forth unto all men, by our good conversation, whose children we are; and that we may adorn and beautify our most holy profession by walking in a Christian course, and in all the sound fruits and practice of godliness, and true religion. To this end, we pray thee, sanctify our hearts by thy Spirit, yet more and more: sanctify our souls and bodies, and all our corrupt natural faculties, as reason, understanding, will, and affections, so as they may be fitted for thy worship and service, taking a delight and pleasure therein. Stir us up to use prayer, watchfulness, reading, and meditation in thy law, and all other good means whereby we may profit in grace and goodness from day to day. Bless us in the use of the means, that we may daily die to sin, and live to righteousness: draw us yet nearer unto thee: help us against our manifold wants. Amend our great imperfections, renew us inwardly more and more, repair the ruins of our hearts, aid us against the remnants of sin. Enlarge our hearts to run the way of thy commandments, direct all our steps in thy word, let no iniquity have dominion over us. Assist us against our special infirmities and master sins, that we may get the victory over them all, to thy glory, and

the great peace and comfort of our own consciences.   Strengthen us, good Father, by thy
grace and Holy Spirit, against the common corruptions of the world, as pride, whoredom, covetousness, contempt of thy gospel, swearing, lying,
dissembling, and deceiving.   O dear Father, let
us not be overcome of these filthy vices, nor any
other sinful pleasures and fond delights, wherewith thousands are carried headlong to destruction.
Arm our souls against all the temptations of this
world, the flesh, and the devil; that ·we may
overcome them all through thy help, and keep on
the right way to life, that we may live in thy fear,
and die in thy favour, that our last days may be
our best days, and that we may end in great peace
of conscience.   Furthermore, dear Father, we entreat thee not only for ourselves, but for all our
good brethren, thy dear children scattered over the
face of the whole earth, most humbly beseeching
thee to bless them all, to cheer them up, and glad
them with the joy of thy countenance, both now
and always.   Guide them all in thy fear, and
keep them from evil, that 'they may praise thy
name.   In these dangerous days, and declining
times, we pray thee, O Lord, raise up nursing
fathers, and nursing mothers unto thy church.
Raise up also faithful pastors, that thy cause may
be carried forward, truth may prevail, religion
may prosper, thy name only may be set up in the
earth, thy Son's kingdom advanced, and thy will
accomplished.   Set thyself against all adversary
power, especially that of Rome, antichrist, idolatry, and atheism: curse and cross all their counsels, frustrate their devices, scatter their forces,
overthrow their armies.   When they are most
wise, let them be most foolish; when they are

most strong, let them be most weak. Let them know, that there is no wisdom nor counsel, power nor policy, against thee, the Lord of Hosts. Let them know that Israel hath a God, and that thou which art called Jehovah, art the only ruler over all the world. Arise, therefore, O most mighty God, and maintain thine own cause against all thine enemies; smite through all their loins, and bow down their backs; yea, let them all be confounded, and turned backward that bear ill-will unto Sion. Let the patient abiding of the righteous be joy; and let the wicked be disappointed of their hope. But of all favour, we entreat thee, O Lord, to shew special mercy to thy church in this land wherein we live. Continue thy gospel amongst us yet with greater success, purge thy house daily more and more, take away all things that offend. Let this nation be a place where thy name may be called upon, and an harbour for thy saints. Shew mercy to our posterity, dear Father, and have care of them, that thy gospel may be left unto them as a most holy inheritance. Defend us against foreign invasion, keep out idolatry and popery from amongst us. Turn from us those plagues which our sins cry for; for the sins of this land are exceeding great, horrible, and outrageous, and give thee just cause to make us spectacles of thy vengeance to all nations: that by how much the more thou hast lifted us up in great mercy and long peace, by so much the more thou shouldest press us down in great wrath and long war. Therefore, dear Father, we most humbly entreat thee, for thy great name's sake, and for thy infinite mercies' sake, that thou wouldest be reconciled to this land, and discharge it of all the horrible sins thereof. Drown them,

O Lord, in thy infinite mercy through Christ, as it were in a bottomless gulf, that they may never rise up in judgment against us. For although our sins be exceeding many and fearful, yet thy mercy is far greater. For thou art infinite in mercy: but we cannot be infinite in sinning. Give us not over into the hands of the idolators, lest they should blaspheme thy name and say, where is their God in whom they trusted? But rather, dear Father, take us into thine own hands, and correct us according to thy wisdom: for with thee is mercy, and deep compassion. Moreover, we most humbly beseech thy good Majesty, to bless our most gracious king James, and to shew much mercy to him in all things. Guide him in thy fear, and keep him in all his ways, working in his soul unfeigned sorrow for sin, true faith in the promises, and a great care to please thee in all things, and to discharge the duties of his high place, in all zeal of thy glory, and faithfulness towards thy Majesty: that as thou hast crowned him here in earth, so he (spending his days here below in thy fear) may after this life, be crowned of thee for ever in the heavens. We beseech thee also, to bless his majesty's most honourable privy counsellors. Counsel them from above, let them take advice of thee in all things; that they may both consult, and resolve of such courses as may be most for thy glory, the good of the church, and the peace of this our commonwealth. Bless the nobility, and all the magistrates in the land, giving them all grace to execute judgment and justice, and to maintain truth and equity. Bless all the faithful ministers of the gospel, increase the number of them, increase thy gifts in them: and so bless all their labours in their seve-

ral places and congregations, that they all may
be instruments of thy hand to enlarge thy Son's
kingdom, and to win many souls unto thee. Comfort the comfortless with all needful comforts. Forget none of thine that are in trouble; but as their
afflictions are, so let the joys and comforts of thy
Spirit be unto them; and so sanctify unto all
thine, their afflictions and troubles, that they may
tend to thy glory, and their own good. Give us
thankful hearts for all thy mercies, both spiritual
and corporeal: for thou art mercy merciful unto us
in the things of this life, and infinitely more merciful in the things of a better life. Let us deeply
ponder and weigh all thy particular favours towards us; that by the due consideration thereof,
our hearts may be gained yet nearer unto thee,
and that therefore we may both love and obey
thee, because thou art so kind and loving unto
us; that even thy love towards us may draw our
love towards thee, and that because mercy is with
thee, thou mayest be feared. Grant these things
good Father, and all other needful graces for our
souls or bodies, or any of thine throughout the
whole world, for Jesus Christ's sake. In whose
name, we further call upon thee, as he hath taught
us in his gospel, saying, " Our Father which art
in heaven," &c.

A PRAYER TO BE USED AT ANY TIME,

BY ONE IN PRIVATE.

O Lord, my God, and heavenly Father! I, thy most unworthy child, do here in thy sight freely confess that I am a most sinful creature, and damnable transgressor of all thy holy laws and commandments: that as I was born and bred in sin, and stained in the womb, so have I continually brought forth the corrupt and ugly fruits of that infection and contagion, wherein I was first conceived, both in thoughts, words, and works. If I should go about to reckon up my particular offences, I know not where to begin, or where to make an end; for they are more than the hairs of my head, yea, far more than I can possibly feel or know; for who knoweth the height and depth of his corruption? who knoweth how oft he offendeth? Thou only, O Lord, knowest my sins, who knowest my heart: nothing is hid from thee, thou knowest what I have been, and what I am; yea, my conscience doth accuse me of many and grievous evils, and I do daily feel by woful experience how frail I am, how prone to evil, and how untoward to all goodness. My mind is full of vanity, my heart full of profaneness, mine affections full of deadness, dulness and drowsiness in matters of thy worship and service; yea, my whole soul is full of spiritual blindness, hardness, unprofitableness, coldness, and security; and in very deed I am altogether a lump of sin, and a mass of all misery; and therefore I have forfeited thy favour, and incurred thy high displeasure, and have given thee just cause to frown upon me, to give me over, and leave me to mine own corrupt will and affections. But, O my dear Father, I have learned from thy mouth, that thou art a God of mercy, slow to wrath, and of great compassion and kindness towards all such as groan under the burden of their sins. Therefore, extend thy great mercy towards me a poor sinner, and give me a general pardon for all mine offences whatsoever; seal it in the blood of thy Son, and seal it to my conscience by thy Spirit, assuring me more and more of thy love and favour towards me, and that thou art a reconciled Father unto me. Grant that I may, in all time to come, love thee much because much is given, and of very love fear thee and obey thee. O Lord, increase my faith, that I may steadfastly believe all the promises of the gospel made in thy Son Christ, and rest upon them altogether. Enable me to bring forth the sound fruits of faith and repentance in all my particular actions. Fill my soul full of joy and peace in believing. Fill me full of inward comfort and spiritual strength against all temptations; give me yet a greater feeling of thy love and manifold mercies toward me; work in my soul a love of thy Majesty, a zeal of thy glory, an hatred of evil, and a desire of all good things. Give me victory over those sins which thou knowest are strongest in me. Let me once at last make a conquest of the world and the flesh. Mortify in me whatsoever is carnal; sanctify me throughout by thy Spirit; knit my heart to thee for ever, that I may fear thy name. Renew in me the image of thy Son Christ daily more and more. Give me a delight in the reading and meditation of thy word. Let me rejoice in the public ministry thereof. Cause me to love and reverence all the faithful ministers of thy gospel. Sanctify their doctrines to my conscience; seal them in my soul; write them in my heart; give me a soft and melting heart, that I may tremble at thy words, and be always much affected with godly sermons. Let not my sins hold back thy mercies from me, nor mine unworthiness stop the passage of thy grace. Open mine eyes to see the great wonders of thy law. Reveal thy secrets unto me; be open-hearted towards me thy unworthy servant. Hide nothing from me that may make for thy glory, and the good of my soul. Bless all means unto me which thou usest for my good. Bless all holy instructions unto my soul. Bless me at all times, both in hearing and reading thy word. Give me the right use of all thy mercies and corrections, that I may be the better for them. Let me abound in love to all thy children. Let my heart be very nearly knit unto them, that where thou lovest most there I may love most also. Enable me to watch and pray, that I enter not into temptation; give me patience and contentment in all things. Cause me to love thee more and more, and the world less and less. So draw my mind upward, that I may despise all transitory things. Let me be so enwrapt and ravished with the sight and feeling of heavenly things, that I may make a base reckoning of all earthly things. Let me use this world as though I used it not. Let me use it but for necessity, as meat and drink. Let me not be carried away with the vain pleasures and fond delights thereof. Good Father, work thy good work in me, and never leave me, nor forsake me, till thou hast brought me to true happiness. O, dear Father, make me faithful in my calling, that I may serve thee in it, and be always careful to do what good I may in any thing. Bless me in my outward estate. Bless my soul, body, goods, and name. Bless all that belongeth unto me. Bless my goings out and comings in. Let thy countenance be lifted up upon me, now and always; cheer me up with the joys and comforts of thy Spirit; make me thankful for all thy mercies. For I must needs confess that thou art very kind unto me in all things. For in thee I live, move, and have my being; of thee I have my welfare and good being; thou art a daily friend, and special good benefactor unto me. I live at thy cost and charges. I hold all of thee in chief, and I find that thou art never weary of doing me good: thy goodness towards me is unstanchable. Oh, I can never be thankful enough unto thee for all thy mercies, both spiritual and corporeal. But in such measure as I am able, I praise thy name for all, beseeching thee to accept of my thanksgiving, in thy Son Christ, and to give me a profitable use of all thy favours, that thereby my heart may be fully drawn unto thee. Give me, O Father, to be of such a good nature and disposition, that I may be won by gentleness and fair means, as much as if thou gavest me many lashes. Pardon all mine unthankfulness, unkindness, and great abusing of thy mercies, and give me grace to use them more to thy glory in all time to come. Strengthen me, dear Father, thus to continue praising and glorifying thy name here upon earth; that after this life, I may be crowned of thee for ever in thy kingdom.   Grant these petitions, most merciful God, not only to me, but to all thy dear children throughout the whole world, for Jesus Christ's sake; in whose name I do further call upon thee, saying, as he hath taught me, "Our Father, which art in heaven," &c.

GLASGOW:

WALTER G. M'LAREN, PRINTER, 257 ARGYLE STREET.

Made in the USA
Las Vegas, NV
28 March 2021